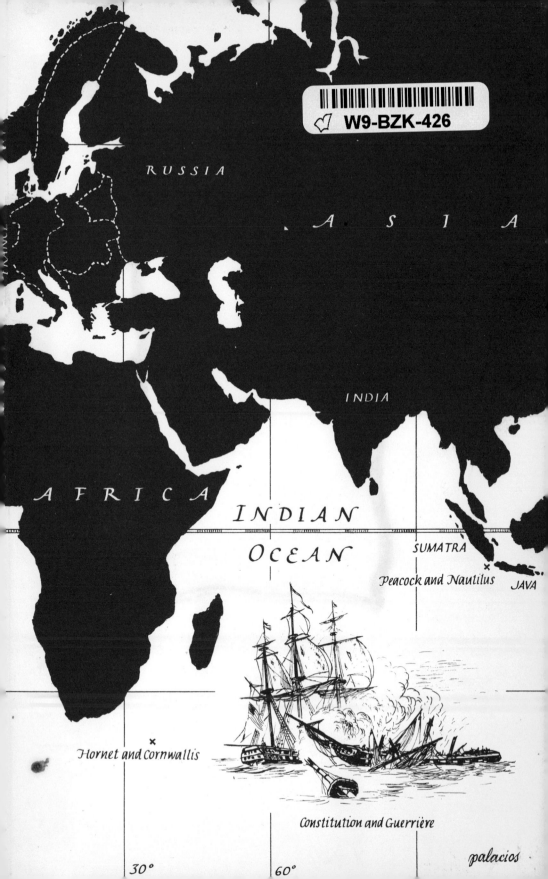

W9-BZK-426

RUSSIA

ASIA

INDIA

AFRICA

INDIAN

OCEAN

SUMATRA

Peacock and Nautilus

JAVA

Hornet and Cornwallis

Constitution and Guerrière

palacios

30°   60°

Mainstream of America Series ★

EDITED BY LEWIS GANNETT

THE AGE OF
FIGHTING SAIL

By C. S. Forester

THE GUN

THE PEACEMAKER

THE AFRICAN QUEEN

THE GENERAL

*BEAT TO QUARTERS

*SHIP OF THE LINE

*FLYING COLOURS

CAPTAIN HORATIO HORNBLOWER
(Originally published in the
three volumes starred above)

TO THE INDIES

THE CAPTAIN FROM CONNECTICUT

PAYMENT DEFERRED

RIFLEMAN DODD and THE GUN:
TWO NOVELS OF THE PENIN-
SULAR CAMPAIGNS (RIFLE-
MAN DODD was published in
England under the title
DEATH TO THE FRENCH)

THE SHIP

COMMODORE HORNBLOWER

LORD HORNBLOWER

THE SKY AND THE FOREST

MR. MIDSHIPMAN HORNBLOWER

RANDALL AND THE RIVER OF TIME

LIEUTENANT HORNBLOWER

HORNBLOWER AND THE ATROPOS

THE NIGHTMARE

THE GOOD SHEPHERD

THE AGE OF FIGHTING SAIL

THE AGE OF
FIGHTING SAIL

The Story of
The Naval War of 1812

By C. S. FORESTER

DOUBLEDAY & COMPANY, INC., *Garden City, N.Y.*

Library of Congress Catalog Card Number 56-7741

THE AGE OF
FIGHTING SAIL

Chapter I

IT MIGHT BE EXPECTED that a belligerent's war aims should bear some relationship to the grievances or ambitions that led to the war. It might even be expected that the belligerent's war plans should bear some relationship to his war aims. Yet history has shown that these relationships are frequently of the slightest; Clausewitz' dictum that war is the continuation of policy by other means is modified by Seeckt's logical addendum that the coming of war marks the breakdown of policy. Moreover, as a war progresses, the original issues tend to become obscured and the war plans more complicated—as need hardly be pointed out to a generation that has seen American soldiers fighting Italians in Africa in a conflict that originated in a boundary dispute between Germany and Poland. Nor need it be stressed that there are frequently profound differences between the real and the ostensible causes of a war, and wide divergences between the real and the ostensible war aims. And, with war contemplated or entered upon, the military ideas of the politicians may differ radically from those of the soldiers and sailors (in the same way as the political ideas of the soldiers and sailors may differ radically from those of the politicians) so that plans and execution may be tortuous or ineffectual or apparently motiveless.

Mr. Madison's message to Congress of June 1, 1812, which

resulted in a declaration of war on June 18, stated the grievances of the United States. The first was the practice of impressment by British ships of war of seamen from American ships. If the men pressed were British subjects, Mr. Madison, without admitting the legality of such action, had been willing to discuss "arrangements" which would render it unnecessary. Regarding the impressment of American citizens—and Mr. Madison affirmed that thousands had been impressed—Mr. Madison admitted no possibility of compromise whatever.

The next grievance was the habit of British ships violating the sovereignty of American territorial waters, and Mr. Madison alluded, but not in specific terms, to such incidents as the engagements between the *Chesapeake* and the *Leopard*, and between the *President* and the *Little Belt*.

In the sixth paragraph Mr. Madison brought up the subject of "pretended blockades," "mock blockades," with particular allusion to the inadequate notice given before such blockades were enforced.

Next came the question of the Orders in Council and their sweeping regulation of all trade with the continent of Europe. Here the matter of pretended blockades was not discussed in such detail; the grievance was that the British government was trying to force trade into particular channels and was adopting a policy which under pretense of the necessities of war favored British trade and handicapped that of America.

At this point Mr. Madison reviewed the negotiations which had taken place up to that date. The actual wording of his message here deserves close study; and close study is further necessary because of the rambling nature of the argument. It reflects all the difficulties under which the two governments had labored; many of them had been greatly increased as a result of blunders in the technique of international negotiation. There had been misunderstandings; some agents had exceeded their powers and others had been indiscreet, and in each case the mutual irritation had been heightened unnecessarily; the irritation is plain in every word.

It was of course impossible to discuss the negotiations with England without discussing those with France. Here it was plain that Mr. Madison had been fooled by Bonaparte; that, for a time at least, the downright lies that Bonaparte had told had been accepted as truths, and the shifts and subterfuges to which Bonaparte had resorted had been accepted as straightforward dealings. Yet it is possible to read into the style and manner of the message a certain uneasiness. Without avowing it to himself Mr. Madison had by now formed a vague, a very vague, suspicion that Bonaparte had been lying and that by that means Bonaparte had maneuvered the British and American governments into their present attitude of hostility. There was almost a hint of regret in Mr. Madison's admission that at one point war with France had been as likely a possibility as war with England.

But now the die was cast; in making his recommendations to the legislature Mr. Madison put his trust in the enlightened and patriotic councils of the nation; and the United States, with naval and military forces as inconsiderable on paper as those of Portugal or Sicily, entered into war with the nation which had for years defied the whole world in arms.

And the avowed purpose of the war was to put an end to interference with American trade and shipping; the slogan "Free Trade and Sailors' Rights" was coined to fit it. It remained to be seen how the United States government proposed to bring it about.

At the time when the final fatal interchange of notes was taking place between England and America, Bonaparte was notoriously massing his troops for an attack upon Russia. He had defeated Russia before; he had defeated every great continental power. Since his seizure of power he had engaged in six great campaigns—Marengo, Austerlitz, Jena, Friedland, Spain, and Wagram—and had emerged personally victorious from every one. From the Balkans to the Arctic and the Atlantic, save for Russia, all Europe acknowledged his suzerainty with the apparently minute exceptions of Sicily and Sardinia, Sweden and Portugal, and a small area in Spain—and even in Spain the close of 1011 witnessed the fall of Valencia, almost the last Spanish city that could defy him, and the surrender of almost the last army that Spain could put in the field. With the approaching conquest of Russia, Bonaparte's power would be seemingly unchallengeable, and England would be forced into recognition of the fact and would swallow the unpalatable pills presented to her.

The last time England had faced a united Europe and a hostile America she had given way, had suffered enormous affronts to her pride, and had signed in 1783 the peace which freed America and limited her own power. It would seem—judging by recent events—that the lesson had been badly learned and a second lesson was necessary, and Mr. Madison was in no way averse to administering it. After the Peace of Paris it was plain that never again could the King of England hope to exert so much influence on the government of his country—tyranny had been put within bounds, and freedom had been enormously extended by the establishment of an independent America. A new peace would clear up much that had regrettably been left unfinished when the old one was signed. The government of England would be further liberalized. The question of the arbitrary use of sea power would be definitely settled. Canada would be admitted to the benefits of a republican form of government, certainly looking to Washington for guidance and possibly owing Washington actual and grateful allegiance. And Europe under the benevolent supervision of Bonaparte would enjoy the belated fruits of the European Revolution which had been fertilized by the American Revolution.

Clausewitz at this moment was fighting in the Russian ranks against the French, and Mr. Madison was not fated to read what Clausewitz had to say about war, nor what his disciples made of his teachings. A total victory of the kind that Clausewitz envisaged was not a wild dream at a time when England was

at war with France. It was a possibility. The total overthrow
of one side or the other had become a more and more likely
result of the conflict ever since the rupture of the Peace of
Amiens, although no demand for unconditional surrender was
made until after the return from Elba. It is doubtful if the American government ever realized this; in the correspondence both
of Jefferson and of Madison the possibility of the invasion of
England and her "moderate republicanization" is contemplated
with equanimity. Prejudiced against the Tory government then
in power, and prejudiced in favor of the French government
with its talk of liberty and equality, the United States government did not realize that England, with all her faults, was fighting for the liberty of the world against a tyranny as crushing
and as treacherous as any that had appeared in history. There
could be no such thing as a moderate defeat of England when
two opposing ideologies were locked in combat, but Madison
believed there could be. He was never disillusioned, luckily for
the world. He might have lived to see, if England had been
defeated, tyranny not only extended throughout the British Isles
and Europe, but reaching out across the Atlantic; a lord of the
world in Paris eying jealously the existence of free speech in
Washington, the Louisiana Purchase repudiated, and a satellite
Spain raising difficulties in Florida in consequence. The Napo-
leonic policy of force and fraud would have found plenty of
objectives in the United States, and it is hardly likely that a victorious French Empire would have paid any more attention to
an American request for free trade and sailors' right than England had done.

Yet for good or for ill, America was at war, and the question
had to be decided as to how the objectives of the war should be
attained. Presumably, if faced by imminent total overthrow,
England would hasten to make peace on any terms with her less
malignant enemy; but action had to be taken in case that overthrow were to be long deferred or to prove impossible of at-
tainment. Then America must make such a nuisance of herself

that her demands would be listened to; and to ensure the granting of those demands it would be well if she were to acquire
something to bargain with in addition to the mere offer to cease
hostilities. The results of the embargo proved that simple economic pressure was not sufficient—at least when exerted only to
the limited extent that the federal government could force its
citizens to apply it. Obviously the next step to take was to attack British commerce, and some months before the declaration
of war Congress had reached a decision which settled, for the
duration of the war, the principal means by which British commerce was to be attacked. A congressional committee had reported wistfully that a small fleet of twelve ships of the line and
twenty frigates would suffice to keep the British navy at a re-
spectful distance from the American coasts (and such a force
would most likely have been strong enough for that purpose),
but the committee had realized that there was no chance of
Congress' voting for such a force and had limited its recommendations to the frigates alone, and the House of Representatives had voted down the recommendation. It had voted down
the proposal to establish a dockyard. All it would agree to was
a minute provision for the purchase of timber. If war was to
come—and war was by then a decided possibility—it would
have to be fought at sea by private enterprise backed only by
the tiny naval force at present in existence.

Nevertheless, this same Congress, at the same moment, had
displayed some insight into the corresponding problem. Privateering, in its opinion, would provide the "nuisance force." To
establish the United States in a bargaining position, it was proposed to rely upon the army, which was to conquer Canada,
and with that objective in view a huge increase in the army was
voted. A present establishment of ten thousand was to be increased to thirty-five thousand; fifty thousand volunteers were
to be enlisted at the same time. Such a force could hardly cost
less than seventeen million dollars a year (the vote for the purchase of timber barely exceeded half a million dollars), and

moreover, as the regular army was far below establishment, the proposed increase of about fourteen to one meant that the force raised could not attain efficiency without months of preparation and further months of training. Little thought was given to the question of how this force was to be recruited, housed, equipped, or trained. And no thought was given to the manner in which it was to be employed, for no steps were taken or contemplated for attaining the necessary naval superiority on Lakes Ontario and Erie. Canada was to be conquered (by "mere marching," Jefferson suggested) apparently by the wishing for it, for five months after the vote to increase the army the Secretary of War blithely reported the number of regular troops as less than seven thousand. Yet, whatever the means available and however nebulous the actual plans, it was already obvious that the war objectives would be best attained by an attack on British commerce and by the occupation of Canada.

On the British side the confusion was not quite so universal, and it was more evident in policy than in execution, as might be expected after the British experience of almost twenty years of warfare. Seeing that England had allowed war to come, it might be thought that her war objectives were maintenance of the present state of affairs, but the conclusion is not quite sound. In the first place, after years of argument with the administrations of Jefferson and Madison, the British government had come to believe that America would not fight in any circumstances, a belief which accounted largely for the aura of unreality which surrounded most of the British proposals. The government did not, or could not, believe that America would fight; and equally important was the fact that most of those people who would have to do the fighting did not care if she did.

The recklessness and highhandedness of British naval officers had an effect as inevitable upon their government as the timidity of their government in judging their behavior had upon them. Captains of British ships of war, very much left to their own initiative while communications remained slow, were eternally plagued by the twin problems of manning their ships and dealing with desertion. A captain whose professional career, whose actual life, depended on the safety of his ship, which in turn depended on acquiring the services of another twenty topmen, was not going to give too much attention to the niceties of international law when he saw a chance of acquiring those twenty topmen. And his breach of international law brought only faint protests from Washington, not strong enough to call down any rebuke upon him from his professional superiors; the vicious circle was established readily enough, especially as the practice of impressment from neutrals—from ships of Bremen or Hamburg, states too feeble to be worth consideration—was of long standing.

There was an even keener edge to the British captain's feelings when it came to recovering deserters. It was not a matter of regaining the deserters' services; as they were mostly hanged, or flogged into idiocy, the deserters were not going to be of further service in any case. But a successful desertion—still more a successful mass desertion—shook the whole structure of discipline in a ship every man of whose crew (as far as years and years of experience seemed to prove) was doomed to live on in hardship and peril until his broken body was cast into a watery grave. The recovery of one deserter, and his spectacular hanging or flogging round the fleet, made a deep impression upon, and was likely to eliminate dangerous thoughts from, the minds of the thousands of seamen who witnessed it. So hungrily was this possibility regarded by admirals commanding squadrons, and captains commanding ships, manned by men at least half of whom would desert if they saw a chance of doing so, that they would go to any lengths short of professional ruin to bring it about. Their professional superiors were in complete sympathy with them, having faced the same problems, and could not fail to influence the Cabinet in their favor; and the Cabinet, convinced by long experience that no outrage would elicit a declaration of war, took no decided steps to check outrages. The

Cabinet was responsible to a country which was fighting for life against a powerful and unscrupulous tyrant; the only sure protection against that tyrant was the Royal Navy, and the Cabinet must needs hesitate before interfering with practices in that navy which high professional opinion deemed essential to its existence.

The navy—and the nation too—was, however, reckless as well as desperate. It had won victories over every major naval power in the world. France and Spain and the Netherlands had all suffered repeated defeats at its hands. Nearly every victory had been won against serious numerical odds. Under the protection of the navy, British merchant shipping and British troop transports sailed with practical impunity in every quarter of the globe despite the hostility of all Europe. To men in this mood, to men without imagination, there was nothing deterrent about the prospect of a small addition to the numbers of their enemies. Denmark had possessed at least five times the naval force, at least ten times the military force, of the United States, and she had been twice struck down and was now reduced to nearly complete impotence, able to offer only the most trivial annoyance to the merchant fleets of England sailing up the Sound almost within cannon shot of her shores. What was there to fear from America?

The merchant fleets of the rest of the world had been swept from the seas. Alien flags, save for that of the United States, were flown only in furtive blockade runners. Men with limited imagination might be tempted to contemplate the prospect of the whole carrying trade, of the whole business of the world, being conducted under the British flag without rival. Prizes were rare nowadays, and men with a greed for gold could eye covetously the rich American shipping. Admirals and captains had built up immense fortunes out of prize money in happy years not so long ago. War with America might make it possible again, and the ignoble motive could well be excused by the plea that every prize brought into a British port would increase British wealth. War with America would certainly put an end to the nagging problem of desertion to American ships. War would teach a lesson to the upstarts who had once taken advantage of England's misfortunes to gain their independence and who now boasted of their liberty. To shortsighted British naval officers and to those members of the British public who were also shortsighted while taking an interest in naval affairs, there was nothing to fear and much that was attractive about the prospect of war with America.

So public opinion in England did little to check the British government in its offensive attitude. It is noteworthy that, when at last convinced that the United States would not flinch from war, the British Cabinet hastily revoked the Orders in Council relative to the blockade of Europe but held fast to the British claim to the right to search neutral vessels for British subjects, so that it may be said that it was on account of this claim, and this claim only, that England was prepared to go to war. It is an oversimplification of the case, however. The basic reason for war was really to be found in the attitude of mind of the two governments and of sections of the two peoples; the mutual irritation was skillfully envenomed by Bonaparte's diplomacy. A few concessions early in the controversy; a few lavish promises made later (even though only paper promises like Bonaparte's —but the British Cabinet was incapable of rising to such heights of ingenuity or sinking to such depths of duplicity); a few well-publicized restraints put upon British naval officers; a few unmistakable evidences of good will; some public appreciation of the difficulties of Mr. Madison's task; perhaps even a mere well-timed sop to Mr. Madison's vanity; any of these might have turned the rising tide of war. But war it was, and England had to fight, and she had to make plans as to how to employ her strength and how to minimize her weaknesses.

There was the first and most obvious move, to be expected of a nation with vast experience of maritime warfare. The London *Gazette*, as soon as certain news of the declaration of war reached the Cabinet, published an order in council, wherein it was ordered that "commanders of H.M.'s ships of war and privateers do detain and bring into port all ships and vessels belonging to citizens of the United States of America." American commerce was to be swept from the seas. Yet that very same issue of the *Gazette* carried an Admiralty order, wherein the commissioners for executing the Office of Lord High Admiral announced that "we do hereby revoke and declare null and void and of no effect all licenses granted by us to any ship or vessel to sail without convoy to any port or place of North America, Newfoundland, the West Indies, or the Gulf of Mexico." The nuisance value of the American declaration of war was admitted in these lines. The valuable West Indian trade had recently been freed from the trammels of local convoy, for the capture of the last of the French islands had deprived French privateers of any base in the Caribbean; Spanish privateers had ceased to be hostile with the commencement of the Peninsular War. Now the whole trade was to be subjected once again to the delays, expense, and inconvenience of convoy. The Convoy Act was all-embracing in its provisions and severe in the penalties it imposed. No British ship could obtain clearance without the local collector of customs being satisfied that convoy was available, and the Admiralty order implied not only that the great outward- and homeward-bound fleets should be escorted but that the inter-island trade which built up the homeward-bound convoys and into which the outward-bound convoys dispersed was immobilized in the absence of vessels to guard it. This meant an inevitable accumulation of delays which no amount of organization could reduce, and it also meant a constant demand for escort vessels in the Caribbean which it was not easy to meet in the face of the other demands for naval force.

During this year Great Britain had at sea, refitting, or repairing 191 ships of the line and 245 frigates and ships of fifty guns; she had several hundred smaller ships of war and she had in hand an extensive building program to increase this force still more. There was a man serving in her fighting fleet for every two hundred men and women and children in her population. And yet this enormous force was stretched very thinly, thanks to Bonaparte's policy of building ships all round the coast of Europe, from Venice to Lübeck. His ships of the line were not greatly fewer than those of England, although their manning was immeasurably inferior; and they had to be watched constantly in case at their "selected moment" they should burst out and gain at least a local superiority over the Royal Navy at its "average moment." With the American declaration of war, vigilance appeared more necessary, for alarmists in England conjured up a nightmare of a French squadron eluding the blockade and reaching an American port. Based there, and with its crews filled up with capable American seamen, it could cause the infinity of trouble—it was thought—that could have been caused by that American squadron of ships of the line for which thoughtful Americans had pleaded in the wasted years of the past. The danger was actually not very serious; relations between the United States government and that of the Empire were hardly cordial, and the friction that would have arisen in any attempt to co-operate between French admirals and American officials would have reduced to a minimum the activity of any blockade-running squadron. In the twenty-two months that France remained a belligerent no effort was made to carry out the scheme, but the Admiralty could not be sure of that; in war the side conducting a nervous defensive is always likely to overestimate the strength, and to underestimate the difficulties, of the potential attacker.

England had much else to be nervous about. She was maintaining in the Spanish Peninsula a British army which represented almost her entire military strength; she was mantaining a Portuguese army; she was maintaining what was left of the Spanish armies, all locked in a life-and-death struggle with the Imperial forces. Her stake there was enormous; it is almost no exaggeration to say that her national existence depended on the integrity of her sea communications with Lisbon. Two thousand ships a year carried to the Peninsula the military stores, the troops, the money—even much of the food for the civilian population—which kept the struggle going. The line of communication curved round the French flank temptingly close to the French Biscay ports; now it must be guarded on the side of the Atlantic from any thrust the American government—or American private enterprise—could contrive to make at it. Of any single sea route traveled by British ships, this was the most vital and the most vulnerable, but there was a vastly important trade with India; British ships sailed to China, to the Philippines, to Australia; British whalers traversed the Pacific, and they must all be guarded against possible raiders. It was not to be wondered at that the Admiralty found difficulty in scraping together a naval force to watch the American seaboard; the strain was so severe as to be almost intolerable.

It was at least an interesting coincidence that relief from the strain made itself felt immediately. Already coincidence had come to Britain's aid. The effects of the embargo and of non-intercourse had been greatly modified because Bonaparte's reckless interference in Peninsular affairs had at that time opened first the Portuguese and then the Spanish colonies to British trade. Now the same *Gazettes* that carried the notices of the American declaration of war and the orders about West Indian convoys carried more heartening news. "In the name of the Most Holy and Indivisible Trinity" it was declared by Their Majesties the King of Sweden and the King of Great Britain and Ireland that there should be between them "a firm, true, and inviolable Peace." There was a hurried and ecstatic announcement that peace had been signed with Russia, too, backed up by an instant revocation of the Order in Council that commanded general reprisals against the Russians. There was the text of the decree opening Swedish ports to British trade. Now the very considerable forces which had been watching Sweden and Russia could be reduced; and, of great importance as well,

Sweden would resume her supply of naval stores at the same moment as America discontinued hers.

The Grand Army had crossed the Niemen. The Imperial hordes, urged on by the Imperial freebooter, were pouring into Russia, destined for Moscow—and destined to retreat from Moscow, such of them as survived. And Wellington had crossed the Agueda, marching out of Portugal with an incomparable British army to free three quarters of Spain from French dominion and to strike the shattering blow of Salamanca that would cause the French military structure to totter on its foundations. It was all in the same week that Bonaparte crossed the Niemen, that Wellington crossed the Agueda, and Mr. Madison crossed the Rubicon.

Chapter II

JOHN RODGERS WAS A MAN OF THIRTY-NINE, nearly forty. He had seen a good deal of war; as first lieutenant of the *Constellation* under Truxtun he had taken possession of the French *Insurgente* after the action which resulted in her capture and in his own promotion to captain at the age of twenty-six; and he had demonstrated his seamanship by taking the wrecked prize into St. Kitts despite heavy weather and a restive mass of prisoners. As captain of the *John Adams* he had fought and destroyed the Tripolitan *Meshouda*, and he had had long practical experience during the Tripolitan War of keeping his ship efficient far from a base. Most important of all, he had had experience of command in chief on active service, holding command of the American Mediterranean squadron three thousand miles from Washington. He was a thoughtful member of his profession, in a navy which was notably inclined to the debate and discussion of professional problems. At the moment of the outbreak of war his name was best known as the captain of the *President*, which, the year before, had cut up the *Little Belt* in an accidental night action off Cape Henry.

For the past two years he had held command, as commodore, of a squadron made up of nearly every ship of war the United States possessed, patrolling, under orders from the Secretary of the Navy, American territorial waters so as to set some bounds on the behavior of the Royal Navy. His stern orders to his captains had reflected his own concern regarding the dignity of the United States and the prestige of the American navy. The appointment was a fortunate one; Rodgers had two years in which to drill his ships in conditions approaching those of active service, to work out, in continual discussion with the brilliant officers under his command, the problems of the coming war, and to evolve and perfect systems of tactics adapted to varied conditions and armaments. In two years of hard work a man like Rodgers could achieve a great deal, despite the fact that during this period of humiliation the United States Navy suffered a steady drain as disgusted officers resigned their commissions or went on half pay. The years of Rodgers' command from 1810 to 1812 must have been far more important in the development of the American navy than the better-remembered "prison school" which David Porter instituted among the captive officers of the *Philadelphia* in Tripoli.

With war declared, Rodgers had to put into action the plans he had evolved regarding the employment of America's naval force. Under his command in New York he had a powerful striking force, the two big frigates *President* and *United States*, the smaller frigate *Congress*, the sloop *Hornet*, and the brig *Argus;* his other frigate, *Essex*, was undergoing repairs. He had received little help from the government in reaching any decision; indeed at one moment Mr. Madison had decided that in the event of war the United States ships would be better employed as floating batteries, and had been persuaded to countermand the order only by the urgent representations of two good captains—Bainbridge and Stewart—who happened to be in Washington.

Official intimation of the declaration of war reached Rodgers in New York three days after the resolution of Congress, but no orders accompanied it. That was only to be expected of an administration that had never displayed any understanding of the problems of sea power. The Administration had indeed gone as far as to request suggestions from several captains, but it had not yet had time to digest them, and the orders eventually issued—almost a week after the declaration of war—show no sign of having been influenced in the least by the recommendations of Rodgers or Decatur or Bainbridge.

But Rodgers did not wait for orders. His ships were ready for sea, except for *Essex*, and he sailed immediately on hearing of the declaration of war—Nelson had said, "Lose not an hour," and Rodgers acted in exactly that spirit. His greatest fear had been lest a superior British squadron should appear off Sandy Hook before he could get away; that was always possible, and Rodgers was fully aware of the possibility. In the two years of his command he had had every opportunity of gathering information regarding the strength of his immediate opponent.

This was Vice-Admiral Sawyer, Commanding His Majesty's Ships and Vessels at Halifax; Bermuda also came within his command, so that he faced the greater part of the American seaboard, and it was the ships of his squadron which had been most prominent in the irritating treatment of the United States. Sawyer's force consisted of the *Africa*, a 64-gun ship of the line (one of the smaller vessels of this class, therefore), of a varying number of frigates, seven or eight usually, and some small vessels. Thus he had considerable superiority of force; two to one, possibly. In Nelson's opinion three frigates were a match for one ship of the line, but it is very much to be doubted whether the *Africa* could have withstood Rodgers' two big frigates—even one of them could have fought her with a chance of success. So unless Sawyer's force was concentrated there was a chance that it might meet with disaster, and in less than two days one of his ships very nearly did. Sawyer's force was not concentrated, and the hope that the powerful American squadron might encounter small portions of it influenced Rodgers' decision to sail at once.

Not only was Rodgers' force strong enough to deal with Sawyer's unless the latter was concentrated, but it was also strong enough to fight the usual kind of escort provided by the Admiralty for major convoys. A typical convoying force would consist of a ship of the line, one or two frigates, and one or two sloops, sufficient to cover the lumbering convoy from the attacks of privateers and capable of dealing with a stray French ship of the line that might evade the blockade. If Rodgers should encounter such a convoy and escort he could deal a shattering blow. If the escort was too strong for him to face with confidence—and not all escorts included a ship of the line—he could count at least on forcing it to form line of battle so that his well-handled ships would have every opportunity of getting in among the convoy. At the least he could inflict serious losses; at most he might wipe out convoy, escort and all; and, of all the possibilities open to him, that was the one most likely to prevail upon the British Cabinet (if it survived such a shock, as was doubtful, or its successor if it fell, as was likely) to come to terms with the American government, and that was the object of going to war.

So it was with the double hope of either catching some portion of Sawyer's force or of intercepting a large convoy that Rodgers put to sea, and it was with both objects in mind that he kept his own force concentrated. In doing so he acted in a fashion contrary to the suggestions of Decatur and Bainbridge, and in a very different manner from that laid down in the orders that did not reach him. The naval officers had suggested a policy of dispersion in varying degrees, with the idea that the wider the American force was spread the greater was the chance of capturing British shipping. They missed the point that very soon American privateers would be pushing out of American ports by the dozen, by the score, even by the hundred. Among this swarm of ships Rodgers' squadron, if scattered, would only constitute five more. They could snap up isolated ships, stragglers from convoys, and so forth, and would do this hardly more efficiently than the privateers. They would be incapable of dealing a heavy blow, and they would be incapable of forcing the Admiralty to maintain guard against such a blow. It might even be thought that captains of United States ships might not possess the specialized knowledge of the ways of British merchant ships that would be looked for by the owners of privateers in their captains; successful commerce destruction calls for familiarity with trade routes and seasonal variations such as might not have come the way of an officer in a regular service. And there was the further point that any increase in Rodgers' numbers, regardless of the increase in his force, added to its efficiency in extending his field of vision. His three frigates in line, ten miles apart with visibility ten miles, could sweep an area forty miles wide; the *Hornet* and *Argus* would increase that width to sixty miles—an important consideration, because even a large convoy covers only a small area of the sea and can frequently be missed by a vessel searching for it. Merely increasing by half Rodgers' chances of sighting a convoy made it worth while taking the smaller vessels along—at least in Rodgers' opinion—as balanced against their chances of effecting captures when cruising independently; and in the event of a convoy being met, they could be, even though of small use in the line of battle, most efficacious in attacking the merchant vessels while Rodgers fought the escort.

Rodgers, as a thoughtful sailor, could not help being aware of a further consideration. A hostile force known to be at sea, and yet with its whereabouts and destination unknown, is a source of anxiety to the enemy and compels precautions disproportionately greater than its strength would appear to demand. Every vital point within its striking distance must be guarded; to make sure of intercepting it, far greater total forces must be disposed over its possible routes. At one time in 1914 there were seventeen British ships of war trying to catch the small German cruiser *Emden*, and that was at a period when cable communication between shore stations made co-ordination of search considerably easier than in 1812. Rodgers knew that during these last few weeks, with the imminent approach of war, American merchant vessels had begun to swarm home, and part of his manifold duties was to ensure their safe entry into American harbors, and he had to do this in the face of a manifestly superior force. His disappearance out to sea with his united squadron was the most effective way of ensuring this. No single British cruiser would gladly remain at a focal point off the American coast when her captain was aware that at any moment Rodgers' topsails might appear over the seaward horizon, cutting him off from escape; no British admiral would gladly leave his cruisers dispersed in situations inviting their destruction in detail. With Rodgers' departure known, there would be urgent British orders for concentration. The net cast to entrap American shipping would be entirely altered in character; the individual strands would have to be made stronger at the cost of making the holes infinitely larger—so large that in the event the home-ward-bound shipping found its way through with remarkably small losses. Rodgers' bold decision to take his squadron far out to sea had a profound effect on the rest of the war.

Parenthetically it may be mentioned that the Administration had sent Rodgers orders in contemplation of the same situation; he left New York before he could receive them, fortunately, although the student of naval history may regret that they did not arrive earlier and afford a lesson in what an intelligent com-mander in chief should do on receipt of orders obviously un-wise. Rodgers was instructed to divide his squadron into halves, to put one half under Decatur's command, and to separate the halves, which were to cruise off and on from the Capes of the Chesapeake and from New York. It was only three weeks after Rodgers' departure that Broke, with the *Africa* and several frigates under his command, appeared off Sandy Hook; if Rodgers had waited for orders and had then gone out in obedi-ence to them—in a fashion as dilatory as the Administration's —Broke would probably have caught Decatur and his New York squadron; if he had not destroyed it he would at least have chased both Decatur and Rodgers into harbor and could have blockaded them in the comforting certainty of knowing where they were.

As it was, Broke, after keeping his squadron concentrated off New York and discovering that Rodgers had disappeared out to sea, was so anxious about the fate of a homeward-bound West Indian convoy which was guarded only by a single frigate that he went off to escort it with his squadron, still, perforce, in one mass. By the time he had seen it safely on its way and had returned to New York he had covered two thousand miles, and six weeks had elapsed; six weeks during which American ships could enter the unwatched American ports. His brief stay off Sandy Hook had been enlivened by the historic chase of the *Constitution;* the *Constitution* escaped, as will be later described, but it is necessary to point out that the knowledge that Rodgers was at sea meant that there was no British cruiser off Boston, whither the *Constitution* made her escape and whence she sailed again, still unobserved, on the cruise which resulted in the capture of the *Guerrière.*

Rodgers' sortie was therefore amply justified, as even Mr. Madison grudgingly admitted in his message to Congress; it remains to recall the details of his voyage. It was only thirty-six hours after he sailed that he had his first opportunity of striking a serious blow, when he sighted the *Belvidera,* a British 32-gun frigate—seriously inferior even to the *Congress,* therefore—which was watching New York and yet had not heard of the declaration of war. Byron of the *Belvidera* was a cautious officer as well as a very capable seaman; he kept away as soon as he made out that five ships of war were approaching. He was under the impression that the American ships had been sent out to chase away British ships of war in American territorial waters, and he had no desire that his ship should figure in another *Little Belt* affair when he was opposed to odds of some ten to one. He turned his stern to his pursuers and set all sail. The wind, which was fresh at the moment of sighting, grew fitful and erratic. They were out of sight of land, so there was no question of the British ship being in territorial waters, but Byron sent his men to quarters and did his best to increase his distance from the powerful force pursuing him. With the dying away of the wind the chase was prolonged; although the American ships were almost within range, they could not close, and Byron, soon after midday—it was dawn when he had turned away—took the opportunity of sending his men to dinner while the ships crept along through the heat, mantaining bare steerage way, all within plain sight of each other and without any communication being exchanged.

Later in the afternoon the wind freshened; the American ships felt the effects first, closing rapidly, and Rodgers in the *President* found himself within range, opening fire at less than half a mile with the two bow guns which would bear, Rodgers himself firing the first shot. The first three shots all hit—a tribute to American gunnery—and did considerable damage. Byron was still in doubt as to whether a state of war existed, but he gave the order to return the fire. Before he could be obeyed, however, an event took place that may have had a great deal of influence on the first result; the foremost main-deck gun in the *President*, above which Rodgers was standing on the forecastle, burst as it fired its second shot. Rodgers went down with a broken leg, and fifteen other men were killed or wounded. Into the confusion and consternation that ensued—although the British throughout the action were ignorant of what had happened—the *Belvidera's* stern guns opened fire.

The bursting of the gun was a disaster for the Americans, but it could have been worse. The American armaments industry at the time was in its infancy, and there had been complaints as far back as the Mediterranean war about the quality of the guns. It was not an easy matter to cast large masses of metal without hidden flaws and air bubbles. At this conclusive indication that their weapons might be faulty the American gunners could excusably feel mistrust of them and could have been chary about firing them, but they maintained their fire without hesitation.

Rodgers' wound was more disastrous, possibly. The *President* had to solve the problem presented to every chasing ship: whether or not it would be advantageous to yaw and turn the broadside toward the target, losing distance but multiplying tenfold the number of guns that would bear.

The problem was not capable of an easy solution by the rules of simple proportion; it was not enough to decide whether the bow guns could or could not fire ten shots during the wasted interval of getting back into range after yawing. The efficacy of each shot increased disproportionately with every decrease in range. Yawing might enable the pursued to draw away for good; on the other hand, a lucky broadside might inflict so much damage on sails and rigging that the chasing ship could close to decisive range before it could be repaired. Wind and sea could vary; darkness would certainly come sooner or later. To reach a correct conclusion observing all the probabilities and possibilities called for a clear head as well as resolution and wide professional knowledge; it is possible that Rodgers, shaken by his recent experience, did not succeed in doing so, although no proof of it was possible at the time.

The *President* yawed and fired broadsides, and it is generally assumed that she should rather have held her course, but that is only an assumption. The *Belvidera* fought a good fight, maintaining an excellent return fire, replacing damaged rigging, fishing injured spars; there was no need to urge the hands to the work, because every man on board was enraged at what he could not be blamed for regarding as an unprovoked, even treacherous, attack made in overwhelming force on an unsuspecting victim. With boats cut away, water pumped out, and everything done to make every yard of distance, the *Belvidera* contrived to escape fatal injury; not one of the other ships of the American squadron succeeded in getting within range. Darkness came down; the wind settled so that it suited *Belvidera's* best point of sailing, and she drew away and disappeared into the night. Three days later she reached Halifax, having taken some American prizes on the way, but the cautious Sawyer, still not sure that a state of war existed, released them and actually sent one of his precious sloops under flag of truce to ask for explanations—incidentally, the information that the *Belvidera* brought regarding the strength of the American squadron also led him to send hurried messages calling in every isolated ship under his command.

The pursuit and the escape had been only a tiny incident in the history of the naval wars of the time. There had been scores of similar brushes between British and French ships during the preceding years. More attention has been paid to the technical details than the occasion warrants. If *Belvidera* had fallen into Rodgers' hands the results would hardly have been important; the American public could not have been as impressed by a chance victory gained by overwhelming force as it was by the subsequent victories of American ships, and the British public had sense and experience enough—the naval history of the French wars is punctuated with records of the loss of single British ships caught by much stronger forces—not to be shaken by the loss in such circumstances of one frigate.

The real importance of the incident lay in the exasperation of the British seamen and officers at what they tended to look upon as a treacherous attack, or at least as one made in ungentlemanly fashion. Rodgers' behavior had been correct enough, and more than once the British navy had taken advantage of a surprise declaration of war to reap a harvest of unsuspecting prizes, but there was considerable ill feeling nevertheless, which was likely to embitter the struggle and make peace less easy to come by. It might have been well had it occurred to Rodgers to give *Belvidera* some definite warning of the outbreak of war before he opened fire. A gesture—unnecessarily chivalrous—would have cost nothing and might have profoundly affected the subsequent relations of the two countries.

When *Belvidera* was out of sight and out of reach Rodgers with his broken leg had to recast his plans. Before he left New

York he had received some vague information regarding the departure of a homeward-bound West Indian convoy a month or more earlier. Rodgers did not want the blow he was dealing to be a mere blow in the air. The capture of a West Indian convoy would be the most effective blow he could deal, and the hope of overtaking this one—by no means a wild hope—reinforced by his fear of being blockaded, helped in deciding him to sail instantly. The ordinary trade route to England from the West Indies took advantage of the Gulf Stream to make northing while in the northeast trade wind belt; it then took advantage of the westerlies to head for the approaches to the Channel. Rodgers with his handy squadron was entitled to hope that he could anticipate the arrival there of a lumbering convoy. Only an hour or two before sighting *Belvidera* he had received information from an incoming American ship that she had actually sighted the convoy four days before and three hundred miles away. His pursuit of the *Belvidera* had hardly distracted him from the necessary course to intercept; repairs to the *President* hardly delayed him a moment. He headed across the Atlantic.

He ran into thick weather on the Grand Banks and carried it with him all the way, with visibility rarely more than five miles and sometimes down to zero, and yet he made a satisfactory passage, fifteen days from the Grand Banks. His hopes were sustained by reports from ships he encountered that the convoy was not far ahead, but in the thick weather that prevailed he did not sight it. He turned back on July 13 when a hundred and fifty miles from the Scillies.

It is hard to believe that he was wise to do so. In not maintaining his course for another day, in not scouring the approaches to the Channel, he was giving up his best chance of dealing a heavy blow. On the open sea a ship—even a convoy—is hard to find, but Rodgers was close to a focal point where shipping was bound to be concentrated. During centuries privateer captains and U-boat commanders made a practice of seeking their prey in the approaches to the Channel. In sailing-ship days even more than in the age of steam certain areas were likely to yield a harvest, for the sailing ship after a long passage was bound to be somewhat uncertain of her longitude, and it was a usual practice to make a landfall by running down the latitude—a westerly sweep along 50° N. often resulted in a raider finding a victim running straight into his clutches. But Rodgers turned away when he had hardly reached the fringe of the area where he might expect to make captures. So far his movements had been bold, well timed, and effective; now they were futile. He had achieved the one objective of disrupting the British blockade of the American coast; he abandoned the other, of damaging British commerce, when it was within his grasp. A few more days of bold action could have been productive of important results. He could have pushed into the mouth of the Channel, even into the Bristol Channel and the Irish Sea. Undoubtedly there was danger in such a course; chance might have taken him into the arms of some heavy British squadron inward or outward bound on blockade service, but it was not a very great chance and he could expect his frigates to be able to escape from ships of the line. He could expect two or three weeks of freedom of action before the news of his presence would result in deliberate movement against him of forces detailed for that purpose by the Admiralty, and then it would be time enough to disappear again. In that two or three weeks he might well encounter a convoy; there could be no doubt at all that he would find plenty of coastwise shipping to harass. There would be long faces in Leadenhall Street and even in Threadneedle Street at the news that a powerful American squadron was scouring the coast. The Admiralty would be at its wit's end to find the necessary ships of the line and accompanying frigates—at the expense of the blockade of the French coast—to form the squadrons to chase him away again, and the possibility of his return would complicate future arrangements for weeks to come.

Rodgers made no attempt to profit by the opportunity he had

made for himself. He turned away, heading south for Madeira
—still in thick weather—before turning westward for home. In
his reports he made such small attempts to explain why he did
not linger in the mouth of the Channel that it seems he attributed no importance to the possibility; he certainly put forward no excuse and deemed no excuse necessary, and it is odd
that a sailor of Rodgers' caliber, who had given much thought
to professional problems, should not have devoted a few lines
in his reports to discussion of this course of action.

It is likely—and the whole tenor of Rodgers' report is in accordance with the theory—that, having set out from New York
in pursuit of one particular convoy, and having for three weeks
urged his course with that objective in mind, Rodgers was so
disappointed at the thought of having missed his quarry and so
exasperated at the continuance of thick weather which had
hampered him that he gave no thought at all to any alternative
activity. He had been three weeks without news from America,
and he could anticipate that it would be longer still before his
return would enable him to hear any. He had left behind him a
powerful British force based within striking distance of the
American coast, and he must have been consumed with anxiety
about what had been happening there. He had made his sortie
in the hope of facilitating the return of American shipping and
in the conviction that this was the best course, but in three
dreary weeks at sea the conviction could weaken. If he returned
at once he would still have been absent for two months or so;
that was time enough for American shipping to reach home,
and in the presence of the enemy he could find fresh employment for his force. By the time of his return the drinking water
of his squadron would be seriously depleted—although that difficulty would not be acute—and he could see no opportunity
for replenishment. One way and another, there were arguments
in favor of recrossing the Atlantic, and Rodgers acted upon
them.

His southward sweep to Madeira opened up the possibility

of capturing valuable East Indiamen, but the faint possibility did not materialize. In his whole voyage Rodgers captured no more than seven small merchantmen. He skirted the Nova Scotian coast to make what observations he could of hostile activities, and with sound judgment he selected Boston as the port to which he should return, and there he dropped anchor after seventy days at sea. Ten weeks without news, having left his country at the moment of coming to grips with a powerful and enterprising enemy; Rodgers' anxiety as he approached must have been intense. He found a city which the day before had been raised from the depths of depression to the heights of exultation.

Chapter III

IN 1812 THE BRITISH NAVY could look back with complacence over a record of victories frequently gained and easily won. Time and time again it had faced numerical odds and had emerged triumphant. At St. Vincent it had faced odds of two to one and had snatched a colorful and important victory. At the Nile it had gone boldly into action against odds of five to four and had won the most crushing naval victory of recent centuries. Nelson at Trafalgar, Strachan at Cape Ortegal, Duckworth at San Domingo had all fought fleets considerably or slightly superior and had destroyed them. In no case had the enemy misconducted himself. Frenchmen and Spaniards, Dutchmen and Danes had fought to the death, unavailingly. Brilliant tactics and bold leadership accounted only partially for the long succession of victories. There had been single-ship actions too numerous to count, and in the great majority of these actions British ships had been victorious, and often over ships of greater tonnage, with more guns and larger crews.

The British public, and even the navy, could be excused for forming the belief that there was something intrinsically superior in British seamanship and perhaps in British material. Ships commanded by British officers could expect victory over ships of comparable force of any other nation. A British captain who avoided action against anything less than a force obviously and overwhelmingly superior did so at his peril; nor did it often happen, for British officers were sublimely confident of victory and went into action with the assurance to be expected of men who seriously believed they represented a chosen race destined to pre-eminence.

There could, in fact, be no denying the present intrinsic superiority of British naval forces over those of Europe. The facts spoke for themselves, even when, as has already been said, allowance was made for the vast professional excellence of the British admirals of that generation. To inquire into the causes of this superiority might be deemed unpatriotic in a people who were prepared to accept the more ready—if actually less tenable —explanation of national destiny, and at the time the inquiry was hardly made. Time had to elapse, and serious histories had to be written, before the causes became apparent to the general public, and even then the public was loath to form the necessary conclusions.

The Revolution in France had gone far to reduce the efficiency of the French navy; too many French naval officers had emigrated, there were too many schisms in French opinion, the French government was distracted by too many anxieties for the French navy to retain the excellence it had displayed during the War of American Independence. Once the British navy had asserted its superiority by a great deal of hard fighting, the superiority became more and more easy to maintain. A fleet blockaded in harbor loses its efficiency rapidly. An equally potent factor was the constant drain of trained seamen, who were steadily combed out to man the ships that sortied. The fierce frigate warfare consumed them by the thousands. Every British capture of a French privateer—and privateers were captured by the hundreds—meant a loss of trained seamen into the British prison camps and hulks. Ten thousand men were consumed in a single night in the holocaust of the Nile. With these constant losses, and with small opportunity of training fresh men, the

French navy was bound to sink farther and farther into inferiority.

Spain had languished for years under the imbecile rule of the Bourbons and the incredible mismanagement of Godoy; her navy was in an unsatisfactory condition from the start, and as soon as she entered the war on the French side it was certain to deteriorate from the same causes as affected the French navy. The Netherlands experienced revolution and emigration and attrition until Camperdown saw the destruction of her navy, a thousand killed and wounded and four thousand prisoners. The balance was bound to swing farther and farther in favor of Great Britain.

After the period of great victories other factors began to assert themselves. The British navy continued to expand as fast as ships could be built and men found, somehow, to man them. In seven years its force was almost trebled, at a time when it was generally agreed that nothing less than three years' service was sufficient to train a seaman, and at a time when wastage, from disease, from the accidents of the sea, and from battle casualties, was very severe; when the mere lapse of time saw the superannuation of seamen who were understandably too old for their profession at forty. Even the large mercantile marine and the relentless use of the press could not supply sufficient seamen; the shortage could be deduced from the constantly renewed royal proclamations offering a bounty of no less than five pounds to any able seaman under the age of fifty volunteering for service—and blood money of three pounds to any informer who would deliver up any able seaman to the press; a guinea to anyone whatever who would persuade a landman to volunteer. In this matter Wellington's victories in the Peninsula had an unfortunate effect, for young men of spirit began to enlist voluntarily in the army, at the same time as the army competed for recruits with the navy in the jails and among the young men in trouble. The standard of manning in the British navy suffered, during these years, a small but important decline.

The ranks of the officers had undergone a similar expansion and had suffered very similar wastage. It was more important that a high proportion of the officers were afflicted with the sense of superiority already mentioned, understandably, even excusably, but unfortunately. The victories had been won; it was even more gratifying to believe that they were the consequence of innate qualities rather than of hard work and brilliant leadership, and it would be certainly less gratifying to believe they were the result of French misfortunes. When service at sea was constant and battle more and more rare, there was a natural inclination to devote more attention to seamanship than to warlike exercises. In the prevailing state of mind the lessons of the war were misread. Nelson had written, before Trafalgar, that no captain could be far wrong who laid his ship alongside an enemy. It was an excellent and well-timed order at a moment when Nelson was envisaging a pell-mell battle against an untrained and disorderly enemy, but it did not embody the secret of universal success, and there could easily be occasions when that action could be disastrous. The untrained French gunners were bad marksmen; if the British gunners were drilled to fire three times as fast, they would score three times as many hits even though they were equally bad marksmen. If there was time left over from seamanship drills (and attention to the outward display which is always likely, in a disciplined service during a period of stagnation, to be accepted as a mark of efficiency) it could be employed in gunnery drills devoted to maintaining a high rate of fire; they were impressive to behold and did not have the disadvantages of actual target practice, in which the gunpowder consumed was likely to make paint work dirty and had to be accounted for to a niggardly and hard-pressed government. If the French—or Spanish or Dutch or Italian—captain they might meet did not have the professional ability or the trained crew to enable him to keep his ship out of harm's way they could count on closing rapidly, when superior rate of fire would decide the battle quickly enough, and in any case they could always board, when superior discipline would assert itself at once. There was not much need to think, and there was no urgent need for battle practice.

On the other hand, the American officers had always realized that war with a European power would find them facing numerical odds; it was inevitable that they should devote thought to discovering means of counterbalancing this deficiency. They had had enough experience of actual war in the Mediterranean to discover the promising junior officers and to acquire a fighting outlook rather than a routine outlook. It was plain to them that they must make the best of what they had. Gunnery must be practiced so that no shot would be wasted; discipline and esprit de corps must be developed to make that gunnery even more effective; small-arms exercises were necessary to fit the men for hand-to-hand encounters. The manning problem was by no means as difficult as in England; liberal pay—fifteen dollars a month—and a moderate disciplinary system made the service attractive, especially when embargo and non-intercourse caused periods of unemployment in the extensive mercantile marine. Enlistment for a definite short period—two years—made it easier to obtain recruits, although the system had its own obvious disadvantages, which had made themselves apparent more than once in the Mediterranean and were to do so again. The proportion of able seamen in the American navy was always remarkably high, which made it easier to devote time to battle exercises.

It gave the American officer time to think about the theory of his profession, too, under the stimulus of the likelihood of encountering superior force. There had been exercises with a plotting board in the Tripoli prison; there were constant discussions of theoretical problems during the long years of tension with England. In these discussions the carronade was pitted against the long gun, the small ship against the big ship, the weather gauge against the lee gauge, two ships against one and one ship against two, American methods against British. When the high average of ability among that generation of American captains is taken into account along with their large professional experience, it might be expected that the British would encounter tougher opponents than they had known in a long while. Pride might meet a fall; complacence might change to dismay.

There have been analogous situations in plenty wherein a stronger military power has encountered humiliation at the hands of a hard-fighting and thoughtful weaker power who compensated by efficiency for numerical inferiority. The defeat of the Spanish Armada in 1588 is an early example, when men of genius like Drake and Hawkins and Frobisher led a small and handy force to victory against a fleet of arithmetically overpowering numbers.

There was complacence regarding the naval situation among the British public in 1914; there were both confidence in numbers and a sublime faith in the superiority of British material and British seamen. The German navy had been built up by men who were well aware that they must encounter sooner or later a navy greatly stronger and who had endeavored to prepare for the struggle by the superior efficiency of their ships and their methods. The British defeat at Coronel is strongly reminiscent of the defeat of the *Guerrière* by the *Constitution;* a weaker force, not too well manned (Cradock's crews were mainly reservists), was annihilated by a highly efficient stronger force handled by a man who knew exactly what he was doing and who was ably supported by subordinates trained to a high degree of co-operation. In the state of the public mind—and of a large part of the professional mind—in England in 1914 Cradock could no more have refused battle than Dacres could have done in 1812. And there were subsequent shocks to British complacency too. The destruction of the British battle cruisers at Jutland, the disproportion of the losses in that battle, and the successful withdrawal of the German fleet from an apparently hopeless situation were harsh reminders to the British public that national security could not be entrusted merely to a large output of the shipyards and a semi-religious confidence in the national destiny; that (it was a difficult pill to swallow) other nations might produce navies in no way inferior man for man and ton for ton, and that intelligent preparation was a better weapon than blind faith.

These are lessons that have to be relearned every few generations and can be profitably remembered at any period in a nation's history. They were remembered in England in 1940, when the highly efficient Royal Air Force, handled by men of great ability, beat back the attack of Goering's squadrons which for years had by their mere existence paralyzed the political thought of Europe. Once again determination and fixity of purpose triumphed over irresolution and change of plan, intelligence and courage over obtuseness and overconfidence, material and personal excellence over numbers.

The material excellence of the American ships in 1812 had its origins in the germination of the navy as far back as 1797. America was well served by her chief constructor, Joshua Humphreys, who combined originality of thought with professional ability, and whose shrewdness and tact enabled him to obtain a fair field for the employment of his other qualities. An act of Congress had authorized the manning and employment of frigates; Humphreys saw to it that the frigates were outstanding in their class, taking advantage of an unwonted vagueness in the financial provisions of the act and of its successors. He built with the avowed purpose of producing a frigate more powerful than any frigate yet thought of, of the dimensions of a not-too-small ship of the line. He mounted in the hull the heaviest armament he could venture to mount, having consideration for the fact that Congress had authorized frigates and not ships of the line. The ample funds of which he disposed enabled him to employ the best possible materials and workmanship. The fact that his vessels did not mount as great an armament as their displacement might justify made it possible to provide living quarters for the crew on a scale more liberal than was the case in other ships of war and still left a margin available for larger space than was usual for the storage of food and water and munitions of war. And his native genius combined with his deep learning to give point to his ideas; he designed hulls and sail plans that excited the admiration of those qualified to judge and instilled a living force into his fighting machines.

There is some similarity between the situation of Humphreys' working within the congressional limitation of American ships of war to frigates and that of the German naval constructors after 1918, who were limited by treaty to the construction of ships under ten thousand tons. They made liberal use of the funds at their disposal. The Germans produced the "pocket battleship"; without regard to expense they made use of every means to cut down weight to crowd as much fighting potential as possible within the arbitrary limit. They made use of every possible innovation. They substituted welding for riveting, Diesel engines for steam. The ships they constructed were viewed with dismay by the other naval powers; they seemed to be the equal in fighting power of vessels of twice their displacement. Naval opinion was inclined to lose sight of another aspect of the case: Germany might have produced a still more powerful naval force for the same expenditure of funds if she had not been held within the arbitrary limits of ten thousand tons. In the same way Humphreys might have produced a more powerful force if he had not been restricted by the word "frigate." Had he gone any farther, dissentient voices in Congress could have complained that what he was building were not frigates at all. He went as far as he could.

Yet America was well served by the persistence of the term. *Constitution* and *United States* were frigates from the moment of their conception; they were not "large frigates" or "extra-powerful frigates." The warring countries used the same language; they were both addicted to the usage of rating a vessel by an arbitrary number of guns when actually she carried more

—wartime exigencies, demanding that every vessel should be crammed with armament to the limits of safety and convenience, had brought that about—and, in the language they used, the term "frigate" had an exact connotation. Ships were not expected to engage out of their class. A frigate could run from a ship of the line without dishonor (although in special circumstances Pellew in *Indefatigable* had destroyed the *Droits de l'Homme*) and a sloop could run from a frigate. But throughout the long French wars British frigates had engaged French frigates of superior force without hesitation and usually with success, and the British public had come to expect similar victories as a matter of course; so, for that matter, had the Royal Navy, and the defeat of a British frigate by a frigate of any other nation was a disturbing blow to the national pride.

The German navy in this matter of nomenclature was less fortunate. The German ten-thousand-ton ships were labeled "pocket battleships," and battleships they remained, even though treaty limitations, after they had been designed, brought about the construction of ships of the same tonnage which, with growing experience and a similar lavish expenditure of money, were more effective vessels of war and yet were called "cruisers." The defeat of the *Graf Spee* at the River Plate was the defeat of a battleship in the eyes of the anxious British public and of the watchful American public and even of the propaganda-fed German public—although this does not decry the brilliant handling by Commodore Harwood, in that battle, of the much lighter British cruisers which won the victory.

It is hardly necessary to recall the military situation of the United States at the time when the news arrived of her first naval victories. General Hull had surrendered at Detroit on August 16; Dearborn and Van Rensselaer had had time enough to demonstrate their incompetence or their impotence or worse. The hope of a prompt and bloodless conquest of Canada had been succeeded by a fear of invasion no more reasonable, and despair was reinforced by suspicion. Rodgers had vanished into the Atlantic, and no one knew what had happened to him; if the American army could fail so disastrously at Detroit, what could be expected of the American navy? The *Constitution* had come into Boston with a tale of a hot pursuit, while off New York, by a British squadron—a tale which would lose nothing in the telling of the narrowness of the escape nor of the overwhelming strength of the enemy who had been evaded but who had already captured an American ship of war, the *Nautilus*. True, the *Constitution* had put to sea again, but could there be any reasonable hope of her achieving anything, seeing what her recent experience had been? And her captain bore the ominous name of Hull; he was indeed the nephew of the coward—or traitor—who had surrendered at Detroit.

Chapter IV

AT THE TIME OF THE DECLARATION OF WAR a large part of the American navy was not ready for sea; the Administration had not been capable of coping with the tiresome details of management. The two-year period of enlistment had proved to be a handicap (effective though it was as a stimulant to recruiting) to a government which was shortsighted and improvident; the crews which had been enlisted at the time of increasing tension in 1810 were due for discharge in 1812, and no steps had been taken in advance to replace them. Captain Isaac Hull with the *Constitution* lay in the Chesapeake at Annapolis collecting a new crew. It was not until three weeks after the declaration of war that he was able to sail, even though he was in a fever of impatience to get away—he, like Rodgers, feared the instant arrival of a superior British blockading force; and the Chesapeake was geographically an easier point to watch by a blockading fleet than the New England coast.

Hull was a man not yet forty. He had served his apprenticeship in the mercantile marine; for two years he had been a lieutenant in the *Constitution* and had won notice in command of a brilliant expedition which had cut out a French privateer on the San Domingo coast during the undeclared war with France. He had been commander of the *Argus* in the Tripolitan War, and now for six years—a remarkably long time—he had been captain of his old ship, the *Constitution*, much of that time at sea. With war declared, he was in no doubt as to the use to which he should put his command. He received the news, which traveled slowly over land, that Rodgers had put to sea from New York, and at the earliest moment possible he headed in that direction in accordance with his orders from the Secretary of the Navy. He had no certainty of Rodgers' plans, but he could be sure that the addition of the *Constitution* to Rodgers' force would not make their execution more difficult. In fact, with *Constitution* added to his squadron, Rodgers could well have thought himself superior in strength to Broke if he had been able to obtain particulars of Broke's force, *Africa* and all. The imagination is heated at the thought of that possible fleet action off Sandy Hook.

But Rodgers was at this moment heading for the Azores from the approaches to the Channel, and Broke was off New York in force. Off where Atlantic City now stands—an almost uninhabited island at that time—Hull sighted, in the afternoon of July 17, when he was five days out from the Chesapeake, the sails of ships of war. They could well have been Rodgers' squadron, if Rodgers were acting in accordance with the orders sent from Washington, which he had not received and which commanded him to cruise to the southward from New York. The wind was weak and variable; the afternoon lengthened into evening, and night fell without contact being made. There were four ships toward the land and a fifth farther out to sea, exactly the number Hull could expect to find under Rodgers' command. Hull was cautious; at nightfall he beat to quarters and kept away from the shore, heading for the more isolated ship.

She was the British frigate *Guerrière*, Captain James Dacres; the other four, of course, were the rest of Broke's squadron. *Guerrière* was rejoining after being separated; she was off an enemy's coast, and a hostile force—Rodgers'—was known to be at sea; in the failing light Dacres was bound to be as cautious as Hull was being. His fears were confirmed when the ship that was bearing down on him in the darkness made lantern signals to him which he could not understand. They were not the British recognition signals. He kept his distance until the first light of dawn, when he edged down upon the stranger, which by now he could not doubt was an American frigate. It was his duty to engage her; if she was of greatly superior force he must at least keep in close touch with her, and if possible disable her to give his consorts a chance to overtake her. He was within very distant cannon shot when he sighted, down to leeward, the rest of Broke's force. He identified himself to them and received no answer, for reasons which are obscure to this day. Likely enough Broke took it for granted that Dacres knew who he was; it is equally likely that Dacres' signals were read by *Belvidera*—probably the nearest frigate— and were not seen by Broke's ship, the *Shannon*, although the *Belvidera* assumed that they had been and left it to the senior officer to reply. Dacres thus found himself within range of a powerful American frigate and between her and four unknown ships—and Rodgers was known to be at sea with five ships. Dacres could hardly be blamed for turning tail and doing his best to extricate himself from a situation potentially disastrous. So the great opportunity of bringing the *Constitution* to action passed in a few minutes. Hull, even though the *Guerrière's* movements puzzled him, could have no doubt that he was in the presence of Broke's squadron and not Rodgers', and he turned his stern to the four ships and made the best of his way away from them. The wind was still light and variable; he could foresee a long chase and he hurried his preparations for it. Cutting away part of his taffrail, he was able to point a 24-pounder and a long 18 directly aft and two more 24-pounders through his cabin windows. Moving these prodigious weights of iron called for great exertions on the part of his men, but they were only a foretaste of what was to come. Already the breeze had died away, and he set his boats to tow the lumbering hulk which was the *Constitution* in the absence of a wind.

Then came the lightest of breezes, and Hull set all sail. The most careful organization and good seamanship were required to get the boats in while the ship was under way; with the enemy only half a mile out of range an accident could be fatal, especially as a pursuer could well, if an opportunity presented itself, leave a boat behind to be picked up by a following friendly ship. For half an hour the breeze held. When Hull had been first lieutenant of this same ship she had won a race with a British frigate and a wager for her captain. After six years of command he knew his ship's best points of sailing; and at the end of her last commission she had been hove down and cleaned and had not since had time to grow foul. He had four frigates after him now, and utter destruction as well in the shape of the *Africa*, hull-up over the horizon astern. Broke himself, in the *Shannon*, caught a fortunate flaw of wind and actually came near enough to try a few long shots, but they fell short. Then the breeze died away to nothing, the ships all lying motionless on a glassy sea in the growing heat of the July sun. Out went the boats again, and the dreadful toil at the oars recommenced.

A signal from Broke had summoned to the *Shannon* boats from the rest of the squadron, all helping to tow his ship forward. It was a dangerous development. At this moment Hull's first lieutenant came up with a suggestion—Charles Morris, who as a midshipman had been the first man to board the *Philadelphia* when Decatur burned her in Tripoli harbor. He had ingenuity as well as courage. Soundings had revealed that the ship was in only twenty-six fathoms of water, a mere hundred and fifty feet. The hands who were not at the oars were now set to work rousing out cables and rope, joining all together. While the long line was being completed a cutter was recalled from towing; a kedge anchor was got out and suspended from a strongback in her, aft—the activity on *Constitution's* deck at this moment must have been something to see. The cable was loaded down into the cutter, and away she went under her oars, laying out the cable behind her. With the cable fully out, the suspending line was cut and the kedge dropped to the bottom. Then in *Constitution* the capstan bars were manned and the ship was hauled by brute force up to the anchor. Meanwhile a second cable had been prepared, a second kedge suspended in a second cutter and sent ahead. As *Constitution* passed over the first kedge and it was hauled up and hung again in the first cutter the second kedge was dropped, the nippers clapped on, and the ship hauled forward without losing the way she had acquired.

Given comparatively shallow water, it was a far more efficient method of propelling the ship than tugging her along by oared boats—given also the necessary seamanship and coolness of head, for the possibility of a small blunder that could cost a fatal ten minutes' delay was more than slight. It was only the ship that was being pursued that could make use of the method at decisive ranges; the four long guns pointing aft from the *Constitution's* stern forbade its use by the pursuing ship as soon as she drew near, because at small distances the pursuing ship's boat taking her kedge forward would come within cannon shot. And it must be remembered that if the *Guerrière* had stayed within the long gunshot of the *Constitution* where she had found herself at dawn nothing of the sort could have been attempted. The *Guerrière* would have kept the *Constitution* from launching her boats while Broke's other ships worked up to her. As it was, *Constitution* managed to draw away from *Shannon* despite the number of boats which were towing the British ship.

An hour of this work and a little wind came; boats and kedges had to be hoisted in. A few minutes of wind and then calm again; out went boats and kedges once more, for another hour's work over the glassy sea, the stillness broken only by occasional cannon shots as the pursuers tried the range and found it just too great, and as the pursued warned the enemy's boats not to come too close. To the southward a cat's-paw of wind was seen creeping over the surface of the sea toward *Constitution's* port bow. The yards were braced round, the boats were warned, and she was ready as soon as the breeze reached her, to gain a few priceless feet before the breeze reached the pursuing ships. The breath of wind was hardly more than a breath; as it died away, out went the boats again, and Hull had to make up his mind to a serious sacrifice. There was the drinking water on board; ten tons of it made an inch difference in *Constitution's* draft, and if *Constitution* drew an inch less she might make a hundred yards' better progress in half a day's work when a hundred yards could mean the difference between safety and destruction; but the sacrifice would have to be made now, at this moment—it would be no use regretting not having made it later on when the ship was under fire. So the water was started and the pumps set to work to pump it overside, ten tons of it; ten days' supply at a minimum ration, which meant that if *Constitution* eventually got away her useful career would be shortened by that time.

Shannon was steadily advancing, towed by a dozen boats; kedging and towing in the frightful heat, *Constitution* just maintained her lead. Another breeze and another calm; this time the breeze just suited *Belvidera's* best point of sailing and she gained considerably—it was *Belvidera* which had outsailed *President* less than a month before. Captain Byron in *Belvidera* began to resort to kedging as well, as long as her boats were out of range of *Constitution's* guns. In midafternoon the breeze returned, and lasted for four blessed hours, only the faintest breeze, but enough to make kedging unnecessary. It brought a charge of labor. Now the sails had to be kept wet, for a wet sail holds more of the wind than a dry one. Water had to be hoisted up from the sea to the towering height of *Constitution's* yards and spilled down the sails. Even in the humidity that prevailed—the humidity that made the labor so exhausting—the rate of evaporation from that area of canvas made it necessary that the work should be hard and continuous.

From midafternoon until nightfall the ships crept along with the breeze, no British ship contriving to gain the half mile which was all that was necessary to open a crippling fire, and then with the setting of the sun the breeze died away again and kedging and towing had to be resumed in the hot night. By midnight the breeze had returned, the boats were got in once more, and the ships crept on through the darkness; not too dark to conceal *Belvidera* gaining a little on them. But with the breeze holding steady although light, *Belvidera* was right to leeward; even though she was abeam of the *Constitution* she would not be able to close unless she gained a much greater distance so that she could tack and intercept. At daylight she made her attempt, coming about in an effort to close. It was a situation that called for careful judgment of time and distance on the part of Hull, because another light frigate, *Aeolus*, had found the breeze to her liking during the night and had closed considerably and was on the weather quarter. Hull waited half an hour and then put *Constitution* about. The half hour following was a time of tense excitement in slow motion as the three ships crept along with bare steerageway, *Belvidera* and *Constitution* just out of cannon shot of each other, *Aeolus* close-hauled, trying to anticipate *Constitution* to windward, every ship keeping the hands at work at the endless labor of wetting the sails, and every captain watching as the bearings slowly altered. A shift in the wind, or a variation in its strength—and anything was possible in that weather—could change the whole situation in five minutes. But as the minutes passed, the bearings of the two British ships as taken from the *Constitution* moved slowly aft. She was drawing ahead of *Belvidera* and weathering on *Aeolus*. The British frigates had made their pounce and had missed.

The wind continued steady, even freshening a little, and the slow race went on as the sun climbed higher in the sky. Soon there was a moment of fresh excitement, when a strange sail came up over the horizon to windward, heading directly for them. She was identified quickly enough as an American merchantman, homeward bound, and there was a possibility that she would sail straight into the British arms. Byron hoisted American colors—to encourage her to do so; Hull promptly hoisted British colors, and one sight of those was enough for the merchantman. He put his wheel hard down and proceeded to claw his way to windward out of reach of the creeping ships.

Constitution gained by slow inches on her pursuers as the hours dragged on monotonously, the sheaves wailing in the blocks as water was hauled up to the yards and spilled down upon the ever-drying canvas, with the yards continually being trimmed to the inch with every small shift of the wind, and while weary men and officers, after twenty-four hours of violent exertion and extreme excitement, tried, during their watch below, to snatch a little rest despite the continuing emotion of the situation. *Belvidera* was now dead astern and a full two miles out of gunshot; the other British frigates were farther off still, and farther to leeward, for *Constitution* had eaten her way up to windward more successfully than they, and the *Africa*, the lumbering ship of the line, was hull down to leeward, in the absence of the strong gale which alone would have given her any chance at all to close with the American ship.

During the afternoon *Constitution* little by little increased her lead; even *Belvidera* was being left not merely behind but to leeward, whether the tantalizing breeze freshened or moderated. The sun was setting and night approaching fast when the first real squall approached. Hull, to windward, had the first warning of it and had all hands at their stations and his orders given before it reached *Constitution*. With the first puff he clewed up, got in his light canvas, reefed his heavy canvas. The squall passed astern, blotting *Constitution* from the sight of the British frigates in the gathering night. Hull sheeted home as the violence of the squall died away; under all plain sail, close-hauled, *Constitution* made eleven knots for some exhilarating minutes. The squall reached the British frigates and passed on, revealing them once again to the telescopes on board *Constitution*. The British captains had not been quite as fore-handed; the British crews not quite as smart. During the interval *Constitution* had both head-reached and weathered upon her pursuers. *Belvidera* was several miles away and two points to leeward now; the wind, blowing from *Constitution* to *Belvidera*, interposed a barrier between pursuer and pursued no less impenetrable than it was invisible.

Even so, the danger was not at an end. In the darkness the wind died away steadily again, with every ship setting more sail the instant it became possible, until *Constitution* once more had every inch of canvas spread, and until once more the weary work was resumed of wetting the sails all through the night, the second night of the long pursuit, the third night of the long encounter. The night glasses trained from *Belvidera* toward *Constitution* had increasing difficulty in picking her out in the surrounding darkness; it had to be regretfully admitted that *Constitution* was still slowly drawing away from them, and at the end of the weary night the beginnings of dawn confirmed the conclusion. *Constitution* was hardly in sight, having run her pursuers down almost over the horizon, and the British squadron was strung out in a long straggling line, with *Africa* far behind; there was no sign of any change in the weather which might make the race even.

Soon the last gleam of *Constitution*'s upper sails vanished over the horizon. Pursuit was hopeless now, with the chase able to alter course without being seen, and Broke called his ships together and abandoned the pursuit. He had gained no credit from the incident; even if—as seems certain—*Constitution* was superior to all the British ships at every point of sailing, there had been found nowhere in the British squadron any ingenuity or inventiveness or moral drive sufficient to overcome that hand-icap in the face of the very high standard of Hull's profes-sional accomplishments and the seamanlike qualities of his crew

—who, it must always be remembered, had had only five days at sea in their present enlistment. Their organization and handling by Hull and his officers must have been excellent; there were numerous periods during the chase when a gain of a mile by any one of the three British frigates would have meant disaster, and a single muddle or mistake or error in seamanship, at a time when every man on board was hard at work, could have brought about the necessary delay.

Now Hull and *Constitution* were free; they had vanished over Broke's horizon, and Broke had to decide what to do next; the disappearance of *Constitution* forced him back at once from a stimulating and active tactical offensive to an anxious and wearisome strategical defensive. Broke knew that Hull and Rodgers were now both at sea; what was going on also at Boston and what had happened in New York during the past few days were hard questions for Broke to answer. But Broke also knew that a homeward-bound West Indian convoy—not the one Rodgers believed himself to be pursuing—had recently left the Caribbean and was now in Gulf Stream waters under the convoy of a single frigate, within easy striking distance of Hull, and perhaps of Rodgers too, whose whereabouts were quite unknown to him. What Broke would have chosen to do, if he had been free to choose, was to break up his squadron and station one ship at least off each principal port of the eastern seaboard. By that means he could intercept the returning American merchant ships; and he could not doubt that American privateers were fitting out feverishly, anxious to get to sea and reap a harvest of British shipping. It was far easier—the experience of many years of continental warfare proved it—to catch them emerging from their home ports than to hunt them down at sea.

He did not dare do anything of the kind; with Rodgers at sea he had to keep his squadron united. The most he could do was to watch one single American harbor. Up to the declaration of war the Admiralty had maintained on the Halifax station what might be thought an adequate force, stronger than the whole American navy, considerably stronger if measured by the simple arithmetic of counting heads; but the first moves of the war revealed the weakness of the apparently adequate force when opposed to an enemy enjoying the advantages conferred by an extensive coast and many possible bases, and commanded by men of the quality of Rodgers and Hull.

In the actual event Broke decided not to watch even one American harbor at the moment. A West Indian convoy was too valuable to risk—Rodgers had reached the same conclusion on the opposite side—and Broke elected to guard the present one rather than blockade New York or Boston or the Delaware or the Chesapeake. The fact that the convoy reached home waters without sighting an enemy does not prove that Broke was wrong, any more than the corresponding fact that Rodgers did not sight a convoy while he crossed the Atlantic proves that Rodgers was wrong. Broke had to balance possible losses against possible gains. He quitted the American coast and the next seven weeks were spent covering the West Indian convoy and returning to New York.

During those seven weeks he encountered another of the difficulties which inevitably plague the commanding officer of a blockading squadron. He could not keep his ships at sea indefinitely. Even if Sawyer at Halifax could find storeships for him, and even if those storeships could run the gantlet of the American privateers, and even if they could guess where he was —all of which was doubtful—his ships would wear out slowly, would grow foul, would need repairs and refitting, and supplies that a storeship could not bring. This tiresome limitation on his freedom had to be dealt with by prevision. Ships had to be sent in one by one, in rotation, to complete with stores and carry out necessary refitting, or else the commanding officer might at length find himself with all his ships unfit for service simultaneously.

Three weeks after abandoning the pursuit of the *Constitu-*

tion, when Broke quitted the West Indian convoy and turned back toward the American coast, he detailed one of his frigates to go into Halifax and fit herself again for a further prolonged period at sea. It was the most economical course he could follow; the frigate would be away from his squadron for the least possible time. She headed for Halifax, he for New York. For three days after parting company the frigate held her course for Halifax without incident but very slowly, with constant head winds. Her name was *Guerrière.*

Chapter V

CAPTAIN HULL had to make decisions as well, the moment Broke's royals disappeared below the horizon astern of the *Constitution*. He might have considered himself free to strike with his powerful ship against any British trade route in the world, except for one annoying factor. He had pumped out ten tons of his drinking water. He had been eight days at sea. One fifth or one sixth of his available supply, then, was already consumed or wasted, and his ship's endurance was diminished in that proportion. He had just sighted every ship of Broke's squadron and he knew just where they were, but that certainty would grow smaller with every passing minute. England would undoubtedly make every effort to blockade the American coast, but the war was yet young, and it was unlikely that reinforcements had even been dispatched, far less likely that they had arrived. He could count with whatever certainty there is in war on an unopposed entrance to Boston, and thither he took his way, arriving a week after losing sight of Broke's squadron. His surmise that no British ship of war would be present off the port proved correct. American ships were returning in large numbers, and—without neglecting his duty to his own ship—he did what he could to spread the news that Boston was at present a safe home port.

But he had no certainty that this state of affairs would endure for long. Broke might at any moment detach vessels to watch the port; there might be new arrivals from across the sea. Even Hull, with his sturdy common sense, fell into the almost inevitable wartime error of overestimating the enemy's strength, ingenuity, and speed of movement. In this case the error had only the effect of stimulating him to greater exertions, not of paralyzing his movements as might have been the case with a more timid man. He completed his ship's stores, wrote his dispatches to Washington, and got away again with the first fair wind. It is worth noting that he had to borrow the necessary money from private sources and that the last orders he had received enjoined him, if he had not met Rodgers, to await further orders in New York.

He had to determine where he would strike his blow. From the moment of leaving port the endurance of his ship would begin to diminish with the consumption of his stores; his blow must not waste itself in the air nor permit of being parried by the enemy. The nearest focal point of the enemy's trade routes was, on the face of it, the one to be aimed at. Broke had been left behind off New York and had not shown up off the New England coast. It did not appear likely, then, that he was coming northward and eastward—this was the moment, as a matter of fact, that Broke was going off to cover the West Indian convoy—and it appeared likely that the enemy's communications with his base at Halifax were unguarded. From Halifax it would be an easy move to the St. Lawrence, whither would be flowing the stream of material and reinforcements that Hull could not doubt was being directed to Canada for an attack on the United States. A campaign that would be of direct assistance to America—and that would not be playing Bonaparte's game as much as it played America's—was naturally attractive to an American officer.

To Halifax he went—it is worth noting that he was off Halifax fifteen days after being in sight of Broke—and there he discovered once more the emptiness of the ocean even when all the ships in the world are at sea. He captured nothing and moved on to the St. Lawrence. The harvest was better here. He ravaged the unguarded shipping until the moment of the next coincidence of the chain which led to the great denouement. He overhauled and captured an American brig with a British prize crew on board. The Americans on board, freed from captivity, could give the information that the British refused to give. Broke was in the vicinity. To Hull it was a natural assumption that *Constitution's* presence off Halifax had been reported to Broke and that Broke was in pursuit of him. Hull decided at once on a fresh move. It was the strategy employed by raiders since naval war began, to strike in one area until the strength of the enemy was directed thither, and then to slip away and start again in a fresh unguarded area. The next nearest focal point was Bermuda, and toward Bermuda he directed his course.

Then came the final coincidence. A month after running *Guerrière's* topsails over the horizon at the end of the historic chase, Hull saw them coming up over the horizon again as she was making her way to Halifax in obedience to Broke's orders. Hull had made the rounds of Boston and Halifax and the St. Lawrence; Dacres had been far out in the Atlantic with Broke and the convoy. Both Broke and Hull had made the incorrect deductions, usual in wartime, from imperfect premises; both had acted on the soundest military principles, and this was the result, this entirely accidental meeting hundreds of miles from land.

There was a fresh breeze blowing when the ships sighted each other in the early afternoon, *Constitution* to windward, *Guerrière* to leeward. Hull could bear down toward the stranger in the comforting certainty that although any sail sighted was likely to be hostile he was in command of a ship that could fight any frigate afloat; if by some small chance he was approaching an isolated British ship of the line, or if the stranger were part of a powerful force, he could keep clear of danger as he had done from Broke and the *Africa*. Dacres' business, as captain of a British frigate, was to investigate any strange sail he might sight, and he was sustained by the knowledge that for years British frigates had fought successfully against any vessel inferior to the ships of the line which frigates could count on evading.

Dacres was a man of twenty-eight; he was the son of an admiral who had captured Curaçao in 1807 and a nephew of a captain who had been Sidney Smith's flag captain at the forcing of the Dardanelles the same year, which helped to account for his promotion to post rank at the age of twenty-two, only two years older than was Nelson at the time he reached the same rank. He had commanded ships for six years; he had seen much service; he could be expected to know his business. With the ships closing fast, he soon recognized the stranger to be a ship of war, and promptly cleared for action. He saw that the ship was American immediately after, and he must have known her to be the *Constitution*—although it is hard to determine the exact moment of recognition—at nearly the same instant; only a month earlier he had had her in sight for three days. The realization made no difference to his determination except to strengthen it. He had no doubt whatever that the enemy was of nominally superior force: seeing that he was to leeward, an attempt at escape was easily open to him. It might have been barely possible for a coolheaded man, well informed and of sound judgment, to be certain that *Guerrière*—in the absence of great good fortune—was facing defeat at the hands of *Constitution*, but Dacres did not expect defeat; even the recent encounter had not convinced him of the quality of the American navy. Nor could he have run away in any case without facing the gravest risk, the positive certainty, of a court-martial. At that moment the captain of any British 38-gun frigate who refused battle with the *Constitution* would have been promptly condemned, not merely by legal process, but by the whole of the professional opinion of the Royal Navy. Dacres' judgment was no more unsound than that of any of his colleagues.

He did not handle his ship unskillfully. He reduced his canvas to "fighting sails" (and observed that his opponent was doing the same), and as *Constitution* came rushing down on him he did his best to cut her up during the important minutes of the approach. But he was opposed to a man whose judgment of time and distance was superior to his. Dacres awaited his coming, with his ship hove to, fired a broadside when he judged the ships were within range, and then put his ship before the wind on roughly the same course as the *Constitution's*, in order to prolong as far as possible the period of the approach, and he yawed first to port and then to starboard in order to present his broadside to the advancing enemy and rake him as he came down. Dacres' eye was not keen enough, or excitement may have clouded his judgment, or his gunners were not well enough trained, or the gunnery control—there was an elementary system practiced at that time in all ships—was inefficient. The first invaluable broadside missed clean; either Dacres underestimated the range or the guns were fired at the wrong moment of the roll. After the first broadside, with *Guerrière* before the wind, her gunners were under the additional handicap that every yaw gave notice to Hull, watching carefully on his quarter-deck, that a broadside was imminent. A small application of helm was sufficient to swing *Constitution* away in order to avoid being raked and to bring about an abrupt alteration in the rate of change of range that baffled the British gunners. A shot or two went home, but so few that Hull, his attention concentrated on the enemy's movements, did not notice them. The occasional shots fired by such of *Constitution's* guns as bore during the approach did no particular damage.

For three quarters of an hour the two ships ran before the wind, *Constitution* steadily gaining on *Guerrière*, until the range had closed sufficiently to be decisive. It was no time now for *Constitution* to delay, when one of those broadsides might perhaps shoot away a spar. Hull gave the order to set more sail. Experience had long proved that in action usually it was best to have the ship under "fighting sails"—topsails and jib, with the royal yards sent down—but there were many occasions when ships went into action with all sail set; *Victory* did so at Trafalgar for a similar reason to *Constitution's* now, in order to reduce the time of the approach. *Constitution* was fully manned, her present crew and officers had been on board for the past two months, and her organization—as the escape from Broke's squadron had already proved—was perfect. Even with the guns' crews standing by there were plenty of men available. The main topgallant sail was set with all the rapidity to be expected of well-trained men, and *Constitution* closed the gap between the two ships in five minutes.

It might be expected that *Guerrière* would counter the move by setting more sail also, but Dacres did not attempt to do so. Most probably he was taken by surprise by the rapid action and had not time for anything further; possibly, discontented with the results of the action at long cannon shot, he was willing to allow the enemy to close. *Constitution* came up alongside, and the traditional action, broadside to broadside, began at once and endured for fifteen minutes. *Constitution's* broadside was far heavier than *Guerrière's*—the respective weights have been calculated at 684 pounds to 556—and the disproportion was accentuated by the fact that *Constitution's* far heavier shot were being directed against the far lighter scantlings of the *Guerrière*, while from the moment that losses began the disproportion increased still more with the greater losses of the *Guerrière*. It seems likely that *Guerrière's* guns were served faster than *Constitution's;* it also seems likely that they were not as well pointed. *Constitution* was badly cut up in her rigging, but *Guerrière* lost her mizzenmast, which fell over the disengaged side and, as it dragged in the sea by its uncut standing rigging, both slowed her down and swung her round. Dacres, in his report and in his defense at his court-martial, ascribed his defeat to this incident; but, judging by the small losses *Constitution* had suffered by that time, the argument appears unsatisfactory. Dacres might have done better service to his country if he had frankly stated that he had been beaten by a bigger ship manned by an efficient crew. As it was, *Guerrière* slowed and turned; Hull, who had already been counting on his greater speed to cross her bows, turned with her and raked her crushingly as she lay disabled. With that broadside delivered, he wore round, his ship being still manageable, to cross *Guerrière's* bows again and rake her with his portside guns, which so far had hardly been in action. Those two broadsides reduced *Guerrière* from a fighting ship to a beaten wreck; there was that much truth in Dacres' plea.

Hull's judgment of speed and distance was not so accurate at this instant. He had shaved across *Guerrière's* bows so closely that her bowsprit reached over *Constitution's* quarter-deck and then caught in her mizzen rigging. The two ships swung counterclockwise, as the way that *Constitution* carried bore her on, dragging *Guerrière* round with her. There was contact between the two ships; there was *Guerrière's* bowsprit as a boarding bridge if either side chose to take advantage of it. But it would be a perilous passage at best in that tossing sea, with the ships plunging and the bowsprit slowly working its way round as they turned. It would be the more perilous because in both ships the boarding parties rushed to the point of contact, forward in the British ship and aft in the American, and faced each other across the gap.

They were only a few feet apart, close enough for musketry to be accurate even with a high sea running. Losses were heavy on both sides, particularly among the officers who started forward to lead their men on. The marines of both countries claimed their victims. Charles Morris, *Constitution's* first lieutenant, whose suggestions regarding kedging had been so effective a month before, was shot down as he leaped upon the taffrail, but his wound was not mortal and he lived to receive his promotion to captain for the victory. Dacres had run forward and climbed upon the hammocks in their nettings on the fore-castle the better to view the situation, and his conspicuous position brought him a wound from a marksman in *Constitution's* mizzentop.

Down under his feet, on the fore part of the main deck which had been so thoroughly swept by *Constitution's* last two broad-sides of grape- and round shot, a few disciplined survivors shook themselves out of their dazed condition and, in the dark of the smoke and timber dust, manned such guns as would bear and were not dismounted, and fired into *Constitution's* stern—into Hull's cabin. So close were the ships that the flame of the explosions, or burning wads, started a fire here, but disciplined men in the American ship, although ignorant of when the next discharge would come to destroy them, extinguished the fire.

There was not time for much firing, nor was there much time for the boarding parties to face each other. The ships swung; they rose and plunged on a following sea, and *Guerrière's* bow-sprit tore free from *Constitution's* mizzen rigging. *Constitution* went on ahead, leaving *Guerrière* behind, still held back by her trailing mizzenmast. Dacres could count now on a few min-utes' grace in which to clear away the wreck and to reorganize his defense, but at that moment both his other masts went over the side, they and their rigging having been badly wounded during the action. The loss of her masts, and of their steadying effect on her roll, made *Guerrière* helpless. She lay in the trough of the sea, rolling frantically and fast, dipping her open gun ports below the surface, first on one side and then on the other; the guns could hardly be loaded or run out. There was just a chance that by setting sail on the surviving bowsprit Dacres could get his ship before the wind so that she could pitch instead of roll, and he actually set about the task; but the spritsail yard was wounded, too, and gave way under the strain, and *Guerrière* continued her frightful rolling in the trough of the sea; it is not pleasant to think of the condition of her sixty wounded as the surgeon and his mates endeavored to work upon them as she rolled. The sea was pouring in through a score of shot holes below the water line; the fallen masts, overside, were pounding against the ship's sides.

Constitution ran before the wind until her crew could reeve new running rigging to replace what had been shot away. The work was done quickly and well. New braces allowed the yards to be trimmed; the fore- and main-courses were set, and, once more under command, *Constitution* wore round and her men stood to their guns while the wind brought the dismasted hulk down within range of them again in the gathering darkness. There was still a British flag to be seen, which seamen had hoisted on the stump of the mizzenmast, but it would be simple slaughter to fire into the helpless wreck. There was nothing dishonorable about surrendering a ship that had fought to the last gasp. Wooden ships, especially ships of the line, could be beaten into helplessness long before they sank, and to continue action in those circumstances meant the killing of unresisting men; it was not until 1914 that a new convention arose —partly as a result of the vastly greater ranges at which naval battles were fought—under which it was deemed disgraceful to haul down one's colors when in a helpless situation.

Hull sent a boat to demand the surrender which he fully expected, and Dacres surrendered, with the approval of his surviving officers. Later one of those latter wrote to a friend, "It was extremely fortunate that the Americans returned to us after we were dismasted." *Guerrière* was sinking; the fact was so obvious that all hands in both ships set to work at once to transfer the wounded to the *Constitution;* and it is an interesting commentary on the standard of seamanship in the two ships that the work was accomplished, in the dark, with a considerable sea running, and with *Guerrière* rolling wildly, and yet without mishap. Seventy-eight of the *Guerrière's* crew of 272 were killed or wounded, nearly thirty per cent; more nearly still with allowance for the ten Americans on board whom Dacres permitted to remain out of the fight. In 1806, when *Guerrière* had been captured off the Faroes by the *Blanche*, her French crew of over 320 men had suffered a loss of fifty casualties before surrendering. *Constitution* had lost less than three per cent of her 456 men, and it would have been less still if Hull had anticipated that lunge of *Guerrière's* bowsprit. She was ready to fight another battle; *Guerrière*, set on fire by her captors in view of the impossibility of salving her, blew up and went to the bottom.

Yet Hull did not contemplate the possibility of seeking another battle nor of continuing his cruise. He had been out less than three weeks, but he had two hundred prisoners on board as well as wounded. A ruthless man determined to stay at sea might perhaps have risked taking a prize or two, or meeting one or two American merchant ships into which he could have put his prisoners. In the twenty-five minutes of firing he had not consumed a third of his ammunition, and his ship had suffered no serious material damage. The arguments in favor of getting to sea from Boston when he sailed had more force still, seventeen days later. Nevertheless, Hull thought of nothing except returning there, and for a very obvious and excellent reason. He wanted America to have the earliest news of his victory.

He turned back, contended for ten days against baffling and unfavorable winds, and entered Boston on August 30, 1812. He could announce himself as the victor in the most important single-ship engagement in the history of his country, and ironically he was never again to hold a fighting command.

Chapter VI

OPINION IN NEW ENGLAND had been strongly against war. Just as during the days of non-intercourse and embargo, some mercantile interests were prepared to evade the law and to continue commercial relations with Britain; at this very time the British forces in Canada were being fed on supplies sent up from America. There was intense dislike—hatred—of Mr. Madison, his Administration, and his principles. The political judgment of many in New England, shrewder in this case than Mr. Madison's, condemned Bonaparte for the unprincipled tyrant that he was; there were patriotic men who felt dismay at the prospect of aiding tyranny in a war against freedom. They knew a dilemma unknown to those who merely desired to make a profit; they were tempted to extricate themselves from it by secession from the Union. Political hatred, commercial interest, and distrust of Mr. Madison's judgment made a powerful combination; and this was in a country whose chief historical memory was one of successful rebellion against authority.

The beginning of the war had been gloomy. General Hull's astonishing surrender at Detroit was a shattering blow to the hopes that had been entertained of an easy—even a bloodless—conquest of Canada. It was a moral disappointment as well as a military defeat, in that it proved that at least some elements in Canada were prepared to fight. It provided a further argument for those people who mistrusted Mr. Madison's judgment. The British government, conducting a war for national existence, and aware of the existence of a potential separatist movement in New England, had no scruples in the matter. It was prepared to make use of any factor, a mere desire to make money or personal jealousy or local jealousy or actual treason, that would simplify its task. In the matter of blockade, in the matter of granting licenses for American ships, and in the matter of trading with the enemy, its policy was not to rouse the antagonism of the mass of the people.

And the mass of the people might be swayed by an active and intelligent minority. There was a lack of the symbols and simplifications that could influence the unthinking; and the news from Detroit could implant the uneasy suspicion that they were on the losing side—and there was an absence of the inspiring leadership which could call forth the determination to see the matter through.

It was into this atmosphere that Hull returned with the news of his victory. He had two hundred prisoners to put ashore under guard. He had sent to the bottom of the sea the *Guerrière*, whose appearance, the cut of whose jib, had been familiar to so many in that seafaring community. He had in his power one of those lordly British captains whose bland—or not so bland—assumption of superiority had irked even an Anglophile society. He had scored a victory over the British navy which had been victorious over every other nation on earth, and he had scored that victory by a bold and vigorous offensive in the face of peril. The news was exhilarating. There could hardly be a croaker to point out that this was no more than a pinprick in the rhinoceros hide of British naval power. When even the well informed could be carried away by enthusiasm, the unlettered or unthinking masses were bound to be influenced yet more strongly. The quite serious danger of a pro-British (or anti-Washington) movement in New England began to decline from its peak, although it remained serious.

A week after Hull's triumphant return, news began to filter through from New York to add to the exultation. Captain Porter had returned in the frigate *Essex* with a remarkable story of successes and escapes. His ship had been undergoing repairs when Rodgers sailed for his encounter with *Belvidera*. The repairs completed, Porter sailed on July 3; at that moment *Belvidera* was back in Halifax, and Broke was not due to start from there with his united squadron until July 5. *Essex* got clear away and headed toward Bermuda as a focal point. Porter's judgment was proved correct, for not far from Bermuda *Essex* sighted, at night, a British convoy—seven troopships carrying British soldiers from the West Indies, where the recent conquest of the French possessions made their presence unnecessary, to Halifax.

The escort was the frigate *Minerva;* she was considerably smaller than *Essex* and might be considered considerably weaker —the question of comparative force is complicated by the fact that *Essex* was armed with carronades, making her much more powerful at short range and much weaker at long range. During the night encounter the question was made more complicated still by the fact that Hawkins in the *Minerva* was never sure that the *Essex* was not one of the three big American frigates which could have shot him to pieces in ten minutes' firing. The night ended with honors even. Porter had captured one transport, with two hundred soldiers; Hawkins had escaped with the other six and his own ship intact.

Porter bore away; subsequent days brought him further prizes, and on August 13 he made an important capture, the British sloop *Alert*. Porter lured her within range by posing as a merchantman, fired two crushing broadsides into her as she tried to make off, and received her surrender—it was hopeless for her to fight, as *Essex* was four times her strength. Porter used her as a "cartel," putting on board of her some of his numerous prisoners, whom he paroled, and sending her with them to Halifax. Another prize awaited him on his homeward way. He just evaded Broke, who was now returning from his escort duty, and he entered New York on September 7. He had taken ten prizes, with more than four hundred men on board, including two hundred soldiers who would otherwise have been destined for the invasion of the United States. He had captured a British ship of war, whose colors he brought in in triumph. He had twice given Broke the slip. It was small wonder that his news swung further the revulsion of feeling initiated by the capture of the *Guerrière*.

Meanwhile Admiral Sawyer was writing from Halifax, dating his letter from the *Africa* and addressing it to Croker, the secretary to the Lords of the Admiralty: "It is with extreme concern I have to request you will be pleased to lay before the Lords Commissioners of the Admiralty the enclosed copy of a letter from Captain Dacres, of H.M. late ship Guerriere . . ." Dacres was writing from Boston, and his letter began, "I am sorry to inform you . . ." Sawyer's covering letter expressed his conviction that *Guerrière* had been defended to the last. He estimated that the *Constitution* was "of very superior force"; he gave no express opinion regarding the propriety of having engaged her, but the tone of his letter left no doubt that he approved.

The British public was as shocked at the news of the loss of the *Guerrière* as the American public was delighted. The last time the British flag had been hauled down in a single-ship action was in 1803, and during the intervening nine years British pride had been gratified and inflated by victories innumerable. The press displayed uncalculating annoyance and dismay. There was even a hint of condemnation for Dacres because he had surrendered and had not gone down fighting, even though professional opinion was on his side on that particular point— as one naval officer wrote, "The blood of every forfeited life would have been upon him."

Even the more sober press was startled and disappointed. The measure of the public interest is displayed in the amount of editorial comment devoted to this one frigate action (the loss of the *Alert* was accepted as one of the inevitable incidents of war) at a moment when events of immense importance were happening elsewhere. Wellington had won his victory of Salamanca and had made his triumphant entry into Madrid. Bonaparte had entered Moscow, and the news that the city had been burned arrived at the same time as Dacres' report; even though acute guesses were being made that Bonaparte was about to be forced into retreat, that imminent possibility was not regarded as compensation for the loss of the *Guerrière*. Brock had defeated and captured Hull at Detroit, but that startling military victory did not salve the national irritation over the minor naval defeat.

Professional opinion in the press endeavored to strike a more restrained note. Naval officers wrote, pointing out the great superiority of strength of the *Constitution;* at first their arguments were handicapped by the use of the term "frigate" to describe the American ship, but later, as public dismay still was evident, they freed themselves from the handicap and wrote about "disguised ships of the line," falling into the other extreme of exaggeration. They pointed out that *Constitution* had fought at an advantage, but they were blind to the argument that this was because she was better handled—it could only be the result of bad luck. They pointed out the weakness of *Guerrière's* crew, with numerous officers and men away in prizes; they refrained from calling attention to the smallness of the damage inflicted on the *Constitution*—indeed, it appears that they could form no idea of how small it was. The court-martial findings aided them in advancing the suggestion that *Guerrière* was in bad condition, that her masts fell from their own rottenness rather than as a result of the enemy's fire. It was not long before they were suggesting that British crews contained numerous untrained men and boys, and then that the American crews were all trained seamen and further included many Englishmen— missing the point (made later very neatly by Theodore Roosevelt) that in that case *Guerrière* lost because Americans would not fight against their own country while *Constitution* won because Englishmen would. The whole question of the presence of British seamen in American ships was very much labored; Englishmen did not like to think that America could maintain an efficient navy without their services.

That was the point which no one in England wanted to admit: that some other nation could fight at least equally well at sea. It was the hour of England's pride; perhaps it was the hour when pride was growing into vanity, when confidence was breeding carelessness. This vanity was of recent growth. During the Dutch wars there had been very few suggestions that Dutchmen as a race were not as efficient fighting men at sea as Englishmen were; on the other hand, the nation took pride in the fact that it had contended victoriously against men who were as good as they were. The French navy of the Bourbon kings commanded British respect, yet now it was a bitter pill to swallow to admit any approach to equality as regards a new and upstart navy.

An anonymous correspondent in the *Naval Chronicle* came near to facing the issue. Writing in November 1812, after the receipt of Dacres' report and before the arrival of any fresh news, he displayed commendable restraint and caution. He alluded to the suggestion that *Guerrière* had been unlucky, and to the frequently expressed hope that other British frigates would be more successful. "I hope sincerely, I have little doubt they will," he wrote; but he went on to say, "But the victory will be dearly bought; we cannot expect an easy conquest," and, in a later passage, "It will be no bloodless conquest, for the Americans have manifestly great advantages, and are manned with *able* seamen"—the anonymous writer was responsible for the significant italics. He pointed out that Sawyer had been given insufficient force to accomplish the double object of watching the American ships of war and guarding convoys, and he did not hesitate to advance the suggestion that the best way to deal with the American nuisance was to swamp the opposition by the immediate dispatch of heavy reinforcements of ships of the line. That was as far as any Englishman could be expected to go, and much farther than most Englishmen were prepared to go; he was clearly of the opinion that the American navy was not to be trifled with, and he was willing to forgo the vainglory of victories against odds in favor of the solid advantages to be derived from the use of overwhelming force. But he was almost alone so far in his opinion; editorial comment in the *Naval Chronicle* was still voicing the professional feeling that "an English frigate of 38 guns should cope successfully with a 44 gun ship of any nation."

It was while this rather depressing correspondence was appearing in the English press that America was not only indulging in the exultation of victory but was responding to its stimulus. Cities and states and government vied with each other in voting honors and rewards to Hull and his crew. Hull was feted wherever he appeared. He was a man of self-restraint and of a patriotism that recognized no limits. He saved his government a good deal of embarrassment by agreeing cheerfully to his supersession in the command of the *Constitution*—the order for that had been made out after his unauthorized departure from Boston and before his return—and he accepted the thankless appointment to supervise the harbor defense of New York. His advice, given in Washington whither he was summoned to make a personal report, directed the enthusiasm of Congress and the new energy of the administration into reasonable channels.

A hurried vote by Congress appropriated funds for the building of a better fleet—four ships of the line and six more heavy frigates. It could not be known whether the lethargy which the British government had so far displayed on the American coast would continue long enough to enable those ships to be completed or to get to sea, but it was worth trying. Meanwhile the President and the Secretary of the Navy turned their attention to the matter of making use of what naval strength was available, and they did so with all the enthusiasm of converts. All the old fears of the growth of a naval caste were forgotten, and so were the gloomy fears which had once led to the contemplation of the desirability of laying up the whole fleet. In sending orders to Decatur and Rodgers they could find a welcome distraction from the heartbreaking news of General Hull's surrender; with a new-won insight into the importance of naval affairs they sent orders to Captain Isaac Chauncey to give up the command of New York Navy Yard and to assume the command on Lakes Erie and Ontario—a decision made in the nick of time which was to affect the whole course of the war. Every day had brought the cheerful news of the return of American merchant ships; with the ships safely in harbor, and with the seamen available for fresh enterprises, they could congratulate themselves on this undeserved good fortune, especially as now they could perceive what disasters might have overtaken them.

This is the moment to devote some attention to the reverse of the medal, even though it involves the proverbially unsatisfactory discussion of hypothetical campaigns. The shortcomings of the American administration have been debated by historians, both American and British; not so much has been written about the failures of the British Cabinet and the Admiralty. Despite long warning of the possibility of war, the precautions taken on the American seaboard were inadequate, and it is hard to believe that they were necessarily so. Sawyer's force based on Halifax was not nearly large enough for the work to be undertaken. As has already been pointed out, it was barely strong enough, when massed, to face the American navy if the latter were concentrated too. There was nothing whatever left over for any of the other duties.

It is readily accepted that with the necessity of watching the French navy, at least until war between France and Russia was quite certain, nothing could be spared from the European

theater to reinforce Sawyer; perhaps it is accepted without sufficiently weighing the arguments in favor of taking increased
risks. Three ships of the line and ten frigates might have been
scraped together and dispatched across the Atlantic in early
1812; in view of the inactivity of the French navy, it can hardly
be argued that such a detachment could have risked greater loss
at the hands of France than was actually experienced at the
hands of America. Three squadrons the size of the one Broke
eventually assembled could have been maintained off the American coast, and if Rodgers on his first sortie from New York
had promptly encountered one and had been driven back into
harbor—or even conceivably had met with disaster—the effect
would have been profound. Frigates backed by ships of the line
could have watched during the summer months of 1812 Boston,
New York, and the Delaware. The returning American mercantile marine could have been captured wholesale, paying dearly
for having hurried to sea in the spring to evade the embargo imposed by the administration. The losses could not have failed
to be demoralizing. One single naval disaster in these circumstances could have been fatal and might not have been unlikely;
if the overwhelming force which captured the *President* in
1815 had been present in 1812 and had achieved a similar success in the opening days of the war (even as it was, only Hull's
seamanship saved *Constitution*), American public opinion
might have forced a dejected administration into accepting a
peace indistinguishable from surrender. Whether the subsequent history of the world would have been the happier would
be a subject for debate far less profitable than the consideration
of the shortcomings of the Admiralty. That consideration is
necessary to reveal the importance of the achievements of
Rodgers and Hull.

Chapter VII

THE LONDON "GAZETTE" of the date August 12, 1812, carried the brief announcement that "Admiral Sir John Borlase Warren, Bart., K.B., is appointed commander in chief of H.M.'s squadron on the Halifax and West India stations, and down the whole Coast of America." It was an important unification of command, making it more practicable to combine the strengths of the squadrons based to the north and south of the United States, and it was the first hint that the Admiralty suspected that large forces might eventually have to be employed, for Warren was an admiral of enormous seniority—he had commanded in chief the squadron that had wiped out Bompart and his unlucky expedition to Ireland as far back as the fatal year of 1798.

The command he was being given was nevertheless more important than anything he had experienced up to date, for in effect he was now made responsible for the conduct of the whole naval war against the American seaboard; he was America's chief enemy. His appointment had been decided upon before much news of the progress of the war had reached England. It was not anticipated that there would be any desperate fighting, if any at all. The admiral needed for the command, in this case, would be (besides being senior enough to command the commanders in chief at Halifax and in the West Indies) a methodical hard worker, capable of carrying out the routine work of distant service without friction—discipline and promotion, reliefs and refits, water and provisions, and all the other innumerable details which commanders in chief had to deal with in those days aided by staffs ludicrously small by modern standards. No one expected that he would have to deal with any serious strategical or tactical problems—nothing to compare, for instance, with those Pellew might have to face at any moment off Toulon—and, as an administrator, he was known to be efficient although somewhat easygoing.

He was, besides, a man of more ingratiating disposition than many naval officers who had fought through seventeen years of war (he was, remarkably, an M.A. of Cambridge University and there are hints in Nelson's correspondence that he was something of a humbug) and he had had a fair share of the diplomatic experience a flag officer was likely to enjoy. Now he was likely to have more, for he was empowered to make contact with the American government and suggest the re-establishment of peace on the basis of the recent revocation of the Orders in Council. The inevitable delays resulting from the difficulty of communication across the Atlantic (which had hampered every negotiation so far) were as much in evidence as ever. Despite the favorable season, he encountered a series of tremendous gales while on his way to Halifax, in one of which the sloop *Magnet* which accompanied him was lost with all hands. Warren's instructions were dated August 6; Monroe's reply was dated October 27. By that time not merely had Hull returned with the news of his victory but Rodgers and Decatur had got to sea again, and no one could tell what triumphs they would shortly report—in fact, at the very time when Monroe was writing his reply the *Macedonian* was on her way to America as Decatur's prize.

Mr. Madison was in no mood for compromise. The revocation of the Orders in Council had removed one source of grievance—provided, of course, that the British Cabinet really meant what it said—but another remained. Warren's letter made no suggestion that the Admiralty was willing to forgo the impressment of men from American ships. Monroe replied that peace was impossible while the Admiralty insisted on its right to impress; more forcibly he took up the perfectly correct attitude that as his government regarded the practice as an outrage it must cease before negotiations could be resumed. Warren had no authority to negotiate on the matter at all; far less could he give any undertaking that impressment from American ships would be discontinued in the event of an armistice. In consequence the move toward peace ended with Monroe's reply. The British government was prepared to go on fighting to maintain a claim which was quite indefensible, while giving way over a matter in which they could advance reasonable arguments in support of their position.

Warren's instructions went far beyond the authority to negotiate for an armistice. The British government was aware of the state of discontent existing in America regarding the policy of the Administration—a brief study of the virulent New England press might give even an exaggerated idea of it—and Warren was ordered to take every opportunity of encouraging and profiting by that discontent. He was empowered to negotiate with any portion of the United States that might want to make a separate peace; he might promise immunity from capture, resumption of commercial relations, local cessation of hostilities, and he set himself to this part of his task with a good deal of ingenuity and skill, even though the moment—if there had ever been one—for encouraging active rebellion had passed before he could take advantage of it.

The situation was complex enough to admit of the exercise of his ingenuity; that it was so was largely Madison's fault. France was at war with England, America was at war with England, yet legally in American eyes France was no more than a neutral in the Anglo-American war. Spain and Portugal were bound in alliance with England by treaties as solemn as the written word permitted, but Madison would not define the attitude of the United States toward these countries; it was not easy for him to do so, admittedly, for the treaty of alliance between Spain and England was signed by the Spanish Regency that was carrying on what was undoubtedly a war of independence against Bonaparte. A false step on Madison's part might well find the United States committed to a war one of whose objectives would be the establishment of Joseph Bonaparte on the throne of Spain in defiance of the wishes of the Spanish people expressed in the life-and-death struggle at present being waged in the Peninsula. Portugal had been wantonly invaded by French armies and thoroughly pillaged before Wellington succeeded in turning them out; was America to pledge herself to action which, if successful, must end in French armies looting Lisbon? The Spanish colonies both north and south of the Isthmus of Panama were growing restive under Spanish rule; America was bound to turn a benevolent eye on any movement toward independence, but such benevolence would be resented by any Spanish government whatever—it would infuriate the Regency in Cádiz, but also Joseph Bonaparte at present in flight from Madrid, the dethroned Carlos IV at present in exile in Rome, and the shadowy Ferdinand VII in prison in Valençay, to say nothing of Bonaparte himself momentarily in Moscow.

In the absence of any public statement of policy the American merchant was left to choose his own course of action. Legally he could still trade with Spain and Portugal (what was illegal was his acceptance of a British license, which was a logical point in a world seemingly devoid of logic) and he might be the more ready to trade as he was likely to be convinced that those countries were waging war defending their liberties against a tyrant—although the feverish trade with Quebec was proof that some of his compatriots did not have any scruples at all. American trade with the Peninsula was of the greatest importance to England. Wellington's dispatches teem with references to supplies from America. "All this part of the Peninsula has been living this year on American flour." "I requested Mr. Stuart to take measures to get corn from the Brazils and from the North American States." Although Wellington's fore-thought and providence made the situation not quite desperate —"I desired that the magazines of the army might be augmented from a stock from three months' consumption to one for six months' consumption"—it became apparent that provisions from America were necessary to maintain the British effort in the Peninsula, despite Wellington's search for other sources of supply in Canada and Egypt and the Barbary States.

This was Warren's opportunity to kill two birds, or three birds, with one stone. From Halifax and Bermuda he began to issue licenses to American ships, giving them immunity from capture while they were engaged on voyages to and from Lisbon. During the periods of non-intercourse and embargo a wide connection had been built up with those merchants who were willing or anxious to evade the regulations of the United States government; it was easy enough to make the new system known to them. The cargoes could be sold to the Portuguese government, or to private merchants in Lisbon. They might feed the Portuguese army or the Portuguese civilian population; in either case it was a burden lifted from the shoulders of the British government, which would have had to undertake the task—and could well have found it impossible—if it had not been performed by American private enterprise.

There was more than a possibility that some of the supplies might find their way into British government hands and might feed British soldiers; some of the flour might be baked into biscuits to feed British sailors who might fight American ships; that possibility did not check the trade that was carried on. We find Wellington writing as early as September 1812, "I am very glad that Mr. Forster has given licenses to American ships to import corn to Lisbon." Wellington was a man of the strongest common sense and of a clear insight into human nature. We find him writing at the same time, pressing that Portuguese ships should be licensed in a similar way to trade with American ports. That would render him less dependent on American shipping; also he warned that there was every chance that American ships, crossing the Atlantic protected by their licenses, would be tempted to turn aside toward the end of their voyage and run the blockade into French ports. It would be well to assume that a man guilty of one knavery could be capable of another.

By the issue of licenses Warren could not only keep Wellington's army fed, he could retain the good will of the American mercantile community. He was sowing the seeds of discord—if any more needed to be planted—between that community and the American government if the latter could ever nerve itself to cut off this profitable business. American ships sailing from American ports carried with them American newspapers and American news; for Warren they constituted an invaluable source of information regarding American public opinion, regarding the movements of American ships of war, and also regarding any attempts to maintain American trade along lines that the British government did not approve of. The New England states were profiting by this system of licenses, while the southern states were suffering from the interference with their necessary seaboard communications. Later a proclaimed blockade of the southern seaboard hampered those communications even worse. There was at least the chance that the sectional favor he was conferring would lead to sectional jealousies and from there to sectional strife.

Warren's astute handling of the situation did not lead to all the advantages that he expected, and it led to some unexpected difficulties, of which the principal one arose from the necessity for payment for the American supplies. Portugal, devastated by war and with much of her manpower conscripted into her army, had little enough to export in return. A little could be done by sending British manufactured goods to Lisbon for sale by Portuguese merchants to Americans, but that did not bridge the gap. All the large balance had to be paid for in cash, in gold and silver. The problem had been exercising Wellington's mind (Wellington fought a series of successful campaigns while acting as his own paymaster general and economic adviser as well as his own chief of staff and commissary general) even before the war began, during the period of the embargo. "The exporters of specie, to the great distress of the army and the ruin of the country, are the American merchants . . . these merchants cannot venture to take in payment bills upon England . . . they must continue therefore to export specie from Portugal." Again, "When the Americans sell their corn in Lisbon they must receive payment in money." In the midst of commanding England's army in a desperate war he was writing such lines as, "The merchants of England will of course send Colonial goods and merchandise where they can sell it with advantage," but even he had to set limits on his activities—"I cannot enter into the detail of sending Colonial goods or merchandise to pay for corn."

The final result was a constant drain of gold and silver from England to America at a time when the British government was at its wit's end to find any supply of the precious metals. England had to endure the troubles resulting from a paper currency, inflation, and a rising cost of living, while Wellington, who needed hard cash to pay his army's way during its constant movements in the Peninsula, had to devote many anxious hours as to how to proportion his limited supplies between paying his long-enduring troops and his Spanish muleteers and buying the vital stores from America. It is hardly necessary to add that the American merchants did not suffer. The troops fell into six months' arrears of pay, the muleteers and the Portuguese middlemen into as much as a year, but the Yankee captains sailed home with the gold and silver which, by the end of the war, gorged the New England banks and was to play an important part in American expansion and in the later development of American industry.

Warren was not to blame for Wellington's money troubles; he carried out his own duties with regard to trade with America with notable tact and ability, but he had other and more difficult duties to perform, wherein he did not find American private enterprise as obliging. From the moment when war appeared imminent, American shipowners had turned their thoughts to privateering. It was an enterprise that could not but appeal to the American temperament and to the shipping interests. Ships and seamen would be idle; the vast British trade offered the prospect of rich prizes. Privateering offered scope for initiative and ingenuity as well as for courage and endurance. It had some of the attractions of novelty and little of the distasteful routine of humdrum merchant voyaging. There would be individual prizes of enormous value, and the chance of taking one added the fascination of a lottery to an already attractive business enterprise; for the seaman as well as for the owner. The chance that the owner might lose his ship and every penny invested; the chance that the seaman might lose his life —or at least spend a considerable part of it in the curiously uncomfortable British prisons—was likely to be forgotten by those imbued with the gambling spirit. So that while one considerable portion of the American community planned to accept British licenses and to earn the steady profits of the Lisbon trade, and incidentally to aid liberty in its struggle against tyranny, another portion planned to go out a-privateering and to give the British a taste of what it was like to have one's commerce interfered with.

There were owners who could form a shrewd estimate of the military situation, who knew how weak were the British forces off the American coast at the outbreak of war, who perhaps could even foresee the powerful influence that would be exerted at first by the American navy, and who hurried to sea every ship in which they could mount a few guns and into which they could cram a few extra hands who were attracted by the prospect of prize money. They could hope that they could make speedy captures before the British counterarrangements began to function—just as Raeder's U-boats reaped a rich harvest off the American seaboard in the spring of 1942.

There were owners who took a longer view, foresaw a time when prizes would be harder to come by, and made plans for a future in which hard fighting and long voyages were to be expected. There were conferences between the speculative owner and his shipwright in which the relative merits of the long gun and the carronade were debated as well as those of the fore-and-aft and the square rig; in which the fighting capacity of the British brigs of war was seriously estimated and a nice balance struck between the size of the crew and the store-carrying capacity of the ship. Speed and handiness were first essentials; speed with which to overtake the prey and handiness to avoid superior forces. The ability to work fast to windward was eminently desirable as affording a means of escape as well as chances to snatch a prize from a convoy without the escort being able to interfere. This was the period of the early flowering of American shipbuilding, although the day of the clipper ship was yet to come; the Baltimore schooner was already famous and combined the necessary qualities of speed and hardiness. Many of the most successful of the privateers—*Rossie* and *Comet*, for example—were schooner-rigged, although brigs and ships also earned dividends. Schooners provided two thirds of the total of vessels engaged in privateering, but rather less than half the tonnage.

An armament sufficient at least to outfight the guns carried by many British merchantmen was also necessary, as well as a numerous crew to overpower the victim when alongside and to supply crews for taking the prizes into port. Hard fighting was not usually expected, but there were owners who strengthened the sides of their ships to keep the shot out, mounted batteries of powerful guns, and sent out veritable ships of war representing a large outlay of capital. They could count then on their ships being able, if the necessity could not be avoided, to beat

off or to overpower a British sloop of war—and there were occasional valuable cargoes, of specie especially, to be found in the
smaller armed ships of the British navy or of the packet services.

As with every speculative enterprise, there were plenty of
people to be found who risked their capital with an insufficient
knowledge of the conditions or with inadequate preparation.
They were liable to come to grief with a finality hardly to be
equaled on the stock exchange or the grain market. From the
moment of the outbreak of war British naval captains began to
report captures. Captain Hockings of the *Dominica*, reporting
to Sir F. Laforey, had "the satisfaction to acquaint you of the
capture of the American schooner Providence, privateer of
Providence," pierced for twelve guns and with a complement
of sixty men. Lieutenant Loch, acting in command of H.M.
brig *Rover*, announced that he had "this day detained the
American schooner, letter of marque, Experiment, Rider master, after a chase of nine hours"—the square rig had overtaken
the fore-and-aft rig in these two cases.

Allowance should be made for the fact that most American
merchant ships venturing out of port took out letters of marque.
They were inexpensive and easily obtained; the ship ran no
additional danger in carrying one, seeing that she and her cargo
were forfeit in any case should she meet a British cruiser, and if
by good fortune she should encounter an unescorted British
merchant ship the letter of marque gave her the right to capture
her if she could. In consequence many of the captures reported
by British ships of "letters of marque" and "privateers" referred
really to ships which were blockade runners first and privateers
second; there were tempting profits to be made in the trade
with Bordeaux and Nantes, as Wellington with his encyclo-
pedic information had pointed out. The figure of 526, as the
total of letters of marque issued during the war, is somewhat
misleading; Warren, on first assuming command, tried to form
an estimate of the figures and was similarly misled. He was ap-
palled by the size of the total he compiled, and his handling of

his limited forces was rendered timid not only by fear of the United States Navy but also by fear of the vast numbers of privateers which threatened the merchant ships he was supposed to protect.

Private enterprise necessarily but curiously reproduced the forms of government ownership in war. The owners selected captains and promoted officers who distinguished themselves; they issued written orders and studied the written reports that came in, while captains grumbled at the stupidity of owners—as did Barney of the *Rossie*—exactly as did the Royal Navy at the stupidity of the Admiralty. It soon became apparent that, with allowance for good or ill luck, the success of a privateer depended very largely on the ability of the captain. There were captains with a flair for their profession, who could find prizes literally by the dozen, while other captains sought for prey for months without result; flair was desirably supplemented by an intimate knowledge, born of experience, of the trade routes and the seasonal variations of commerce and of the ways of merchant captains both in convoy and proceeding independently; it was in this that privateer captains could be expected (and experience confirmed the expectation) to excel naval officers. Hardihood and ingenuity and energy were called for, boldness in cutting out prizes from protected anchorages, perseverance in shadowing a convoy, prudence in avoiding risks.

Very soon there were captains with reputations, whose services were sought eagerly by anxious owners, and the feverish operations of war eliminated the unfit with Darwinian certainty. Two German governments were to observe similar developments in two world wars; in their attacks on commerce they were to find that the majority of sinkings was effected by a minority of U-boat captains, while their most successful surface raiders were captained by men with experience in the merchant service.

It was while the first wave of privateers was at sea that Warren took up his command; and it was on his arrival at Halifax that he was greeted with the disquieting news of the capture of the *Guerrière*. He was obviously shaken by the reports of the losses suffered by the British merchant ships he was supposed to protect, and embarrassed by the need to take precautions against the American navy, for Rodgers and Bainbridge and Decatur sortied from Boston and disappeared into the Atlantic less than two weeks after his arrival and before he could take measures to watch the port. To Warren the American privateers seemed ubiquitous, and it was impossible to scatter his forces to guard all British shipping from them when at the same time he had to maintain squadrons sufficient in strength to face the American frigates, possibly united in one mass.

In a very brief time Warren became aware of how unhappy may be the lot of a commander in chief. Bitter communications began to pass between him and the Lords of the Admiralty, with Warren demanding continual reinforcements while Their Lordships pointed out that he had at his disposal twenty times the force of the American navy and had apparently achieved nothing; privateers were taking prizes, *Constitution* and *President* and *United States* were out in the Atlantic, and other commanders in chief in other areas were complaining that their arrangements for convoy and supply were being disturbed by American intruders who should have been kept quiescent by Warren.

The most sensitive point in the whole British system of communications was already feeling the rude contact. Wellington wrote to his government from Madrid as early as August 13: "I have heard of war being declared by America, and I beg to draw your Lordship's attention to our communications by the packets. We may depend upon it that the mouth of the Channel and the coasts of Portugal will swarm with privateers." Wellington was a man of remarkable prescience; in this letter he went on to point out the necessity for the squadron blockading Brest to make detachments to guard the communications between Finisterre and the Channel, and for the admiral at Lis-

bon to have sufficient small craft under his command to guard
the coasts from Finisterre to Gibraltar. Wellington at this moment was in the heart of the Peninsula; he was co-ordinating
the movements of half a dozen allied armies besides his own,
and he was observing the behavior of French forces of four
times his strength gathering to attack him. On that day he wrote
to his cavalry commander about the condition of the horses; he
wrote a long report about the recent skirmish at Majalahonda,
and to a divisional general regarding an error in his pay; all this
while actually directing in person the assault upon the Retiro.
The fact that he found time to write as well about the naval arrangements over a thousand miles of sea is a proof of the importance he attached to them.

In later letters he reiterated his warnings. "The navigation
of the coast of Portugal and Spain is of the utmost importance
to us." "Surely the British navy cannot be so hard run as not to
be able to keep up the communication with Lisbon for this
army!" "I hope they [the Admiralty] will adopt some measures
to give us a secure and easy communication along this coast."
Yet his requests and recommendations went unsatisfied. We
find him writing, "I have the honor to enclose a letter . . . containing the report of the capture and ransom of the Canada,
horse transport, by an American privateer, with a detachment
of the 18th light dragoons and other troops on board." "Unfortunately some vessels were taken on the coast of Portugal,
which had on board the equipment for the troops." "Ammunition required for the army has lately been delayed at Lisbon for
want of convoy." "You cannot conceive the inconvenience to
which we are put for want of the sea communication with Lisbon." "I am certain that it will not be denied, that since Great
Britain has been a naval power, a British army has never been
left in such a situation." "If they only take the ship with our
shoes, we must halt for six weeks."

When Wellington, with his sanguine temperament and military wisdom, was writing in this strain; when American priva-

teers were capturing British cavalry and delaying vital movements by impeding the transport of musket ammunition, it can
the more readily be understood how indignantly the Admiralty
was writing to Warren regarding his failure to hem in American naval enterprise. The indignation was the more violent because, although, as has been seen, Wellington had foreseen the
difficulties, they came as a great surprise to the British government. The Cabinet, and its professional naval advisers, had
grossly underestimated the nuisance value of the American
naval effort. Had they been gifted with better judgment they
might have been less obstinate over the question of impressment. The inconvenience to the navy which might have been
experienced if the principle had been abandoned would have
been trifling compared with the actual loss and inconvenience
experienced with the outbreak of war, and the guilty irritation
occasioned by that realization vented itself on Warren's unfortunate head. No one, not even Wellington, spared time or
thought to give him a word of praise for having at the same time
maintained the vital supply of food to the Peninsula. Everyone
was so busy complaining because one section of the American
community was capturing the British soldiers' horses and ammunition and shoes that no one congratulated Warren on the
fact that another section was busy supplying them with the
bread without which they could not have fought at all.

It was inevitable that heads should be demanded and scape-
goats found; inevitable, too, that Warren should for the moment at least succeed in directing the indignation down to his
subordinates. By the end of 1812 a couple of significant paragraphs appeared in the London *Gazette*. "Sir Edmund Nagle,
Knt., to hoist his flag in the Antelope, as commander in chief at
Newfoundland, vice Sir J. T. Duckworth." "Rear-admiral
Cockburn to succeed Vice-admiral Sawyer as commander in
chief on the Halifax station." And so Sawyer, who, after all,
had contrived to place a superior force where it actually made
contact with the *Constitution* before she had done any damage

at all, and who had contributed much to make the licensing system effective, paid the penalty for the errors of his superiors. The blow of his recall was softened for him by a handsome address presented by the city of Halifax thanking him for his "polite and ready attention to the desires of his Majesty's subjects."

American privateering had proved itself offensive beyond all expectation; it is possible that it might have been more offensive still. Certainly there were disadvantages regarding the system, of which the harassed British government was not aware. It skimmed the cream of American seamen; Hull had no sooner taken up his new appointment in New York than he complained that such was the rush to enter into and to fit out privateers that he found it hard to find seamen for naval vessels or workmen for navy yards. It consumed stores and supplies of which the navy felt the need. Competition between individual shipowners was likely to accentuate shortages and force up prices. But these serious disadvantages were only indicative of others, and any attempt to remedy all or any of them confronted the administration with problems which it was peculiarly unfitted to solve.

Privateers sought profits; the national welfare was only incidental. Other privateers were business competitors and only secondarily brothers-in-arms. It could easily happen that a successful owner would endeavor to preserve his trade secrets and to keep his knowledge of the enemy's methods to himself. Undoubtedly he would seek prizes of commercial value; and the facile argument that the greater the commercial loss to the enemy the greater the effect on the war did not hold water. The capture of a homeward-bound East Indiaman would mean enormous prize money, and long faces in the City; but the capture of the coasting brig with Wellington's twenty tons of shoes on board, although it would mean small prize money, would immobilize England's one army in the moment of victory. There could be little doubt as to which capture would have the greater effect in inducing the British government to consider peace on America's terms; unfortunately there could be little doubt as to which capture a privateer captain would endeavor to make —unless he was both exceptionally patriotic and well informed, and prepared to ignore his owners' demand for dividends and his crews' clamor for prize money. Even in the Royal Navy there were continuous hints and complaints that captains and flag officers were tempted to neglect military duties in order to seek prizes, although the orders they received were backed by all the machinery of the Articles of War and with the death penalty looming in the background.

The question of discipline in privateers was always a serious one. The ship's articles gave the captain considerable powers, and many captains were able to use those powers to the full, yet there were exceptions. Although there are accounts of desperate actions fought by privateers, there are plenty of accounts of only feeble resistance being offered and sometimes none at all— more than one English captain reports coming alongside an American privateer to find the decks deserted, the whole crew having run below. The cynic may wonder at the strange quirks of human nature which lead men to give their lives for something as unsubstantial as the honor of their service while they are not prepared to risk them for solid cash, and yet, while wondering, the cynic must admit the existence and the power of those motives; the man who has struck a bargain to go privateering is likely, when faced by the imminent and unimagined danger of hard knocks, to plead misrepresentation and to regret and to go back on his purely commercial bargain.

The privateersman, even the veriest landsman, having entered in return for a share in the proceeds of a voyage, was likely to arrogate to himself the rights of a shareholder and to claim a voice in the management, especially with the tradition of the town meeting behind him; the tendency was almost inevitable and subversive of discipline, and it called for leadership on the part of the captain—and successes as well—to counteract it. The best of privateering captains had to make allowance for the possible restiveness of his crew in conditions of disillusioning hardship and disappointment.

Only the most radical measures on the part of the administration could have minimized these disadvantages of the privateering system. A great organization would have been necessary to supervise the whole effort, backed by compulsory powers, and neither the organization nor the powers could have been voted in the temper of the American people and the American Congress during 1812, whether before or after the outbreak of war; nor could Mr. Madison's political ideas have made it possible for him to ask for them. The federal government neither could nor would have undertaken the necessary management of the whole shipping industry, the rationing of materials of war, the enlistment—almost inevitably compulsory, sooner or later—of the whole body of seamen into the federal service, the subjection of those freeborn citizens and their captains to military law, and the direction of their activities onto trade routes selected by the government. Even after two years of war the federal government could not assume or ask for such powers; the farthest Mr. Madison could go was to ask the agreement of Congress to a small incursion of the federal forces into the commerce-destroying business. He received a grudging assent to the construction or purchase of schooners to be employed as naval vessels under naval command for the express purpose of harassing the British mercantile marine; but the war came to an end before the scheme could be tested.

It was a development noticeable in most campaigns conducted against sea-borne commerce. French corsairs had frequently combined in the past into squadrons under such men as Jean Bart and Duguay-Trouin; by 1918 the German submarines were beginning to employ combined tactics which foreshadowed the "wolf-pack" tactics adopted by the Germans a year after the outbreak of war in 1939. Wolf packs of fast and handy ships under the command of men of the caliber of Perry and Porter might have made important contributions to naval history, and certainly they would have contributed an insupportable addition to the load on the shoulders of Sir John Borlase Warren.

Ships of war under naval officers were more likely to do damage to the enemy for yet another reason. They would not hesitate to destroy their prizes, nor would they hesitate to take prizes which they would have to destroy in view of any difficulty of getting them into a safe port. The privateer, if he saw no chance of making a profitable sale of a prize, would not run the slight risk of making a capture; there was always the chance that the ship he was pursuing might be a disguised ship of war or a fully manned vessel which would make a desperate resistance, and the risk was simply not worth taking if there was to be no monetary reward. In consequence, the menace of the privateer could be dealt with not merely by direct action but by cutting off his market, in the same way as police action against thieves includes the prosecution of the receiver of stolen goods. Close blockade of the American coast would make it less likely for the captured ships to be run into American ports; close blockade of other coasts would similarly impede the entry, and subsequent sale, of the prizes there—privateers endeavored not merely to send their prizes into French ports but especially into Norwegian ones, for Norway, in the topsy-turvy state of the world at that moment, had been an enemy of England since the attack on Copenhagen in 1807, because the King of Denmark was also King of Norway.

But Norway was not a very opulent market for the sale of British ships and cargoes, even allowing for the comparative ease with which the blockade could be run via Denmark to Dutch and German ports. And—to anticipate—the conclusion of peace in Europe rendered these markets neutral, and the purchase of prizes from a belligerent was held to be a breach of neutrality. If this was the case, the only market left for the privateer was the United States, and though the privateer might

count on running the blockade—otherwise he would not be in
the business—he could not rely on a slow merchant prize doing
the same. He could transfer to his own ship any valuable cargo
of small bulk that he might discover, bullion or silk or spices,
but the capacity of his ship was limited and it was those particular cargoes which were best protected. The last resource
was to "ransom" his prize, to let her go under promise that her
owners would pay money on account of her not being destroyed, and it was not to be expected that the British government would allow this system of encouraging the activities of
the privateer to endure for long. It was illegal for British owners to pay ransom bonds—in the same way as it is illegal to com-
pound a felony by buying back stolen goods—and although the
practice was indulged in it meant another discouragement to
the privateer which the government vessel did not experience.
At a late stage of the war the American sloop *Peacock* (this is
to anticipate again; it has not yet been told how that name appeared in the American navy lists) destroyed twelve out of
fourteen prizes, sending in the other two with the accumulated
crews. She herself effected her safe return to New York after
a voyage remarkably similar to those made by several German
commerce destroyers during the two world wars.

Chapter VIII

THE UNITED STATES NAVY had met with some petty disasters. *Nautilus* had sailed into British hands off New York. The British frigate *Barbadoes* had contrived to overtake and capture the American revenue schooner *James Madison* making her way toward the presumably happy hunting grounds of the West Indies from Savannah. Lumley of the *Narcissus* reported the capture of the U.S. brig *Viper* off Havana—it is worth noting that Lumley's laconic report of four lines yet contains the interesting information that *Viper* had been there seven weeks without making any captures. *Viper*, having been designed as a schooner, had been re-rigged as a brig by Tingey, Humphreys' uninspired successor, who was mainly responsible for the progress of gunboat construction, and it may have been this that made her slow enough to fall a victim to *Narcissus*.

Before Lumley captured *Viper*, her sister ship *Vixen*, another converted schooner, had been captured by H.M.S. *Southampton*, also in West India waters, and also after an unprofitable cruise—she had been out five weeks without capturing anything. But from this comparatively insignificant encounter stemmed a long series of events which were to affect the history of the world, by coincidences comparable with the two encounters between *Guerrière* and *Constitution*. For *Southampton* headed for Jamaica with her prize; they took the Crooked Island Passage and a strong current set them to the westward farther than they allowed for. From Conception Island there runs a long reef extending for eight or nine miles which at that time was not charted. Both vessels ran aground in the darkness; *Southampton* sank at once and *Vixen* soon afterward. All on board managed to save themselves, including the captain of the *Southampton*, who was exonerated by a court-martial when he was tried for the loss of his ship.

So far it is an old story—the unusual current and the uncharted rock; courts-martial in a score of navies have heard it told, and many have taken a less lenient view than did this one. But history was in the making, for the captain of *Southampton*, thus acquitted, was Sir James Lucas Yeo. His court-martial took place in February 1813; after that he was available for further duty, at the very time when Warren, with the responsibility for the Great Lakes added to the already considerable responsibility of conducting the whole naval war against the United States from Halifax to Surinam, was looking round for an officer of some seniority to act there as a local commander in chief under his orders. Yeo was available and was given the command "of all the naval forces on the Lakes in Canada." The appointment of a commander in chief whose principal qualification was the fact that he had just lost his ship constitutes a great part of the explanation of subsequent events on the Lakes.

A month before Yeo captured *Vixen*, Captain Whinyates of the Royal Navy was addressing to Warren a letter beginning, "It is with the most bitter sorrow and distress I have to report to Your Excellency . . ." Whinyates was captain of the brig *Frolic;* he had brought far on its homeward way the trade from the Gulf of Mexico, when in mid-Atlantic, beyond Bermuda, he met with bad weather that did a good deal of damage aloft to his vessel. He was busy on the work of repair when a strange sail came up over the horizon, and Whinyates very properly sent the convoy ahead while he held back to investigate the stranger.

Master Commandant Jacob Jones was by no means a young man (he was forty-four) and had had until now a career by no means distinguished. He had practiced for years as a doctor and he had dabbled in the law before he became a midshipman in 1799; he had had a good deal of sea duty, was promoted lieutenant in 1800, and had then seen service in the Mediterranean without gaining any glory. Indeed, his experience had been such as might not have helped him to further employment, for he had been involved, as second, in a duel; he had had a bitter argument with one of his captains (Murray) and had, as lieutenant in the *Philadelphia*, been taken prisoner to languish with the others in Tripoli prison, where he had only scope to practice what he remembered of the medical profession. But seniority brought him promotion and the command of the sloop *Wasp*, which he had held for eighteen months, nearly all that time at sea—at the moment of the declaration of war he was actually in a French port, having been sent there with dispatches.

Returning, he found his way clear to New York (Broke was covering the West India convoy whose existence so complicated the strategical situation for the British) and was ordered out again at once in the wave of exultation following the arrival of the news of the capture of the *Guerrière*. He got out just before Broke appeared off New York again, made an unprofitable cruise toward Boston, came into the Delaware to replenish, and started out again at once, heading this time for the Gulf Stream trade route. Three days out he encountered a gale which did his ship some small damage and left the sea running high. Before his lost jib boom could be replaced he sighted Whinyates' convoy in the darkness of midnight; with the rising of the sun he identified the ships on the horizon to leeward as merchantmen. Between them and his own ship lay a man o' war brig, identifiable easily enough as such although her main yard was down. She hoisted Spanish colors, for Whinyates, very properly concerned about his convoy, had decided that was the best method to employ to lure the stranger down to investigate and bring him within range.

Jones did not need to be lured. With his sailor's eye he had no doubt as to the nationality of the vessel in sight, and he moved in at once for a fight. Having regard to the relative positions of all the ships, it was probably the best plan, to destroy the escort first and, having won a quick victory, to pursue the convoy second. If that was the case it might be argued that Whinyates' best plan was to refuse battle and, by steadily interposing between the raider and the convoy, to await the moment when his opponent's impatience would give him the opportunity to engage at an advantage. In the general strategical situation it was obvious that time was on his side—in fact, an enormous reinforcement was not far over the horizon at that very moment. But no British captain could dare to avoid action against any force approximately equal, and no thought of doing so crossed Whinyates' mind. He expected a victory, although after the event he could hardly say so.

Both ships shortened sail for action as they closed on the tossing sea. *Wasp* was a fine vessel, fast although hard to handle; owing to the peculiar conditions regarding the naval appropriations in 1805, at the close of the war with Tripoli, there had been no need to spare expense when she was built in 1806. She was as well found as any vessel could be, and she had been in commission for well over a year. *Frolic* was a typical British gun brig, one of scores constructed in yards whose resources were strained to the utmost. The type was a necessary one but represented the inevitable unsatisfactory compromise when a vessel has to be designed to fight, to be seaworthy, and to have long endurance, all on a minimum displacement and at a minimum expense. Few men in the Royal Navy had a good word to say for the gun brigs, which rolled terribly and were greatly overcrowded, but they had to be employed.

Neither vessel made any attempt to maneuver; it was Jones's business to close and have done with the fight as soon as possible, and Whinyates was ready to oblige him; in his own words, "both vessels being within hail, we hauled to the wind, and the battle begun." Both vessels carried a main armament of carronades, short-range weapons even under good conditions. In the sea that was running—the wind was still blowing strong—it might be expected that the artillery practice would be poor. On the contrary, it was surprisingly good. In sixteen minutes the *Wasp* was badly cut up aloft, but her stouter scantlings minimized what damage she received below. *Frolic* was battered more badly; her losses were heavy and her damage aloft was serious.

The ships neared each other until from being within hail they were close alongside; they were rolling until their gun muzzles were sometimes under water and the spray flung up between the ships drenched them both, and amid the spray and smoke and confusion the gunners, bending with their rammers as they loaded, felt the outboard end of their rammers strike the side of the other ship across the gap as the ships rolled toward each other. *Wasp* was gaining on *Frolic*, her bows were ahead of the other's—neither ship could attempt to maneuver now, so badly was the rigging cut up—when at last the ships came together. *Frolic*, her bowsprit across the *Wasp's* deck, received the coup de grâce of her raking broadside. Along that heaving bowsprit the *Wasp's* boarders scrambled onto *Frolic's* forecastle.

There was no more fighting. Whinyates was holding himself up for he was too weak with a wound to stand without support. All his officers were wounded and some dying. Of his men, at least half, perhaps three quarters, were dead or wounded; their ship was too battered ever to fight again. Thirty-two-pounder carronades, accurately pointed, could work fearful damage in a frail wooden ship crowded with men. *Frolic's* guns had not been as accurately pointed; *Wasp's* loss was only a fraction— an eighth, perhaps—of hers. Making every allowance, the American gunnery had been far more effective than the British.

The British had fought a desperate fight without flinching, as was to be expected. Whinyates in his report attributed his defeat to the loss of his main yard during the gale before the battle, and it was an argument in his favor. If he had not lost it *Frolic* might not have rolled quite so violently during the action; *Wasp* might not perhaps have drawn quite as rapidly ahead. Yet the disadvantage by no means accounted for the decisiveness of the defeat. British ships had fought French ships under worse handicap and had won often enough. The new enemy was more dangerous; that much at least had to be admitted by the exasperated Royal Navy.

Jones put a prize crew into the *Frolic* and stood by her while the effort was being made to re-rig her. It was then that a strange sail appeared over the horizon—H.M.S. *Poictiers*, 74, bound from Halifax to Bermuda, commanded by Sir John Beresford, brother of that Sir William Beresford who, under Wellington, was commander in chief of the Portuguese army. Beresford needed no urging to head toward the two strange sails lying hove-to on the wild sea; there must have been violent debate on the quarter-deck of the *Poictiers* as officers stared through telescopes and tried to decide what had been happening, until at last it was grudgingly agreed that what they saw was a British ship prize to an American. *Frolic* was immediately overhauled and recaptured; *Wasp* lasted very little longer. She had been badly damaged aloft, and the weather conditions—a rough sea and plenty of wind—were ideal for a ship of the line in pursuit of a much smaller ship.

Jones hauled down his colors as soon as he was overtaken; the convention of a later age would have dictated that he fight to the death, but in those more merciful times there was no shame whatever attached to a surrender in the face of overwhelming force. Beresford took his prizes to Bermuda, where he wrote his report to Warren in the terse style favored by the Royal Navy after an easy success. "I have the honor to acquaint you, that H.M.'s ship, under my command, has this day captured the American sloop of war Wasp of twenty guns. . . ." A later line in the report had some significance: "I have thought it my duty to collect the Frolic's convoy, and to see them in safety to Bermuda." Beresford did not dare to let the convoy go on without escort; it had to wait until one could be found for it. By that much the loss of the *Wasp* found a compensation; the loss of a single brig of war out of England's immense navy was inconsiderable otherwise. Professional comment in the British press regarding the action was neither as passionate nor as lengthy as might have been the case, partly because the capture of the *Wasp* was a partial salve to hurt feelings, but mainly because professional attention was engrossed in the reports of other actions that arrived in England at nearly the same time. They called up the real storm.

In the United States the news arrived earlier by comparison. The American commissary general of prisoners and the British general agent for prisoners had already made arrangements for a system of exchange of prisoners—neither side saw any reason for making war any more uncomfortable than necessary—and Jones and his men found themselves in New York, sent in by cartel, less than a month after the action. They were feted and entertained and rewarded; the loss of the *Wasp* was forgotten in the thought of the victory gained first. That helped to keep public spirits high—and also the spirit of the Administration— until the arrival of still more intoxicating news.

Chapter IX

WARREN'S ESTIMATE of the relative importance of the different aspects of his duty caused him to employ so much of his force on commerce protection that he had none to spare to watch that considerable portion of the United States Navy that had entered Boston. The orders that Washington sent to Boston under the stimulus of the defeat of the *Guerrière* needed no reiteration. Rodgers and Decatur were in a fever to sail again, and sail they did, as early as October 8. The Administration's orders were based on the suggestions Decatur had made previously, and not on Rodgers' practice of the earlier voyage. The four ships were not to act in one mass; they were to cruise as two separate pairs of ships, doubling the chances of finding prizes—the smallness of the number of prizes taken by Rodgers' large force on his preceding cruise presumably influenced the decision. Rodgers, however, was so anxious to miss no opportunity of striking a heavy blow that he actually delayed the sailing of his own detachment (*President* and *Congress*) for several days until Decatur was ready. Rodgers had in mind the possibility of finding outside Boston some small detachment of the British navy. He wanted to fight a battle, and this was only partly because of his savage desire to humble the Britishers' pride. He was even more desirous of forcing Warren into keeping his ships concentrated in large bodies where they could do the least harm to American commerce.

There was nothing to oppose his exit, however, although it was not by so very much that Rodgers missed Beresford and the *Poictiers*—if that encounter had taken place a red and significant page of naval history would have been written, although no one can guess at its purport. Two days out from Boston they caught a glimpse of a British frigate, the *Nymphe*, but she ran at the first sight of the overwhelming force and got clear away; her report that Rodgers was at sea again added vastly to Warren's troubles. Three days out from Boston nothing had been encountered, and Rodgers obeyed the order to separate. He himself with *President* and *Congress* made a vast circular sweep of eleven thousand miles, to the southward of the Azores, to the Cape Verdes, and back via Bermuda. Three weeks after sighting the *Nymphe* he sighted another frigate, the *Galatea*, with two vessels in convoy. One ship was captured, while *Galatea* and the other managed to prolong the pursuit until nightfall and then escaped in the darkness. After that Rodgers encountered literally nothing. The year was over by the time he returned, and in all that time he had sighted only five sail of English ships, and of those he had captured only two. It was the clearest proof of the emptiness of the sea even when it carries a thriving commerce, although Rodgers in his disappointment expressed the hope that it was a proof that British commerce was feeling the effects of the war. Incidentally it was an indication that Rodgers did not have that flair for commerce destruction which characterizes the successful corsair. Intellectual sailor though he was, he did not possess the intimate knowledge of the movements of trade—nor the good fortune—of the American privateer captains. Two prizes would hardly have balanced the pay and maintenance of his squadron had it not happened that one of the two was a West India packet, snapped up during the first days of the voyage, with nearly two hundred thousand dollars in treasure on board. Prizes usually averaged—as the many years of experience of the Royal Navy demonstrated—about twenty-five thousand dollars apiece, so that even with the capture of this ship Rodgers' success was not as great as could have been hoped for. It was a second blow in the air that Rodgers had delivered.

Yet it seems that Decatur was of much the same opinion as Rodgers regarding the area which should be attacked. When he parted company he, too, headed in the general direction of Madeira; *Argus* turned south toward the South American coast to sweep a different area. A fortnight after parting company Decatur sighted his first sail, far out to windward, with a fresh breeze blowing. Captain John Carden was, in obedience to Admiralty orders, taking his frigate *Macedonian* to reinforce the West Indian station. She was a comparatively new ship and had been newly refitted. From this point of view she was a more efficient ship than the *Guerrière*, whose exact equal she was in statistical strength, save that she had a slightly more numerous crew. In the same way *United States* had a few more men and a slightly heavier weight of broadside than the *Constitution*, for, owing to her exceptionally powerful construction (for which she paid in the matter of speed), she mounted 42-pounder carronades on her quarter-deck and forecastle—guns which, within their limited range, would have a prodigious effect on the frail timbers of a frigate.

Stephen Decatur, her captain, was at this moment—even allowing for Hull's recent victory—the most observed of all the officers of the United States Navy. He had been a marked man practically from the moment of his first joining, as midshipman in this same ship; his promotion had been rapid, so that he was first lieutenant of a frigate at twenty-two, with a ship of his own soon after. He had fought in a famous hand-to-hand action against Tripolitan gunboats, and by his brilliant boarding and burning of the captured *Philadelphia*, with almost no loss, he had justified his superiors' confidence in him and won his captain's commission. Now he was thirty-three; he had been captain of the *United States* for two years—during which time, according to a well-authenticated story, he had once met Carden and discussed with him *Macedonian's* chances of success if pitted against an American. Since the outbreak of war he had accompanied Rodgers on the first cruise; his ship and his men were in as good fighting condition as ever they could be.

Carden was a captain of great seniority and considerable experience, his promotion following the capture of the French *Immortalité* after a hard fight with the *Fisgard*, in which he was first lieutenant; this was part of Warren's action against the French invasion of Ireland in 1798. He was not yet aware of the defeat of the *Guerrière*, and there is no way of knowing if the knowledge would have affected his actions. At his first sight of the *United States* he mistook her for the *Essex*, which might possibly have made him more ready to accept action; but, like Dacres, he could hardly have declined it in the current temper of the Royal Navy, although with his windward position he might easily have avoided action with the slow-sailing *United States*. In any event, he came boldly down, determined to fight.

Decatur had the reputation in his service of a fiery-tempered man—his career had been punctuated with fights and duels—but he brought his ship into action with a coolness and a wariness that could only have been the fruit of prolonged consideration in earlier years. As the ships neared he wore round in an attempt to gain the weather gauge but was balked as Carden put his helm to port and headed him off; in those conditions Carden could hardly have lost the weather gauge (if he wished to retain it) unless by gross miscalculation. Decatur wore round again, and the two ships passed on opposite courses at long cannon shot. As they did so the *United States* fired two broadsides from her 24-pounders; the first fell short, but the second did some damage; the *Macedonian's* 18s remained silent—it was long range for them and it was best to save the first broadside for a more decisive moment.

Carden had to wear his ship round, and promptly, if he

wished to retain the weather gauge; he did so, and found himself still to windward but somewhat astern of the *United States*. Decatur's maneuvers had been peculiarly successful, he was inducing his enemy to close in conditions most unfavorable to the British ship. Carden was trying to get close alongside; Decatur, by keeping a little off the wind, was not merely able to prolong the period of the approach but was also able to bring many more guns to bear than Carden could as he bore down. It was a skillful use of the leeward position against an opponent ready to join battle; the French navy at the height of its efficiency had practiced a very similar maneuver against the British in several fleet actions during the American Revolutionary War, more than once deliberately choosing the leeward position on this account. In a fleet action it could only inflict on the enemy a damaging repulse without gaining a decisive tactical victory; in a battle between single ships it was likely to be most effective against an obliging enemy.

Macedonian endeavored to close; *United States* meanwhile cut her up most dreadfully, the American guns being handled very rapidly as well as accurately. Not only were *Macedonian's* spars and rigging shot to pieces, but terrible damage was done on her deck. Her losses were frightful—a hundred, more than one third, of her ship's company were killed or wounded. Her own fire was almost ineffective; she succeeded in shooting away her opponent's mizzen-topgallant mast and in doing some small additional damage to her spars and rigging, but hardly any shots struck home on the *United States'* hull. The total of American casualties was only twelve.

Halfway through the action Decatur backed his mizzen-topsail to allow his enemy to close, and employed that interval of lying hove-to to inflict crushing damage as his already crippled opponent crawled gamely toward him; in any case, *United States* with her greater beam was a far steadier gun platform than the *Macedonian*. The British ship actually never succeeded in getting close alongside; the shortest range during the action was long range for grape—a hundred yards or more, never the "half pistol shot" which was the traditional range for close action.

By the time the British ship had crept to the closest she ever attained she was a beaten wreck, her mizzenmast and fore- and main-topmasts gone, a dozen guns disabled, and several shot holes below water line. Decatur had only to fill his mizzen-topsail again to draw away from her. His ship was under perfect command; he could take up a raking position and continue the slaughter; the British were astonished that he did not. But Decatur had stayed cool throughout the action. He had only to indicate his ability to rake and to demonstrate his complete fitness to continue the action, and Carden surrendered, having been granted an interval in which to reach a full appreciation of his own helpless position, and in the distressing belief that he was the first British captain to haul down his colors to an American; it was cold comfort to hear about the loss of the *Guerrière* while standing a prisoner on the *United States'* quarter-deck.

Decatur had fought a remarkably clever battle; Carden a stupid one. Carden was submitted to a long and rigorous court-martial when he was exchanged; it took place in Warren's flag-ship, the *San Domingo*, at the end of May 1813, after the news of the further loss of the *Java* and before the capture of the *Chesapeake*, at a moment when the Royal Navy was sincerely anxious to ascertain the reason for the successive disasters it had undergone. Even so, the inquiry failed of its purpose. The evidence brought out clearly enough the fact that *Macedonian* had never succeeded in closing with the *United States*, and that served to distract the attention of the court. It was necessary for the honor of the navy (and it was also most necessary for the defense in proving Carden's personal courage) that there should be no question whatever of any flinching from action. In consequence most of the time and attention of the court was consumed in establishing the fact that Carden had endeavored to get to close quarters while retaining the weather gauge; the

discussion was not made any easier by the complete bewilderment of everyone concerned regarding Decatur's tactics. No
one really could understand why Decatur had not met Carden
halfway and engaged broadside to broadside to fight it out as
any member of the court would have done in similar circumstances. The fact that Carden and most of his officers were of
the opinion that in that event *Macedonian* would at least have
inflicted more damage on her opponent did not clarify the problem in the minds of the inquirers, who could not bring themselves to admit that an American captain had acted with more
judgment than they themselves possessed. The very evident
facts were too unpleasant to be given attention; *Macedonian*
had been not only outmaneuvered but outfought; not merely
had she fewer guns but she had inferior gunners. These admissions could not be made, either publicly or in the minds of the
officers who constituted the court. By preference the court,
while a little cool regarding Carden's earlier maneuvers, devoted
its attention to the courage of Carden and his ship's company,
which no one need ever have doubted. It found that there was
not "the most distant wish to keep back from the engagement"
and that everyone concerned, "in every instance throughout
the action, behaved with the firmest and most determined
courage, resolution, and coolness, and that the colours of the
Macedonian were not struck until she was unable to make
farther resistance." Carden was "most honorably acquitted ac-
cordingly," while the court expressed its admiration of his "gal-
lantry and good conduct" and the "highest approbation" of
the support given him by his ship's company.

Macedonian ended the action by no means in the sinking condition that was noticeable in the *Guerrière* when the latter surrendered, which gives, by comparison, some color to the plea
that *Guerrière* was a rotten ship with rotten masts; *Macedonian*
had lost an even greater proportion of her crew than had *Guerrière*—and so had probably been hit more often—but two of her
lower masts were still standing and she was not in instant dan-

ger. Decatur sent a prize crew on board; the weather was kind, and sufficient repairs were effected to justify an attempt to sail the prize to America. Of all the captains in the United States Navy, Decatur was the most sensitive to the imponderable factors of morale and prestige; a British frigate brought in as a prize was worth two destroyed out of sight of the American people. His direct course back to the New England coast kept him out of the track of the English squadrons, and Warren had not yet applied himself seriously to the difficult and tedious task of watching the ports to the northward and eastward of New York. Decatur came through without difficulty, and Warren heard with dismay from American newspapers that *Macedonian* had sailed into Newport with the Stars and Stripes flying over the British ensign; Decatur reached New London at the same time. The moral effects of the victory can be discussed in a later passage; for the moment it only remains to be added that *Macedonian* was brought down Long Island Sound for refit at New York, to be designated the command of Jacob Jones, a captain now after his victory over the *Frolic* and his exchange.

Chapter X

CAPTAIN WILLIAM BAINBRIDGE at the age of thirty-eight had had a career astonishingly varied even for that age and his profession. He had hauled down the American colors far back in 1798, when, as lieutenant in command of the schooner *Retaliation*, he had been caught by two French frigates. As captain of the *George Washington* he had been forced to carry the Dey of Algiers' tribute to the Sultan of Turkey—an unpleasant experience for which the only compensation was the distinction of first showing the Stars and Stripes at Stamboul. He had had the bitter experience of surrendering again when his frigate *Philadelphia* ran aground under the fire of the Tripolitan gunboats; he had endured a long captivity whose monotony was relieved only by his being in constant danger of his life; he had had many years of experience as a merchant captain; he had made a hurried return to America from St. Petersburg when war threatened, arriving just in time to put some stiffening into Madison's decisions regarding the employment of the navy, and he had fallen heir to the command of the *Constitution* when Hull was petulantly deprived of it after his hurried departure from Boston and before his victory over the *Guerrière* was known.

When Rodgers sailed out from Boston the squadron allotted to Bainbridge was not ready for sea, even though *Constitution* had returned at the end of August. The sloop *Hornet*, Master Commandant James Lawrence, was in Boston, also under Bainbridge's command; *Essex* was refitting in the Delaware, and the Secretary of the Navy's orders put her as well under Bainbridge's command, despite the difficulties of communication. Bainbridge was anxious to get to sea; there was no way of knowing if a fair wind at Boston meant a fair wind in the Delaware; he could only sail at his first opportunity, having made by letter a rendezvous with Porter in the *Essex*, which circumstances were to dictate should never be kept.

Constitution and *Hornet* left on October 26, 1812—it grows monotonous to mention that they met with no opposition; at this date Jacob Jones was a newly taken prisoner in Bermuda, Rodgers with a king's ransom in his hold was seeking unprofitably for further prey in the eastern Atlantic, and Decatur's prize crew was laboring at the refitting of the *Macedonian*. Bainbridge had every intention of keeping his command together; the orders he had received from his government, and which he interpreted in his instructions to Porter, were based on what Decatur had suggested, a midway course between Rodgers' advice that the navy should be kept massed as much as possible, and Bainbridge's own to the effect that it should be dispersed over the seas. With a sloop of war in company, a heavy frigate's efficiency was much increased, as the sloop extended the frigate's horizon—it was a frequent British practice to attach a sloop to a cruising ship of the line—while on detached service a sloop of war was not greatly a more efficient commerce destroyer than the privateers that were pouring out of American harbors.

Bainbridge's first desire was to get away from the American shore where, logically, there was the greatest danger of encountering British ships of war; he proposed to solve the problem of water supply by filling up at the Cape Verdes—a Portuguese possession and therefore, in American eyes, neutral. By doing this he would be re-equipped for a long cruise (food was more easily replaced from prizes and in any case was carried in larger quantities) with the advantage of being already far from his home port. To balance against this was the very serious risk of encountering a British ship of war and the certainty that the British would hear very soon about his visit. They were risks that any raider had to run, and once he was over the horizon again it would not be easy for the British to guess whither he had gone. On either side of the narrow neck of the South Atlantic lay two important objectives, the Brazilian trade on the one hand, springing largely from Rio de Janeiro, and the East Indian and China trade on the other, coming from the Cape of Good Hope and calling at St. Helena. Bainbridge seems to have had in mind successive thrusts, first at one and then at the other.

He reached the Cape Verdes and filled up with water without incident; there was no sign or news of *Essex*—Bainbridge could not even know if she had succeeded in escaping from the Delaware. The outward-bound trade route slanted over toward Brazil in accordance with the prevailing winds. He followed it, but diverged to his rendezvous at Fernando de Noronha, desolate and almost uninhabited islands two hundred miles from the Brazilian coast which merchant shipping avoided. That was why Bainbridge had selected it as a rendezvous; he could wait there without fear of being reported—a mid-ocean rendezvous was unsatisfactory in those days when longitude could not be determined accurately.

So far he had made an excellent passage, far better than the worst for which he had necessarily allowed in his instructions to Porter. The disadvantages of a system of distant rendezvous were immediately apparent. Bainbridge was faced by the need for waiting for thirteen unproductive days for the *Essex*, which might not arrive at all. Naturally he could do nothing of the kind, not with British shipping rounding the shoulder of Brazil almost within reach. He visited the Portuguese authorities—Fernando de Noronha was a penal settlement—and announced himself as the captain of H.M.S. *Acasta*. The Portuguese jailers hardly knew America was at war, they were incapable of telling

one ship from another, and Bainbridge's information was good
—*Acasta* could just possibly be in the vicinity. They accepted a
letter addressed to Yeo of the *Southampton* (Yeo had been
wrecked in Crooked Island Passage two days before) and agreed
to deliver it when called for. The letter was noncommittal, but
in secret ink it contained orders for a further rendezvous for *Essex*, and Porter, arriving a fortnight later and posing as Yeo, actually collected the letter and deciphered it. He did not find Bainbridge at the new rendezvous, however. Running down toward
it, well offshore, he passed Bainbridge almost in sight engaged
in most important business unknown to him close in land; he
went on, found no one at the rendezvous, and eventually proceeded on the independent voyage which was to lead to fame
and eventual disaster.

Bainbridge had found the British sloop of war *Bonne Citoyenne* in Bahia and sent in a challenge for her to fight Lawrence
in the *Hornet*, an equal match. The British captain sensibly
refused; his ship was loaded with the gold and silver of which
England stood in so much need for her subsidies to her allies—
and to pay American merchants—and it would have been a
poor gamble to risk a tenfold stake on an even chance. He
also feared that, if he came out and fought and won, Bainbridge
would not be able to resist the temptation to interfere, but he
certainly should have kept his thoughts to himself and not have
expressed them, as he did, in his reply. Bainbridge celebrated
Christmas off Bahia and then left Lawrence to watch the *Bonne
Citoyenne* while he himself cruised offshore in the *Constitution*,
seeking prizes. He found, not a merchant vessel, but a ship of
war.

Back in May 1811 the Royal Navy, ranging the seven seas in
the world-wide war against Bonaparte, had made contact with
a squadron of French frigates off Madagascar. There had been
a most desperate action, in which the French *Renommée* was
captured; she was reported by her captors as being "of the first
class, of forty-four guns," and she had been beaten into a per-

fect wreck, losing well over one third of the 470 men who manned her. When she had been rendered seaworthy again she was sent home in charge of a prize crew and refitted; she was also renamed—she became the *Java*, to commemorate the recent conquest of that island from the Dutch. The same official statement from the Admiralty office which announced the appointment of Sir John Borlase Warren, in August 1812, contained numerous appointments of captains, and among them was "H. Lambert, to the Java." Lambert, like Bainbridge, had known disaster and captivity and court-martial, and victory too. As far back as 1805, when captain of the *St. Fiorenzo*, he had captured the French frigate *Psyche*. Later, when captain of the *Iphigenia*, he had been involved—as a junior captain and so not directly responsible—in one of the petty disasters of the period and had been compelled to surrender his ship, after a fierce defense, following an unsuccessful attack on Mauritius. The capture of Mauritius released him, his court-martial absolved him of blame, and this was the new command that had been given him. Since August 12 Lambert had occupied himself with collecting a crew; he had received orders to take out a reinforcement to the East India station.

He sailed at the beginning of November, having on board the new governor of Bombay (General Hislop) and his staff, some supernumerary officers and a draft of a hundred seamen, and various civilian passengers. In addition he had a load of copper for ships building in India and various other material. The *Java* was a crowded ship, and she was not sailing on a warlike errand; it can be easily understood that no great pains had been taken in making a warlike vessel out of her as she took her peaceful way across the wintry Atlantic. She had followed the usual outward-bound course far to the westward; crowded as she was, she would have to touch at a Brazilian port for water before starting back again with the southeast trades for St. Helena to deliver her first batch of dispatches. It had been a long passage, seven weeks so far; they had crossed the line and celebrated Christmas and then came another pleasant distraction—an American merchant ship, the *William*, had run into their arms and had been snapped up. She represented small but welcome prize money. Lambert put a prize crew on board and took her along with him as he headed into Bahia. Land was actually in sight when yet another distraction hove up over the horizon. Bainbridge had placed himself across the path of the outward-bound India ships, but he had hardly expected the present development.

Constitution was somewhat to the southward of Bahia when Lambert sighted her. He sent in his prize and went on to investigate the strange sail, postponing the run on shore which his passengers had expected to enjoy in the next hour or two. The strange sail kept away; Bainbridge did not want to fight in waters which were neutral by American standards. Lambert sent up the recognition signals and received no intelligible reply; the stranger was not British, Spanish, or Portuguese. Moreover, he was flying a signal which made no sense—the American recognition signal. Immediately afterward telescopes in the British ship made out something more—a broad pendant flying from the main-topmast head. She was a commodore's ship of war, then; she could only be an enemy, and almost certainly an American. Lambert beat to quarters. Bainbridge was by now nearly sure that the newcomer was neither Spanish nor Portuguese. As she came running rapidly down on him he saw the British colors, and all doubt was at an end.

Lambert was to windward; he could refuse action, and a safe retreat into neutral waters was open to him. He was aware of what had happened to the *Guerrière*, and although he did not know as yet that he was looking at the very ship which had defeated her, he could be in no doubt that this one was of the same class. But he went into action without hesitation. In his favor could be pleaded—as was actually put forward at the court-martial—the argument that even if he were defeated he might well inflict enough damage to compel his enemy to return home and leave this area where such profitable pickings were to be found. His French-built ship, newly refitted, was very fast and came down rapidly on the American, both captains judging the distance and gauging the wind as they neared. Once more the British ship was to windward and the American to leeward, but in this case both captains fought a skillful battle, each wringing the utmost advantage from their relative situations. Parry met lunge and riposte followed parry, with the two captains handling their ships like fencing foils. With opponents equally matched, neither could gain a tactical advantage; the approach period ended with the ships within close range and neither had scored a tactical point. The superior speed of the British ship—both had reduced sail to "fighting sails"—was very evident; there was the continual danger that she might cross *Constitution*'s bows and rake her, but Bainbridge coolly countered by setting his main course and forecourse, big sails which long experience had shown were usually better kept clewed up during action. *Java* was no longer able to forereach on the *Constitution*. The risk of setting the additional sail was early minimized; the balance of victory was already inclining rapidly in the American's favor.

In battle, particularly in battle at sea, to him that hath more shall be given and from him that hath not shall be taken away even that which he hath. The superior weight of the *Constitution*'s guns inflicted more damage than *Java* could inflict; the more the damage, the greater the disproportion. The superior American gunnery multiplied it; the superior American protection from shot multiplied it too. In a hard-hit ship, losses among the gun's crews slowed the rate of fire; losses among division officers—five midshipmen were killed and four wounded in the *Java*—meant that the guns were not handled with as much precision, nor were such important matters attended to as the reduction of charges as the guns grew hot; even the death of the wretched powder boys meant that those charges were not brought up as rapidly or as evenly from the magazine. Morally, the men in the suffering ship could be shaken by their losses and the men in the victor cheered on by the sight of the damage they were doing, although there was no faltering on the British side. *Java* was suffering much more heavily than the *Constitution*.

Java shot away *Constitution's* wheel; Bainbridge had to handle his ship by the aid of orders shouted down through a grating to men at the relieving tackles hauling the rudder round by direct action. *Constitution* shot away *Java's* jib boom and the end of her bowsprit, leaving her headsails dangling. In the next maneuver *Constitution* was less handicapped by her disability than *Java* was by hers—or was better handled; *Java* hung in stays for a period of two broadsides in the absence of the headsails to force her round, and those two broadsides were fired, raking, into her stern—the balance tilted more rapidly than ever after that. Lambert could see that he was being beaten in the gunnery duel; if it continued, his ship was lost. He could try to board; the attempt might bring victory and could bring no worse defeat. The sailing master who had been assisting him with advice in the handling of the ship was wounded at his side and carried below as Lambert gave the order. *Java's* helm was put over to bring the ships together. Then her foremast fell and the lunge was slowed. The stump of her bowsprit just brushed the *Constitution* as she swung; she went on round, hardly manageable, and was raked again, and then again, *Constitution* crossing first her bows and then her stern, at the closest range under Bainbridge's cool handling—so close a range that Lambert fell wounded by a musket shot, one more on the list of victims of American individual marksmanship that would include such illustrious names as Brock and Ross. The maintopmast fell, and then the mizzenmast; for the moment the two ships were side by side, and the flame from the guns set on fire the rigging trailing alongside and the burning wreck had to be cut away. It was apparent to Bainbridge that *Java* was beaten, even though the British, and the first lieutenant, Chads, who had succeeded to the command, did not know it yet. Bainbridge drew away from his battered opponent and set his men to work at repairing the damaged rigging.

The British actually set to work too, in the midst of the frightful chaos left by *Constitution's* broadsides. They cut away the trailing wreck. Half the main yard was left; they loosed part of the main course to give them steerageway and then, toiling through the wreckage on the booms, they unearthed a spare topgallant mast, which they proposed to rig as a jury foremast; the original foremast had crashed down through forecastle and main deck. But while they entered upon this inordinate labor Chads's attention was called to the condition of the mainmast. It had been wounded, and at the same time so many stays and shrouds had been cut that it was tottering —the ship, deprived of so much of her top hamper, was rolling deeply without its stabilizing influence, and the mainmast could not endure the additional strain of the rag of sail it was carrying. It was about to fall, and with the ship before the wind it would come down inboard on top of everything else unless prompt action was taken. Chads put his helm over and cut away the weather shrouds in the nick of time. The mainmast went over the lee side to be cut loose, and the ship was left dismasted and rolling wildly.

By this time *Constitution* had completed her repairs and was filling her sails, moving inexorably in upon her victim to administer the coup de grâce. Chads sent his men back to the guns, a dozen of which were disabled. Weary men sponged and loaded and strained at the tackles. But it was of no avail to man the guns if they would not bear. *Constitution's* bows were pointing across those of the *Java;* in a few moments she would be pouring in a raking fire to which there would be no chance whatever of replying. *Constitution* was within speaking-trumpet range, and Chads hailed to say he surrendered.

Night was at hand when an American lieutenant came on board to take possession; Bainbridge had been twice wounded, seriously enough to incapacitate him as soon as the need to keep on his feet had ended. *Java* continued to roll frantically, while the water gained steadily through her numerous leaks despite unremitting labor at what pumps had survived *Constitution's* fire. *Constitution* lay by her through the night and next day. Bainbridge decided the wreck was not worth saving, or in his wounded condition he could not face the international complications that would ensue if he brought a captured British frigate into Portuguese waters. He ferried the prisoners across to his own ship and then set the dismasted hulk on fire. So the last day of 1812 was marked by the burning of the *Java*.

There are conflicting reports regarding the losses, but it is clear enough that *Java* lost about one third of her crew in killed and wounded; it is also worth noting that even with a hundred supernumeraries on board her total ship's company was considerably less in number than the French crew she had carried at the time of her first capture. *Constitution* had been far harder hit than when she had fought the *Guerrière*, or than *United States* had been when she fought the *Macedonian*. Lambert and Chads had fought a better battle, yet Chads inexcusably omitted to destroy the signal codes and the dispatches, which fell into Bainbridge's hands. Chads himself had been wounded, which may help to explain it, and possibly *Constitution's* return to the fight took him by surprise; a few moments of delay in surrendering, while he dropped the codes overboard, would have exposed his ship to another raking broadside.

Bainbridge decided to return home. He complained in his later reports of the *Constitution's* decayed condition, which may have influenced him, and so may his losses, and so may the damage his ship had received. He probably felt hampered by the presence of his thirty wounded. He must have been aware of the need to report his victory, for he did not know of the capture of the *Macedonian*, while he did know of the disturbed state of public opinion in New England and of the disturbed state of Mr. Madison's mind. Decatur just before had reached a similar conclusion, but Decatur had the additional incentive of a prize to bring home. Bainbridge might have done better to stay out; he could have completed with water at San Salvador and left his prisoners there—as he actually did—and then have reached across to St. Helena to attack the East Indian shipping in that neighborhood. *Constitution* out at sea and south of the equator was worth far more than *Constitution* in port and with a blockade to run; a six weeks' further cruise might have been most profitable, but Bainbridge was a clear-thinking man and it would be rash to impugn his judgment.

The prisoners were put ashore at San Salvador under parole; Lambert died there of his wounds. Bainbridge spent five days filling up with stores and putting his ship to rights before sailing for home. The British prisoners noticed that he did not trouble to "fish" his wounded masts—apply a splint to strengthen them at the point of injury—and drew the conclusion that *Constitution's* masts were those of a ship of the line and damage done by a frigate's shot could be ignored; there was a good deal of truth in it. Lawrence in the *Hornet* was given orders to maintain the blockade of the *Bonne Citoyenne*, but Bainbridge had picked up the news from the Portuguese that there was a British ship of the line cruising in the vicinity and Lawrence was warned to make sure of his own safety. In any event, *Hornet* was to return in April. With these orders given, *Constitution* sailed on January 6 and after a tedious passage she reached Boston on February 27 without any interference by British ships of war; Decatur had reached harbor with *United States* and *Macedonian* nearly three months before.

Just three weeks after Bainbridge entered Boston astonishing news came to him from Martha's Vineyard. Lawrence and the *Hornet* were there. They had slipped in there as the nearest unwatched point on the United States coast, not daring to try to round Cape Cod lest foul winds should delay them for even a day or two. For everyone on board was on a minimum ration of water—two pints a day—and suffering extremely. It was not to be wondered at, as *Hornet* had 277 souls on board instead of her normal crew of 150. The balance was made up by a few Americans from a recaptured prize, a few British merchant seamen from another prize, and the survivors of the crew of H.M. gun brig *Peacock*, now lying at the bottom of the sea among the shoals of the Guiana coast. Not only was the *Peacock* sunk, but *Hornet* had on board twenty thousand dollars in gold and silver, taken out of a British packet.

Lawrence had carried out his orders exactly. He had watched the *Bonne Citoyenne* for several days after Bainbridge's departure. He had eluded the attack of H.M.S. *Montagu*, 74, which, having appeared as the Portuguese had warned might happen, had driven him into territorial waters. He had slipped out again the very next night and headed north and east along the Brazilian coast. The treasure had been taken from the English brig *Resolution*. He went on, investigated the coast of Dutch Guiana—in British hands at the moment—and from there to the coast of British Guiana, resolved that if no prospect of prizes presented itself he would try his luck in the West Indies before heading for home.

There was shipping visible here. He chased a brig into the shoal waters at the mouth of the Demerara River, sighted another at anchor inside the bar, and was beating round to get at her when still another sail made its appearance to windward. The two vessels headed cautiously for each other. Lawrence made her out to be a brig of war; he cleared for action and laid his ship as close to the wind as possible to gain the weather gauge.

The stranger made no attempt to avoid action but hurried to meet the enemy, as was the duty of every ship of the dominant navy when chance brought an opportunity of engaging any hostile ship of approximately equal force. The *Peacock* was a gun brig of the same type and quality as the *Frolic*, somewhat more lightly armed; the *Hornet* was somewhat more powerful than the *Wasp*. The wind was light but steady; the sea was smooth, offering a perfect battleground where chance and accident would have small play. No ship, it is apparent now, ever stood in toward more certain defeat than did the *Peacock* on that day; it was not so apparent then.

William Peake, the lieutenant in command, was a man with some reputation. He was one of a family many of whose members were serving in the Royal Navy, but no special favoritism had speeded his career; as first lieutenant of the *Lively* he seemed to have proved himself to be at least not an incompetent officer. Yet such he was. It was only the feeblest fight that he put up, even though he fought to the death. His ship's gunnery was pitifully poor, and the tales told about him, to the effect that he devoted the energy of his crew to perfecting the outward appearance of his ship rather than toward acquiring fighting efficiency, probably had some foundation in fact.

Lawrence was a bold and vigorous officer who had been Decatur's second-in-command when the *Philadelphia* was burned in Tripoli harbor. He was adored by his men, who had been long under his command—*Hornet* had shared in Rodgers' first cruise to the eastward at the beginning of the war, and Lawrence had been under Rodgers' influence and supervision during the important months of exercise before war began. He was an accomplished sailor with a well-drilled crew; he was, moreover, a man with a grievance. Morris, Hull's first lieutenant, had been promoted to captain as a reward for the capture of the *Guerrière*, immediately before *Constitution* and *Hornet* had sailed on the present voyage. The promotion had carried Morris over the heads of the master commandants, of whom Lawrence was one, and the disproportion of the reward was the more marked because Lawrence had received no step in promotion as a result of the *Philadelphia* affair. He was burning to distinguish himself, and the encounter with *Peacock* gave him the opportunity.

Each ship had a main battery of carronades; there could be no question of maneuvering at long range. They rushed at each other; the *Hornet* managed to gain the weather gauge and the ships exchanged broadsides, passing on opposite tacks. Peake wore the *Peacock* round, perhaps with the idea of crossing his opponent's stern, but Lawrence was too quick for him and the *Hornet* too handy. The American, wheeling round over the blue sea in the flaming sunset, came up against the *Peacock's* quarter and shot her opponent to pieces in less than fifteen minutes. "Eggshells armed with hammers" was an expression employed in a later age to describe a very different class of ship, but it applied well enough to the present antagonists. The fragile sides of a gun brig could be torn to pieces in no time by the smashing fire of heavy carronades at close range.

That was exactly what happened to *Peacock*. She was reduced to a sinking condition while her masts still stood. Almost one third of her crew were killed or wounded, her captain being killed. Her first lieutenant hailed to say she had surrendered; water was pouring in fast through her shattered sides and she sent up a distress signal immediately after. The prize crew sent on board tried to save her; they anchored (one mast went over the side at that moment) and tried to plug the shot holes and heave the guns overside, but she sank so rapidly that some men, both British and Americans, were trapped below and drowned. Sinking as she did on a comparatively even keel and in shoal water, her foremast head remained above water, and a lucky few saved themselves by racing up the shrouds ahead of the pursuing water; the rest found themselves afloat in the shattered boat and on the wreckage that drifted off the booms.

Hornet had suffered remarkably little damage. *Peacock's* first broadside had gone high, cutting up her rigging and inflicting a few casualties, and after that it is doubtful if *Peacock* scored one single further hit; likely enough, with *Hornet* against *Peacock's* quarter, *Peacock* had not more than a gun or two that would bear, and the crews of these would be most exposed to the *Hornet's* fire and may have been wiped out. It was a most decisive and convincing victory over an opponent by no means impossibly inferior in force. But the bigger ship had been better handled, her gunnery was better, and possibly she had better luck; those factors—as in most single-ship duels— multiplied each other, with the result that the damage inflicted on the one side was ten times as great as the damage on the other. That is obvious enough now, but it was by no means so obvious then. The public in America and England could only be aware that once more comparatively equal forces had met and once more a crushing, a preposterously one-sided victory had been won by the Americans. Not one such victory, or two, but five.

Chapter XI

THE BRITISH REACTION after the first bewilderment was creditable, as was to be expected of a nation that had risen to dominion at sea only after a good many hard knocks. There was a moment of numb despair; the *Naval Chronicle's* editorial comment on the news of the loss of the *Java* was simply, "The subject is too painful for us to dwell upon." There was some alarm. Early in 1813 there occurred off Sierra Leone a single-ship action between a British frigate, *Amelia,* and the French *Arethuse,* in which the French stuck to their guns and fought one of the most desperate drawn battles of the war, *Amelia* actually losing more than half her crew—far more than half her officers—while *Arethuse* succeeded in beating off her assailant. It appeared as if the French navy was taking heart from the American victories; perhaps even learning something of American methods, and a vigorous and well-handled French navy could still be a grim menace to British national security while American privateers were causing such severe havoc to British merchant shipping.

Nevertheless, calm and objective thinking soon became apparent in professional circles. There was little heard about the intrinsic British superiority. The *Naval Chronicle* drew the correct deduction from *Amelia's* experience, that the French sailor had long gone into battle "with a persuasion, founded on long experience, that his antagonist must be victorious." It spoke of "superstitious terror" and saw the necessity that "the spell be restored"—a remarkable piece of clear thinking on the part of a naval officer. It even perceived the weakness of the British naval staff system (where hardly staff or system existed) and protested against the "ministry of clerks" which could not rise to the occasion when "a new and troubled scene is opened." It demanded intelligent and bold action, so that America should "feel the real weight of the British trident." Meanwhile Wellington, deep in his plans for his amazing campaign of Vittoria, had been thinking along the same lines and even indulging in strong language most unusual in his correspondence: "I have been very uneasy about the American naval successes. I think we should have peace with America before the season for opening the campaign in Canada, if we could take one or two of these damned frigates."

Now that the twenty-year-old spell of continuous victory was broken, it was possible for the Royal Navy to think more clearly. There were still some hysterical moments—the claims in the ecstatic American press (and even in Mr. Madison's public announcements) that *United States'* and *Constitution's* victories had been won over equal force goaded British naval officers into refutations quite as extravagant; but for several months the Royal Navy indulged in serious stocktaking. Now there were fresh admissions that the manning was unsatisfactory. One officer came out with a bold denunciation of "the brutal horrors of the press"—a quite astonishing attack on an institution which was as nearly sacred as three centuries could make it. Another (a captain) minced no words when he wrote, "The American men of war are much better manned than ours" and went on to discuss "the poor creatures who are to be found in every one of our men of war." Another wrote of the British ships as "now manned by a very small proportion of able seamen, and the remainder filled up with good, bad, and indifferent, viz, ordinary seamen, landsmen, foreigners, the sweepings of Newgate, from the hulks, and almost all the prisons in the country." Yet another wrote, "Our ships have the dry rot, and their inhabitants have the mania of apathy and discontent."

The remedies suggested were equally astonishing. Correspondent after correspondent took a fling at the disciplinary system. One of them—and he described himself as an old man —declared frankly that "the code of punishment should have been obliterated by a system of encouragement and rewards," and went on to say, "The number of lashes inflicted on board a ship is not a sure criterion of her state of discipline." Another recommended "a legislative restriction of corporal punishments." The dictum was more than once quoted that flogging ruined a good seaman and made a bad one incorrigible.

Several writers commented adversely on the heartless principle of not paying any seaman a single penny until his ship was paid off; this was supposed to discourage desertion, because a man might be considered less likely to run when by so doing he forfeited his accumulated pay. The obvious answer to this was that seamen deserted even with several pounds owing to them. Similarly the equally heartless—and extremely unhealthy—system of denying men any shore leave whatever (to impede desertion) was also assailed; men still contrived to desert, and the price paid in suffering and discontent might well be too high. A certain and generous pension after long service might be found to reduce desertion.

One correspondent made the point that "we should cherish a more decisive feeling of professional attachment, that soldiers and sailors, whether in the ranks or in the waist, may have a greater identity of self and more rational principle in the cause"; this, be it noted, was long before any naval officer had heard the words "indoctrination" or "morale." There were powerful pleas for the better education and better treatment of the lower deck. The anecdote was often quoted—and fathered on Wellington—of the army officer who, when asked his opinion of naval discipline after a voyage in a British ship of war, replied, "Everything goes like clockwork, but, sir, I would not command an army on the same terms you do your ship, for the Crown of England. I have not seen a smile on the face of any individual since I have been on board her."

When admissions like this were being made in the public and professional press it was obvious that the service was undergoing a serious moral shaking-up. Yet, as other correspondents pointed out, moral and disciplinary reform could only partly solve the manning problem. The quality of recruits was poor "on account of the vast number of ships at this time in commission"; England possessed more ships than she could efficiently man. She had to keep every ship at sea that she possibly could—it was well known, for instance, that Pellew in the Mediterranean commanded a force smaller than the one he was blockading in Toulon—and England had to compromise, unsatisfactorily, between numbers and quality. Every ship, therefore, had the minimum crew for efficiency, and that crew of a minimum quality, and the minimum was hard to decide upon and was likely to be proved a sub-minimum in encounters with American ships.

More than one correspondent took the navy to task for its system of gunnery and gunnery training. "American seamen have been more exercised in firing at a mark than ours." "We are not allowed a sufficient quantity of powder in one year to exercise the people one month." Somebody sharply demanded that a strict inquiry should be held to determine how American gunnery arrangements differed from the British, whether they had fixed ammunition. "Are their rammers, sponges, worms, wads, shot, crows, handspikes, cartridges, tubes, powder horns, or tackle different?" The suggestion was made that British officers who had been taken as prisoners into American ships might answer these questions. The whole question of fixed ammunition was discussed—even to the point where it was proposed that cartridges containing two shot should be prepared for work at close quarters—as well as the questions of rope rammers versus stave rammers, and double-ended rammers versus single-ended. The necessity for the training of gun captains was stressed, and out of this discussion arose debate regarding the best method of discharging guns, whether by port-fires or by gunlocks or by quick match—the correspondents were well aware of the intrinsic difficulty in taking aim that arose from the delay between the decision to fire and the explosion of the charge. From here on the transition was easy from the practical suggestion to the fantastic. It was recommended that ships be rearmed with long-short guns that would be a compromise between long guns and carronades, with the virtues—but more especially the defects—of both. It was seriously put forward that the sweeps—the long oars—that were issued to small ships of war (and even to frigates) should be doubled in length for more efficient use in action, and not only during a calm, for apparently the writer believed that the dismasted *Macedonian* could have brought her guns once more into action if she had been provided with such sweeps. The British marines should be rearmed with rifles and trained to go aloft to pick off American officers—Lambert's death had made a deep impression, and it was forgotten, or unknown, that Bainbridge had been wounded in the same action; nor was it realized that rifles were nearly as rare in United States ships as in British ones, for distorted memories of the War of Independence made every American a rifleman in the British estimation.

Yet on one point the cranks and the hardheaded were agreed, and the point was insisted upon in every letter written; American naval strength must be destroyed. The Stars and Stripes must be swept from the seas, and America must be taught—and the world must be taught by her example—that no naval power could ever with impunity venture to pit itself against England.

The Admiralty roused itself; convulsive efforts had been

made ever since the arrival of the news of the loss of the *Guerrière*. Ship after ship was dispatched to reinforce Warren's command, and the British newspapers obligingly announced their sailing for any American sympathizer to read so that he could remit the news to Washington. The loss of the *Guerrière* brought about a very similar reaction as the defeat of Cradock off Coronel in 1914. Until the bad news came it seemed quite definite that nothing more could be spared for the new seat of war—in 1812 the Royal Navy was entirely occupied in watching the French, and in 1914 it was watching the High Seas Fleet. But defeat changed the estimates. Ships of the line could be sent to Warren, in the same way that it was found possible to spare two battle cruisers from the Grand Fleet to deal with Von Spee. But 1812, unluckily for Warren, did not bring any victory comparable with the Falkland Islands. The reverses, and the losses among the British mercantile marine, went on. Warren failed to lock the stable door even after the first horse had been stolen.

The British press in February 1813 listed the force that was directed against America. Under his personal command Warren had no fewer than fifteen 74s, a 50-gun ship, fifteen frigates, and twenty sloops and brigs. Stirling on the Jamaica station had four frigates and twelve sloops and brigs. Laforey at the Leeward Islands had a 74, four frigates, and sixteen smaller craft. Nagle at Newfoundland had a 50, two frigates, and six smaller craft. Dixon on the Brazilian coast had a 74 and two frigates and two brigs. It was an astonishing exertion; Nelson had won the victory of the Nile with not much more than half this strength. There is irony in the thought that if this effort had been made six months earlier—if, as has already been pointed out, Rodgers had met with disaster on his first sortie from New York—the war would certainly have taken a very different course. The effort could have been made, even allowing for the relief afforded later by the declaration of war against Bonaparte by Russia and Sweden; that it was not made in time was on account of the British Cabinet's false estimates regarding America's warlike intentions, regarding Bonaparte's naval strength, regarding the American navy's dash and enterprise, and regarding the rapidity of the conversion of the American mercantile marine to privateering. Once the mistakes had been made, it was hard to make up for them. The conflagration had not been smothered at its beginning, and it was now almost out of hand.

Warren fought the opening months of the war handicapped by having—he believed—to take precautions regarding his rear. It was a general expectation that Bonaparte would take advantage of the distraction afforded by the American war to send out his fleets and break through the blockade. While Warren was trying to parry Rodgers' thrusts he was also trying to be ready for the unannounced arrival in the American theater of war of a dozen French ships of the line which could destroy in detail any cordon he ventured to extend. Both Warren and the Admiralty that instructed him overestimated the readiness of the French navy to take the sea, nor could they guess at the extent to which the Russian campaign was draining French resources—and the extent to which it was occupying Bonaparte's attention to the exclusion of his naval interests. Wellington with his astonishing prescience guessed the truth as early as December 1812—before the effects of the retreat from Moscow were known—when he wrote to Admiral Martin, commanding on the coast of Spain, "If Bonaparte is wise, and has money, he will send out a large fleet. He has no money, however, and he must have found before now that a fleet cannot be equipped and maintained, as he maintains his armies, by requisitions on the unfortunate country which is made the seat of war." Few men, however, were gifted with Wellington's insight and acute ability to sum up his enemy's weaknesses; if the British Cabinet had been so gifted there would not have been room in the same letter of Wellington's for his dry comment, "Government appear to be at last making a serious effort to get the better of the American navy, which might as well have been made before."

Warren was also, under the instructions sent him by the Cabinet, handicapped by the hope of a speedy peace. The British government, anxious not to make the struggle too bitter while Warren was negotiating, held back the proclamation of general reprisals against America until the middle of October. It was not until the end of November that a commercial blockade of the Delaware and the Chesapeake was determined upon, and not until February 1813—thanks to the delays in communication—that it was put into force. Even ships bearing British licenses were liable to capture when sailing from these waters, and the blockade was gradually extended in the one direction to Montauk and in the other to the mouth of the Mississippi.

In the meanwhile the news of the various defeats of British ships arrived to harass Warren and embarrass the government. The public outcry no less than its own fears forced the Admiralty into new measures of the widest variety. The unsatisfactory manning of the British ships was tacitly admitted. A determined effort was made to scrape together drafts that would reinforce every frigate on the American station with a lieutenant and fifty men, while at the same time orders were given that none of the three large American frigates was to be fought by less than two British frigates—an order that did not make it easier for Warren to intercept the American privateers. At the same time the Admiralty tried to send to sea ships that could be matched against the big frigates. The type was already known—examples had been seen in all navies during the past fifty years. This was the razee, a ship of the line with one deck removed—a number of 74s were hastily cut down in this fashion. The criticism might be advanced that a 74 would be far more capable of dealing with a frigate without being subjected to this alteration, but the critics (and they were many—the professional press was flooded with letters on the subject) could be answered by the arguments that the razee did not need nearly as large a crew, handled better, particularly in regard to working to windward, and drew appreciably less water. Undeniably she would have the massive scantlings and heavy guns of a ship of the line—and of the American frigates—but undeniably she would have the faults of any hybrid or adaptation; the critics roundly condemned the type as "mules."

Nor was this the only construction program taken in hand. Orders were hurriedly given for the building of six large frigates, and, in view of the perennial shortage of oak, particularly oak of suitable growth, they were to be built of fir—a remarkable volte-face, in view of the fact that before the war broke out one of the British expressions of contempt for the American navy was that it was composed of "fir-built frigates." The principal objection that had been advanced concerning fir for ships of war was that it splintered badly under gunfire, thus adding to the casualty list. Now a study of the American casualty lists seemed to prove the theory unsound; it was still almost impossible to admit that the American ships had been hit so little that the theory had not yet been tested.

The three big American frigates were "spar-decked"; where contemporary British frigates had only light gangways along the sides of the ship from quarter-deck to forecastle, the Americans had a solid deck that could carry guns, with the advantage of superior command and additional protection to the main-deck guns in the event of falling spars. The spar deck could not be hastily installed and employed; it was an intrinsic part of the original design, dating from Humphreys' plan to build the largest possible frigates that Congress would permit; large displacement and plenty of beam were necessary if guns were to be mounted so high above the water line. The two-decked 50-gun ships of the various navies of the world were already obsolescent, hardly a dozen remaining in service. On their small displacement living conditions in two decks were extremely hard, and the lower-deck guns were so close to the water that they could not be served when any moderate sea was running. Even the 64, which had long taken part without question in the line of battle (the *Africa,* which had helped pursue *Constitu-*

tion, fought at Trafalgar in 1805), was not regarded with favor nowadays; it was generally agreed that a 74 was the smallest practicable ship on two decks. It had already been gravely pointed out by apologists innumerable that *Constitution* and her sisters had the dimensions of a 74. But they were "spar-decked frigates," and they had been victorious. England must build spar-decked frigates, cost what they might—the closest analogy in recent history that comes to mind is the issue to the British (and American) armies of spiked helmets as a result of the victories of the Prussian army in 1870. The spar-decked frigates were built, and built of fir, but they received no real test in action; and the heavy losses suffered later by the *Chesapeake* and the *President* occasioned a revulsion of feeling with regard to fir. There had not been wanting, at the time of the wild discussions arising from the American victories, a body of opinion that had even objected to the use of teak in warship construction on account of its tendency to splinter.

It can hardly be overstressed that the huge construction and reconstruction programs undertaken by the British government were the result of the employment by the United States of only three large frigates, which might have been thought scarcely to merit the attention of a navy with over a hundred ships of line actually at sea. It was a remarkable example of the "nuisance value" of the American navy; the prospect of the expense and the exertion involved could have been deemed an important factor in persuading the British government to incline toward peace—if peace had been made at that time. Good fortune had played its part as well in the American success, the good fortune which on three occasions brought British frigates singly into action against the Americans, but it must also be stressed that American professional skill was a factor of the highest importance; Hull's professional skill that carried the *Constitution* clear of the British squadron so that the war did not open with a naval disaster, and the professional skill of Decatur and Bainbridge as well as of Hull that made the three frigate victories so overwhelmingly decisive.

But there was no chance of peace at present. America was intoxicated with victory, and the British blood was up. Along with the reinforcements that poured in to Warren came orders reiterating over and over again the need to bring home the war to America; and Warren, while still concerned over his necessary defensive measures, had now to devote serious thought to the problem of taking the offensive, to decide upon how best to hurt a sprawling and undeveloped country that presented no obvious target for attack.

Blockade had already been instituted, and the published lists of captures were growing longer and longer. The items were worth study: schooner *Lively*, of 78 tons, from St. Bartholomew, bound to Boston, laden with molasses and sugar; brig *Phoebe*, of 200 tons, from Civitavecchia, laden with brandy, oil, and juniper berries; schooner *New Foye* from New York, bound to Boston, laden with sugar, earthenware, varnish, and other articles; schooner *Polly*, of 85 tons, from Charleston, bound to Boston, laden with rice, cotton, shoes, and tanned leather; schooner *Eliza*, of 90 tons, from Philadelphia, bound to Boston, laden with pig iron, 16 nine-pounders, gin, flour, dry goods, and sundry other articles.

There were two hundred more names in the first published lists, and the lists were supplemented by others from month to month. The American mercantile marine was losing ships at a rate not far short of the British, although considerably less in tonnage; proportionately the American losses were enormously greater, being sustained by a much smaller mercantile marine. Blockade and capture were reducing America's sea-borne commerce to a minute figure; and at the same time American privateer captains were reporting having sighted and dogged enormous British convoys, of two hundred or even three hundred sail. Sometimes they succeeded, especially in thick or stormy weather, in snapping up a straggler or two from these gigantic fleets; sometimes they had sorrowfully to report that the escorts had been so powerful and so vigilant and so well handled that they had not succeeded in effecting a single capture. It was very obvious that despite the numerous successes of the privateers, despite the five victories, British commerce was not being perceptibly diminished, while America was already experiencing at least inconvenience if not actual suffering. Not only was the transoceanic commerce almost at an end, but the coastal trade was being seriously impeded, and in the America of that period the coastal trade was of extreme importance.

The alternative to transferring goods by sea along the vast length of the American coast line was to send them by wagon over roads notoriously ill maintained. It took ten times as long at least; the transportation charges are hard to estimate at this present time, but a fair estimate would be that they were a hundred times as great; at least equally important was that the facilities for maintaining land communications simply did not exist to the extent necessary. There were not enough wagons or draft animals in the country to take the place of the highly specialized and long-established coastal trade. Boston had to do without its earthenware and varnish from New York and its leather from Charleston; foodstuffs accumulated and spoiled on the quays of Baltimore while the governor of Rhode Island complained bitterly of the shortage of flour at Newport. The intoxication of victory was likely to be succeeded by a reaction not unusual.

A curious note of depression was struck by the publication of the replies of Captain Charles Stewart—Captains Isaac Hull and Charles Mims concurring—to inquiries addressed to him by the Secretary of the Navy at the request of a committee of Congress. The whole correspondence was published and was reproduced in the British press. Charles Stewart (he had an infant daughter next year, Delia Tudor Stewart, who was later to transmit his name to his grandson, Charles Stewart Parnell) wrote much good sense on the usefulness to the United States of a squadron of ships of the line with ancillary frigates and sloops. He suggested that the ships of the line should be as superior to the ordinary 74 as the *Constitution* was to the average frigate, in order to be sure of victory in a single-ship action—he proposed building 76s, "in honour of the year of our Independence." He gave some excellent advice regarding the establishment and maintenance of dockyards. But he ended his message with an odd and depressing postscript. The United States Navy, he wrote, was already (November 1812) experiencing difficulty in finding men for the ships of war because the seamen were aware that they might find themselves in frigates pitted against ships of the line "and cannot but feel a degree of reluctance, at entering the service, from the evident disparity."

Stewart was, of course, stressing the need for ships of the line, but it is hard to believe that he was deliberately misrepresenting facts in order to make his point. He was fulfilling an important duty in giving his professional advice to his government and he was very much in a position to know the truth, since he was at that moment fitting U.S. frigate *Constellation* for sea at Washington. He may have been misled by the shortage of seamen resulting from the competition of the privateers, he may merely have let his pen run away with him, but his letter stands to this day—it appeared in its entirety in the British press in May 1813, greatly to the encouragement of the British public, which felt confirmed in the contempt for American seamen which it had entertained before the war began and which had tended to diminish with subsequent events.

Stewart eventually succeeded in manning the *Constellation;* he took her round to Annapolis, and from there, on the first day of February, he headed for Hampton Roads en route for the open sea. But as he came down the wintry Chesapeake, with Yorktown under his lee, a group of strange sails came into sight ahead, beating close-hauled into American waters. There was no mistaking what they were, unbelievable though it appeared.

Two ships of the line, three frigates, and two sloops; they could only be British.

Warren, under the constant prodding of Admiralty, had at last felt strong enough to take the offensive and had furthermore worked out a plan which he hoped would, when put into effect, carry the war home to America. In his flagship, the *San Domingo* (the name dated from Duckworth's victory off that island in 1806), and with his second-in-command, Cockburn—a man of a very different stamp, harsh and overbearing—accompanying him, he set out from Bermuda in January, Cockburn arriving just in time to head off Stewart and the *Constellation*. Stewart turned and fled at a moment when the smallest delay would have been fatal; he was somewhat in the situation of a man descending from his bedroom to discover unexpectedly an armed band entering his entrance hall. Stewart had to decide at once where in all the innumerable inlets he would find safest refuge, having regard to the weather conditions at the moment. To turn back meant beating to windward and a prolonged chase wherein anything might happen. He was just able to turn aside and head for Norfolk.

He kedged his way up the river—the tidal inlet—with the flowing tide to help him. Cockburn still had a long beat to windward and he was ignorant of the depths of water with which Stewart was familiar. He could only follow cautiously, and soon the tide turned, night descended, and he was constrained to anchor, while Stewart was furiously active strengthening his position. There were some of Mr. Madison's gunboats available, useful at last in this situation, if only to provide guns and men. Cockburn had no troops with him and needed time for reconnaissance; his best chance would have been an attack at the first dawn with the few hundred men, marines and seamen, which his squadron could have provided. He held back, wisely enough; his best chance was a poor one unless Stewart's men flinched. After that the enterprise of cutting out the *Constellation* presented growing difficulties.

Yet Warren and Cockburn were free to range the whole Chesapeake, having provided a small force to watch *Constellation*. They could penetrate wherever a frigate could float and to nearly every point where a launch could carry a six-pounder. The spreading waters of the Chesapeake were a most important link in the internal communications of the United States. Pathetic items began to appear in the long lists of captures effected by Warren's command—American sloop *Nancy*, from Hampton, laden with oysters; American pilot boats *Ulysses* and *Hornet*; schooner *Betsy Ann*, from Alexandria, bound to Boston with flour; the pilot boat *Flowing Cann*, merely carrying oysters from Hampton to Norfolk; the *Independent*, from Richmond to Norfolk, with tobacco and hemp; schooner *Accommodation*, also from Richmond, bound to Norfolk—but she was carrying whisky. The British command of the Chesapeake was disrupting the internal trade of the United States; it was as significant that the women would find no oysters in the market and the men no whisky in the taverns as it was that state executives were complaining about the shortage of the necessities of life.

There was even further significance in the presence of British ships here; with Hampton Roads as a safe anchorage from which they could issue out to sea, and with the Chesapeake denied to American ships as a refuge if sighted at sea when making their way along the coast, the coastwise trade was much more liable to effective interruption than it had been when merely subject to attack by cruisers off the coast. There was the Portuguese brig *Cidade da Lisboa*, carrying oranges and lemons from her name town to New York; the sloop *Solon*, from North Carolina, carrying corn to Boston; and the *Theresa*, from Boston, with sundries for South Carolina. The losses were appalling, for these quoted captures were minor items in lists running to hundreds of names; once more the student tries to imagine what would have been the effect if a squadron of ships of the line had entered the Chesapeake in July 1812 instead of in February 1813; if the topsails of British ships had been visible from Philadelphia at the same time as the news arrived of Hull's surrender, for British ships of war forced their way up the Delaware as well.

This was only the first muttering of the storm which was breaking over the United States and which took both administration and public by surprise. At the moment when Cockburn was on his way to the Chesapeake the crew of the *United States*, victorious over the *Macedonian*, was landing at the New Slip in New York, having made their way thither via Long Island Sound. With a band at their head they marched, "amid the loud huzzas of their fellow citizens," along Pearl Street, Wall Street, and Broadway to the City Hotel, where a reception by the corporation awaited them, and a welcoming speech by Alderman Vanderbilt, and a display of transparencies, and a dinner, and toasts innumerable, the final one being "To the American Eagle—may its wings cover the ocean, and its claws grab the ships of the King of England." It was easy to foresee a revulsion of feeling when the news should arrive—as it did within a matter of days—that the ships of the King of England were cruising without danger within striking distance of the American capital.

Cockburn acted with considerable energy. He sent his boats where his ships could not penetrate. One of Warren's reports (dated from "Annapolis, Chesapeake"!) told of sending the boats of the fleet fifteen miles up the Rappahannock, where they boarded and captured four armed schooners—a privateer and three letters of marque—manned by heavy crews totaling over two hundred officers and men, the British loss being only thirteen; undoubtedly the Americans flinched, and undoubtedly the demoralization resulting from the arrival of the British in the Chesapeake was considerable.

Cockburn pushed on northward into the farthest extremity of the Chesapeake, striking at the communications between Baltimore and Philadelphia; today the Chesapeake and Delaware Canal runs close to the scene of his operations. He had no troops with him at present, save for a small detachment of artillerymen, but he had a rocket boat and several craft of small draft, mostly prizes he had previously captured, and with his marines and a detachment of seamen he could scrape together a force of some four hundred men. He made a feint at Baltimore, occasioning considerable alarm, and then struck at the other side. There was militia to oppose him, but badly led and quite uninspired even though Washington was only a day's ride away. The tiny landing parties met with almost no resistance, the militia abandoning their positions the moment an attack was launched; in one battery a hundred and thirty stand of small arms were picked up after having been thrown away by the men supposed to use them. Cockburn reached all the objectives ("foundries, stores, and public works") assigned to him by Warren's orders. He destroyed a foundry ("the Cecil or Principio Foundery, one of the most valuable works of the kind in America") on the outskirts of Havre de Grace, along with government depots of provisions and military equipment; he burned a dozen sail of coasters, and vast stores of flour, sending one party far up the Susquehanna, all this at a cost of less than a dozen wounded.

He had been faced, from the moment of his arrival, with the problem of dealing with civilian opposition. It was not only militiamen, and certainly not only militiamen in uniform, who fired on his landing parties. It was not in human nature, and certainly not in American human nature, to refrain from taking a shot at red-coated marines landed on a mission of destruction in a country whose Constitution declared that "the right of the people to bear and carry arms shall not be infringed." The laws of war had not yet been codified. It was understood, however, that a man who fought without a uniform was liable to death if caught, his house was liable to destruction, and even the village or town from which he came; but the invading regular troops, on the other hand, were bound to respect civilian life and property. Moreover, there was an occasionally accepted ruling—later incorporated in the Geneva Convention—that a people might be permitted to take up arms in a spontaneous uprising; a year or two before, Wellington had maintained this point in correspondence with Masséna regarding the status of the un-uniformed Portuguese militia. In essence, therefore, the ultimate policy was decided by the commanding officer of the invading force. Cockburn deplored the "useless rancour" of the inhabitants in opposing him, and burned houses and towns where such opposition was offered him. He congratulated himself, and felicitated Warren, on having achieved his object, for Charlestown submitted to him without opposition and he was assured that "all the places in the upper part of the Chesapeake" had adopted the resolution that neither guns nor militiamen should be suffered there. On the surface the policy of reprisals had succeeded, but it is doubtful whether it had conduced toward the ultimate end of the invasion, which was to prevail on the American people to agree to peace.

In the prevailing state of sullen resentment Cockburn had to decide on another question of policy, closely allied to the matter of reprisals. Like every naval officer of the time, he was faced with the chronic problem of the supply of drinking water and with the nearly as urgent problem of the supply of fresh provisions. He could hardly be expected to detach ships to his base hundreds of miles away to fill up with water, nor could he expect his men to live on salt meat when they could see cattle browsing on shore and hear cocks crowing. Yet the parties he landed to fill up his water casks were always liable to have shots fired at them; his efforts to buy fresh provisions were not very successful. He maintained that it was inhuman to deprive his men of drinking water, and he was quite sincere in his protestations that he was offering genuine value for livestock. He did not make allowance for the irresistible temptation his landing parties offered to the local man with a rifle who had heard nothing about the resolution of the towns to make no resistance and who would have cared nothing, whatever he heard. And Cockburn tried to buy cattle with bills on the British Treasury; he was an able and active officer, but he displayed complete ignorance of the people he was fighting if he expected a Maryland farmer to part with his herd in exchange for bills redeemable in London at some vague future date. Wellington was dealing with the similar problem in Spain and France by paying handsomely in gold and silver—even taking care to have supplies ready of the actual currency of the country in which he found himself—but Cockburn had no gold or silver to spare, partly because Wellington had all the available supply. Refusal to sell, in Cockburn's eyes, was a hostile act. He was justified then in seizing provisions without payment, and that, even in the chaotic state of the laws of war, justified armed resistance; resistance justified reprisals, and the vicious circle was started again at the moment when he thought the country was pacified.

This was also the moment when it had been demonstrated, by the most convincing proof possible, that the enormous American flotilla of gunboats, constructed at considerable expense during the preceding decade, was of no use whatever for the purpose for which it was designed. The highest hopes had rested on it—save in the judgment of experienced seamen—and both President Madison and President Jefferson had believed that it would preserve American coasts from insult. Now the gunboats proved their uselessness even here, in the ideal circumstances of the sheltered waters of the Chesapeake. They had several brushes with British ships, once or twice in calms when they had every advantage, and they never scored a success and often suffered loss. Their failure was necessarily a blow to the national pride; even the general public could not forget the vaunting claims that had been put forward for them a few years earlier, when the Administration had flattered itself that it had discovered a means of achieving national security at a bargain price.

Warren by now had received a reinforcement of troops, a couple of companies of Canadians for use as light infantry, a battalion of the 102nd Regiment (the high number was a proof that it was a unit very recently raised), and additional artillery, and he had a good general in command—Sydney Beckwith, who had commanded a brigade of the famous Light Division with distinction, and whose face bore the scars of the wound he had received in his last action, at Sabugal in 1811. The British had lately evolved a successful system of amphibious warfare; during the preceding year, while Wellington was waging the Salamanca campaign, a small infantry force carried on shipboard had cruised up and down the Biscay coast, landing here and there, keeping the whole area in a turmoil and pinning down an immensely superior French army of occupation. Small Spanish armies, hotly pursued by the French, had also been repeatedly shipped from one point to another by an intelligent employment of sea power, and although there had been one or two petty disasters—in one of which Lord Blaney was captured —the principle was well established that a small force employing the mobility conferred by the command of the sea could be used effectively against a long coast line.

The Admiralty plainly had taken the lesson to heart, as appears in its new instructions to Warren. What the Admiralty did not understand, however, was that there were few suitable objectives in the Chesapeake for a force of two thousand men. In Spain there had always been the French communications at which to strike, and innumerable isolated garrisons, and there were nearly always Spanish guerrilla forces within call to act as a useful reinforcement. Beckwith could look for no such assistance in the neighborhood of the Chesapeake. He dared not entangle his small force in very large towns like Baltimore or Philadelphia; there was in fact only one target at which he could aim—the *Constellation* up the Elizabeth River—and this was as obvious to Stewart as it was to Beckwith. The consequence was that when he struck his blow (Stewart had left to take com-

mand of the *Constitution* and Gordon commanded at Norfolk)
he had none of the advantages of mobility and surprise.

Craney Island, guarding the mouth of the Elizabeth River,
had been fortified, batteries thrown up and guns mounted, and
the navigation was difficult. The American seamen stood to
their guns and the militia were inspired by their example. Beckwith and Warren so disliked the situation that they called off
the attack when it had hardly begun. Warren's very extensive
naval experience had included one abortive amphibious operation, that on Ferrol as far back as 1800. He had been in command of the naval forces on that occasion as well, and the
memory could easily have influenced him, although the Ferrol
landing ended in a fiasco rather than a disaster. It was equally
so here; the total British losses were only eighty killed,
wounded, and missing; it was by no means the bloody reverse
which the Americans believed it to be, but it was the belief and
not the facts that was important. The redcoats had launched
an attack and had failed, and the knowledge was a powerful
stimulant at a time when depression was extreme. Until that
moment there had been no apparent limit to the British domina-
tion of the Chesapeake, but now the seemingly invincible had
been turned back.

In consequence the further operations were not of such great
importance. Beckwith, in default of any better objective, turned
against Hampton and captured the place after a neat maneuver.
He demonstrated against the front of the place with his ships'
boats and his rockets while his main body, having already
landed ten miles away, marched against the flank. The operation was well timed and the American militia fled as raw troops
might be expected to do on discovering their flank turned by a
powerful force. They threw away their muskets and left their
guns behind as trophies for Beckwith—and the colors of the
James City Light Infantry—but there was nothing left for Beckwith to do save to blow up the useless batteries and re-embark
his men. The ineffectiveness of his effort was obvious even to

the men who ran away. Beckwith and his force would have been far better employed in Wellington's army, which at that moment was marching through the Spanish sierras toward the victory of Vittoria.

It might even be said that they had done actual harm; for some of the British infantry, bursting into Hampton after their successful assault, got out of hand—it was traditional in all armies at that time that an assaulting army should be rewarded by pillage when successful—and turned to looting and outrage before Beckwith could beat them off. The tales of the sack of Hampton lost nothing in the telling and, exaggerated though they were, they helped to inflame American resentment—they helped to stiffen the defense of New Orleans nearly two years later.

Meanwhile Cockburn, untrammeled by transports, maintained his tireless activity. He pushed up the James and the York and even up the Potomac. The frigate *Adams* lay just beyond his reach at the moment, but a gunboat was captured in a tributary of the Potomac, a revenue cutter in the York, and unfortunate coasters everywhere; it was an odd aspect of the laws of war that anything that floated, down to the most insignificant skiff or ferryboat, was legitimate prize of war to his squadron, while the cows that watched him from the fields were legally safe from him as long as they remained on dry land.

Cockburn was suffering serious losses even though his movements were hardly opposed. His men deserted at every opportunity, and as summer advanced and the water became warm enough for swimming, opportunities were constant. A man needed not to be a specially good swimmer, when his ship lay anchored in the York, to venture to lower himself quietly overside and free himself forever from the lash and the rope, from hardship and indignity. Even non-swimmers—probably in the majority—might well think the attempt worth making, using a barrel stave for support, when the reward would be a fresh start in the land of opportunity. It seems most likely that it was the losses from desertion which led Warren, before the summer was far advanced, to withdraw most of his forces from the Chesapeake. He continued to maintain there at least one ship of the line and enough small craft to make all movement by water hazardous; but the withdrawal was a decided indication of an intrinsic weakness in the Royal Navy at the time.

Chapter XII

FIELD MARSHAL THE MARQUIS OF WELLING-
TON was in temporary and uncomfortable headquarters in
France, in the foothills of the Pyrenees; he had been marching
and fighting all day, and he would be marching and fighting
again tomorrow, against a vigilant and equal enemy. But there
was to be no leisure for him that evening, for the mail arrived
from London (some of it a month old, owing to unfavorable
weather in the Bay of Biscay) and he had to sit down and answer it, as usual with his own hand, with no trained staff to
assist him. His principal correspondent this evening was Lord
Bathurst, Secretary of State for War and the Colonies, and the
most important letter that Wellington had to answer that evening dealt not, as one would expect, with the campaign he was
waging in France, but with the war in Canada. Six years of victory had by now constituted Wellington as principal military
adviser to his government, and he was pestered with inquiries
on every conceivable military matter. It is notable that in the
difficult circumstances in which he found himself, without maps
or books of reference, while reports came in to him from the
outposts, he wrote the best military appreciation of the Canadian
situation that was to appear on the British side during the war,
in this letter, which will bear continual reference.

"Any offensive operation founded upon Canada," he wrote,

"must be preceded by the establishment of a naval superiority on the Lakes. . . . The defence of Canada and the cooperation of the Indians depends on the navigation of the Lakes." After these very definite statements he went on to lay down some important principles regarding offensive operations against America which are not of concern in this present chapter but will demand consideration later. For the moment it is only necessary to note that the ablest military mind in the British service was entirely convinced of the necessity for naval superiority on the Great Lakes.

The early operations in 1812 had made this abundantly clear to the American government. Brock, commanding on the British side, had acted with energy, taking advantage of the naval superiority he possessed on Lakes Huron and Erie. Striking rapidly first at one point and then at another, he had secured Mackinac—and thereby the adhesion of the Indians to his cause —and had forced, or persuaded, Hull to surrender at Detroit. Brock's death in the skirmish at Queenston was a disaster to the British cause, although its importance was not realized at the time; Brock was a man of drive and personality as well as of military insight, and there was no one with these qualities found to replace him. Although a soldier, it is likely enough that had he lived he would have brought enough pressure to bear on the naval authorities and would have given them enough assistance for the British to retain their command of the Lakes. The circumstances in which Sir James Lucas Yeo became available for appointment "to command all the naval forces on the Lakes in Canada" have already been noticed. He was not a man of fiery energy, nor a man of tact. He was subordinate to Warren, who was in charge of the conduct of all operations against the United States, and Warren was not the man to infuse energy into Yeo, especially as he had his attention already occupied in watching the American navy, guarding against American privateers, and attacking the American coast line. Yeo was allotted a small force of officers—four commanders, eight lieutenants, and twenty-four midshipmen—but when the question of a supply of seamen arose it was never seriously considered.

As has been pointed out so often already, lack of seamen constituted the greatest wartime shortage from which England suffered at this time. Warren, enduring the continual chiding of the Admiralty for the shortcomings of his force in the Atlantic, was not likely to weaken his crews by drafts; nor were the authorities in England, confronted at every turn by demands for seamen which they were quite unable to satisfy, likely to make special provision for a distant and not apparently particularly vital area. And desertion, the curse of the navy, was a continual menace; invaluable seamen were not lightly to be sent to Canada where they would have every opportunity of disappearing either into the back country or across the frontier into America. Lastly, the manning of his command was part of the duty of every naval officer. Yeo was expected to make his arrangements on the spot, and little consideration was given to the impossibility of recruiting seamen on the Lakes, however drastically he might employ the press gang.

The first phase of the war on the Lakes ended in 1812 with both sides watching each other across Erie and Ontario, with no decisive action having been taken, and the British holding a precarious naval superiority which had not been boldly employed by the Canadian officer in command at that time. America entered upon the second phase with several advantages. Her land communications with Lake Ontario were better than the British, thanks not only to superior roads but to a denser population and to convenient river and lake transportation; and whatever sources of manufactures she possessed were in touch with these communications. Yet this was not of as much importance as that an active and able officer was put in charge on the Lakes and was given a free hand. Captain Isaac Chauncey was already a man of mark in the United States Navy; his very first commission was antedated in order to give him seniority enough to be Truxtun's first lieutenant in the *President*. He had

THE AGE OF FIGHTING SAIL

preserved a high reputation since that date as a sea officer and as an organizer—his varied experience including a period of civilian employment while on furlough in the pay of John Jacob Astor. For the past several years he had been displaying talent of a high order in command of the New York Navy Yard. It may have been the coincidence that he was occupying this post at this moment that was responsible for his new appointment, or perhaps the whole credit for it may be given to the Administration. American was singularly fortunate in 1812 in commanding the services of so many accomplished forty-year-old captains, just as she had been fortunate earlier in possessing the remarkable galaxy of talent which won her her independence and established her as a nation. It appeared now as if, in Chauncey, America had another officer worthy to rank with Hull and Decatur and Rodgers. It was not until Chauncey was submitted to the actual test of war that it became apparent that although he possessed in a high degree the good qualities necessary in a quartermaster general he did not possess those of a commander in chief.

Chauncey flung himself into the business of building up naval strength on the Lakes with astonishing energy, foresight, and managerial skill. He had two independent bases at his disposal and two independent lines of supply, via Pittsburgh and the Allegheny to Lake Erie, via the Hudson and the Mohawk to Lake Ontario. The British communications with Lake Erie were almost entirely dependent on their command of Lake Ontario, and so the latter lake was of the greater strategical importance; victory here would reduce the British on Lake Erie to near impotence. Chauncey was therefore bound to concentrate his attention upon Lake Ontario; American activity on Lake Erie was a fortunate result both of the existence of the other line of communications and the arrival of another able officer, Oliver Perry, to whom Chauncey could delegate the responsibility.

There was everything to be done; of all the materials necessary for a fleet, only the timber was available—and that was standing in the forests, still growing. Blocks and cordage, nails and cables, not to mention guns and powder and shot, canvas, cartridges, and tools, all had to be remembered, obtained, and transported. Chauncey took his first long step toward the creation of his fleets by appointing a remarkable trio of shipbuilders —Eckford and the brothers Brown—whom he sent up to begin construction while he busied himself with purchases and transportation. There were difficulties in plenty, disease and disaffection, the unsuitability of the available harbors, chronic shortage of necessary materials, obstruction by sullen governors of New England states. The skilled labor which was available in New York, shipwrights and riggers and carpenters, had not only to be persuaded to accept employment on the Lakes but had to be carried there, fed, housed, kept warm and healthy (as far as possible), and protected from attack by the English, while the seamen had to be recruited in the face of the competition of the privateers.

Chauncey's appointment took effect on September 3. On October 9 his subordinate, Elliott—Perry had not yet been appointed—by the aid of seamen sent up by Chauncey and newly arrived in the nick of time, was able to pounce on two British brigs on Lake Erie and capture one and destroy the other. On November 6 Chauncey himself was flying his pennant on Lake Ontario, momentarily in superior force, looking into Kingston and taking prizes. On November 26 he launched the *Madison*, a 590-ton corvette; the trees from which she was built were still standing at the time of his appointment. Then winter closed in and active operations were suspended, but the building race continued under difficulties.

The winter ended and spring began, and even before the breaking up of the ice came the test of Chauncey as a naval commander in chief. He had demonstrated his organizing and administrative abilities, but the rest of the war was to show that he did not possess the further peculiar and rare qualities

that would have given effect to the others. He had it in his
power to strike the first blow. He was personally brave; he was
undoubtedly energetic. Now he had to decide where to strike.
Toward the western end of Ontario was the town of York—
known nowadays as Toronto—and at the eastern end was
Kingston. Both were naval bases; both sheltered ships completed or under construction. With the British communications
by land extremely difficult, York depended for its supply upon
Kingston. The capture of Kingston would cut off York—and
Erie and Huron, too, for that matter—from all resources. For
that matter, so would the capture of Montreal at the head of
navigation on the St. Lawrence, but at that particular moment
an attempt upon Montreal was impracticable. The question in
April 1813 was whether to assail Kingston or York.

The advantages to be gained by the capture of Kingston, and
either its destruction or its permanent retention, were obvious.
They were plain enough to General Armstrong, the newly
appointed Secretary of War; they were plain to Chauncey;
they were almost plain to General Dearborn, commanding on
the New York frontier, who would have to supply the necessary troops—he disposed of almost ten thousand men. With
Kingston in American hands, York would fall almost of itself;
certainly nothing would reach Lake Erie, and the British land
forces in the Niagara peninsula would be dangerously isolated.
Early in the year Chauncey actually formed the opinion that
with a thousand men Kingston would be captured.

But as the moment for decision arrived, timidity began to
replace boldness. It was coming to be realized how complete
had been Bonaparte's disaster in Russia, and Dearborn nerv-
ously conjured up pictures of England diverting her strength
from Europe to America and hurrying battalion after battalion
across the Atlantic. Chauncey came to agree with him. They
could hardly be blamed for their inaccurate predictions about
European affairs; although they knew that Wellington was
back in Portugal and the Russians had only reached the eastern

frontier of Prussia, a sudden collapse of the Empire was perfectly possible. But they fell into the error of overestimating their enemy's strength and facilities. If England acted exactly as they feared; if British troops were available in a condition ready for immediate embarkation; if they were shipped at once and their voyage was rapid; if the Canadian militia was fully equipped, ready and willing to move; if transportation for them existed and if Prevost were making full use of it—*if* all this were happening the British might be present in Kingston in overwhelming force by the time an attack could be launched. There might be as many as eight thousand men there.

Even with winter restricting movement Chauncey and Dearborn had ample sources of information. Deserters came in from the Niagara front at the one end, and information could be gathered from spies acting under cover of the smuggling trade with Halifax at the other, and gossip and trade went on across the whole length of the St. Lawrence in between. Yet with all these facilities—or perhaps because of them, as despondency always can find confirmation of its fears—Chauncey was utterly misled. The British troops at Kingston numbered six hundred men; Chauncey's and Dearborn's estimate of a possible eight thousand was even more fantastically exaggerated than some of McClellan's estimates in 1862.

In consequence a minor objective was selected. A blow struck at York might perhaps just succeed before the British could reinforce the place with their uncounted thousands; and the blow was struck with a promptitude and a vigor that set the imagination to work regarding the possible consequences had it been directed at Kingston. Chauncey took eighteen hundred troops on board at Sackets Harbor and sailed as soon as ice and weather would permit. Three days carried them the length of Ontario. Dearborn was sick with strain and anxiety; Zebulon Pike took command of the troops, landed them outside the town, and had little difficulty in pushing the garrison out of the place. The previous anxieties vanished as it became

apparent that the garrison numbered no more than a few hundred. The blowing up of the British magazine in the course of
the evacuation occasioned a good many casualties—Pike was
killed—which in turn inflamed the American soldiers at the
same time as they were excited by the fighting and by the military destruction which they were ordered to perform. A frigate
on the stocks was burned; the accumulation of naval and military stores was either destroyed or carried off. The public
buildings were burned as well, including those which housed
the legislature of Upper Canada, of which York was the capital.
Inevitably there were some looting and some outrages, after a
successful assault and with the commander on the spot dead and
his senior still on shipboard. The treatment of York was one
item in the list of outrage and counteroutrage which helped to
embitter the war.

Chauncey sailed away when the destruction was complete.
He was in an exalted mood, which was not lowered by the discovery that he had missed the most important prize of all; the
Prince Regent sloop of war had by coincidence sailed from
York just before his arrival and was now in Kingston to reinforce the squadron there. It was still possible to have improvised
and to have carried out an attack on Kingston, but even with
the information gained by the capture of the British commanding officer's papers Chauncey and Dearborn were not to be
diverted from carrying out the next step of the campaign they
had planned. Chauncey believed that the capture of York had
given him undisputed command of the lake, and in that belief
the troops were transported to the Niagara peninsula, where
in a series of fierce skirmishes they succeeded in pushing back
the British from the Niagara River, setting free some vessels of
the Erie squadron which had been shut in on the far side of the
peninsula, an appreciable success.

In the midst of his exultation, however, Chauncey suddenly
received the news that at the far end of Ontario the British
whom he had believed to be reduced to impotence had sallied

out from Kingston and were assailing his base at Sackets Harbor. It was dreadful news; a little more resolution on the part of Prevost and Yeo (the latter had arrived at Kingston immediately after the fall of York) might have resulted in a disaster as serious as Chauncey could have occasioned at Kingston. Chauncey had hurriedly to defend his base, and from now on the naval war on Ontario was waged in seesaw fashion, with each side building feverishly and securing or losing command of the lake alternately with each accession of strength, construction growing more and more ambitious, until at last Yeo hoisted his broad pennant in a ship of 100 guns.

Time after time the opposing fleets were in presence; there were repeated skirmishes but never a pitched battle. Yeo and Chauncey were men of similar temperament regarding decisive action. Each of them had a material viewpoint; each was anxious to conserve his strength and dreaded the future. Conditions never suited the commander who had the initiative at the moment. The one who had the superiority in long guns thought his adversary would benefit by his superiority in carronades; each at different times complained about the sailing qualities or the handiness of the vessels under his command; the wind was unfavorable, or the military situation on land called for restraint afloat. Each for some months fought with half his attention fixed on Lake Erie, until Perry's battle there relieved the one of anxiety and the other of hope.

At the end of the war Yeo could point to the fact that for two years he had maintained sufficient control over the lake to enable British troops to keep the field in the Niagara peninsula for the whole period; what could be noted as a credit on the British side could be noted as a debit on the American. Chauncey had more to gain by victory and less to lose (on account of his better overland communications) by defeat. It was in the spring of 1813 that he had his greatest opportunity, and he let it escape him. An attack upon Kingston then might have been decisive. Destruction of the vessels there and of the shipbuilding facilities would have given him a lead in the ship-building race which he could hardly have lost, and that lead would have been vastly increased if the project of holding Kingston by a military force had been attempted and carried through successfully. The student can occupy his attention with the hypothetical campaign for a moment. Pike with two thousand men, having occupied the place, could have counted on at least several days in which to endeavor to make themselves secure before the British could send up enough troops to form the siege. There was timber for palisades and blockhouses, and guns in plenty; above all, there would be open communication behind them by water. They might have maintained the place for weeks, perhaps for the whole summer, during which time all British operations higher up the Lakes would have been at a standstill and the British land forces there forced into a painful and difficult retreat. That is as far as, or farther than, it is profitable to explore the possibilities.

Chapter XIII

THE NEW ENGLAND COAST was being watched by British ships of war, although a commercial blockade had not yet been proclaimed. There were ships of the line to support the frigates, and in addition to them there were now British privateers to harass American shipping. Years of command of the sea, and the conquest of the French and Dutch colonies, had begun to make privateering a not too profitable enterprise for the British until the American declaration of war offered fresh prizes. Now they clustered along the New England coast, inter- cepting returning merchant vessels, snapping up coasters, and more than once achieving success in cutting-out enterprises well worthy of the British tradition.

The American people could hardly do more than merely endure the insults and the losses with resignation, or with fur- ther outcry against Mr. Madison. Rodgers, with the *President* and *Congress*, sailed out of Boston again on April 23 and van- ished beyond the horizon, having to be careful to avoid the British watchdogs. The *Chesapeake* had come in on April 9 after four months at sea, during which she had taken only three prizes. The representatives of the federal government in Boston were inefficient or lukewarm—it has already been mentioned how Hull had had to borrow funds to enable him to get to sea again. It had taken three whole months to replenish Rodgers'

ships. Now there were difficulties with the *Chesapeake*. Cash
was wanting. Her crew could receive neither wages nor prize
money and, with the two-year enlistment of most of them coming to an end, only stayed by their ship in the hope of receiving
their money. Their captain had been unpopular; the senior
lieutenants were sick. Lawrence received the command on his
promotion after his destruction of the *Peacock*, but, ambitious
of distinction though he was, he tried to decline it. Men were
hard to find, officers even more scarce, and money quite unob-
tainable. The Navy Department insisted on his retaining command and repeated to him the orders already given to his
predecessor; he was to get to sea and attack the British communications in the Gulf of St. Lawrence—every government
department shared the prevailing anxiety regarding the accumulation of force in Canada. The orders were explicit but not
peremptory; Lawrence could exercise the discretion that every
captain may, and should, employ in the event of finding himself under orders to proceed to sea with a ship, in his opinion,
inefficient.

There was further reason for the exercise of discretion. Two
British frigates were watching Boston, close enough in to be
readily recognizable to pilot craft venturing outside. Rodgers
had escaped them without a battle, deliberately avoiding action
even though his force could be considered superior, for the
intellectual Rodgers considered his ships could be better employed in attacking British merchantmen than in an action
which, even if successful, would almost certainly result in a
compulsory return to port to refit. One of the British frigates
was Broke's *Shannon*, arithmetically only slightly inferior to the
Chesapeake; she and her captain were of good repute in the
Royal Navy, but she was not marked down in the American
Intelligence as a superior vessel. She was mainly known for
having exchanged a few shots with the *Constitution* and then
allowing her to get clear away. The other frigate was *Tenedos*,
but soon after Lawrence arrived to take command she disap-

peared, and only *Shannon* remained. On the day that Lawrence completed his officers and crew *Shannon* was visible lying hove-to beside Boston Light.

The influences that worked upon Lawrence have to be guessed at, for he died without writing about them. He was an active and ambitious man; he still cherished a grievance, for, despite his promotion to captain, Morris, late first lieutenant of *Constitution*, was still senior to him. He had very recently won a victory over a vessel of equal force, and he had received adulation on that account that may have disturbed his judgment. He may have been so exasperated with the difficulties he had encountered in Boston that he sailed out as the quickest way of putting an end to them. His irritation at the sight of the British frigate in American waters may have goaded him into action. Broke, as it happened, had sent in a letter to him challenging him to action—a polite letter of which every word was calculated to draw an attack—but Lawrence never received it. The fact that he did not is worth special note, as most of the contemporary British accounts take it for granted that Lawrence's sortie was a direct result of the challenge; as it was, it can be definitely discounted altogether as playing any part in Lawrence's decision. The absence of the *Tenedos* was the result of Broke's having sent her away in accordance with the promise made in the challenge, and her disappearance may have influenced Lawrence. One passage in Broke's letter is worthy of special note, even though Lawrence did not read it; Broke mentions that he is running short of provisions and water and must soon return to his base. Lawrence might have had an unopposed exit if he had waited, even without being dependent on darkness or thick or stormy weather.

It is clear enough that Lawrence went out to fight, and it must be presumed that he went out confident of victory. He could hardly have been so exasperated as to invite defeat in preference to any alternative; nor could the American situation have appeared so gloomy as to call for relief by an honorable defeat—the capture in the St. Lawrence of a transport or two laden with redcoats would have been a far more certain stimulant. His difficulties and annoyances may have clouded his judgment, but it is hard to avoid the conclusion that Lawrence had no doubt of adding a sixth comparatively easy victory to the preceding American five. He did not delay a day or an hour; he had a full crew, of mixed quality, with a solid nucleus of trained fighting men and a considerable admixture of raw hands and foreigners; and the moment his last officer came on board—two of his lieutenants were midshipmen with acting appointments—he cast off and hurried to sea. He was comparatively new to his ship, and half his officers and many of his men were quite new, with their bags and hammocks lying on the deck where they were deposited as the men were distributed to quarters. The recklessness of his sortie is hard to explain. In going out to certain battle he was deliberately contravening his orders to proceed to the St. Lawrence; he could more profitably have disobeyed orders by waiting a few days to give his ship's company time to settle to their duties.

Broke in the *Shannon* saw him coming and stood away under easy sail. Assuming that Lawrence had received his challenge, he was heading for the rendezvous off Cape Ann which he had suggested; he would not fight close in to Boston, where, if his ship were to be disabled, he might find himself not only on a lee shore but subject to attack by small craft. He was anticipating action with confidence; his crew were exercised in gunnery as well as in seamanship to a degree unusual in the Royal Navy at this time, and he had held his command for six full years. He noted that *Chesapeake* had three ensigns flying; presumably Lawrence had hauled down the white flag bearing the words "Free Trade and Sailors' Rights" which he had flown in harbor. If it had been still flying Broke could hardly have failed to remark on it. The wind was gentle—Broke left his royal yards up throughout the action—and the sea comparatively smooth. There were several hours of daylight left, and there was no need to hurry matters. Broke headed to a point well out to sea, between Cape Cod and Cape Ann, thereby disappointing the sight-seers who had accompanied *Chesapeake* out of Boston in small craft. Then he hove to and left the rest to Lawrence, even leaving to him the choice of the lee or the weather gauge.

Lawrence chose the weather gauge; he had sent down his royal yards and had had plenty of time to make up his mind on how to conduct the battle. He had decided on immediate engagement at decisive range and plunged into close action, the two ships running before the wind within hail of each other. Broke had made no attempt to make the approach difficult or expensive for his opponent. If ever two ships came together on equal terms, it was the *Shannon* and the *Chesapeake*. It is hard to believe that Broke had gauged the capacity of his enemy and his enemy's ship so accurately, but it is certain that he knew his own and that of his ship. The broadsides the two ships exchanged were terribly destructive, causing severe damage, mostly to the hulls, and occasioned dreadful losses to the crews; but after only a few minutes' firing many things happened at once. *Chesapeake,* forging a little ahead, lost the use of her headsails and, coming up into the wind in consequence, presented her quarter to her opponent. The half-raking broadside she received swept her quarter-deck. The men at the wheel and the sailing master were shot down, and Lawrence himself was shot through the body by a musket shot fired—so tradition says —by the lieutenant of the Royal Marines on board the *Shannon*, who thereby did something to end the demand to arm the marines with rifles. Momentarily helpless, the *Chesapeake* fell back with her quarter against *Shannon's* bow. There was a furious exchange of small-arms fire. One third of *Chesapeake's* men were dead or wounded, including the first lieutenant as well as Lawrence and the sailing master. The second lieutenant was down with the main-deck guns and did not know he had succeeded to the command. The senior officer left on the upper deck was a midshipman, for the third lieutenant had left the deck in circumstances that later called for debate and a court-martial. There was still some opposition in the smoke and the confusion—a chest of musket cartridges went off at that moment on *Chesapeake's* deck—and the *Shannon's* boatswain, who was trying to bind the two ships together, had his arm cut off. But the Americans were leaderless and disordered by heavy losses; the British in those mad seconds were well led and did their work with remarkable efficiency. In the fore- and maintop, officers and men actually ran out along the yards, and from their precarious perches killed their immediate opponents and opened a demoralizing fire on the enemy below them.

Broke led his boarders onto *Chesapeake's* quarter-deck and dashed forward. He survived a pistol shot fired at him by the American chaplain, cut him down, burst through the opposition offered by the American marines, and reached the forecastle at the moment when the unfortunate second lieutenant arrived there from below. There was no time to organize any resistance there, even though a cutlass stroke went through Broke's hard hat and stripped much of his scalp from his skull. The Americans in the forecastle were killed, wounded and flung down the hatch-way, and the British found themselves in full command of the *Chesapeake's* decks at the same time as Lawrence, down below and mortally wounded, was saying, "Don't give up the ship." But the mischief was done. Men below hatches were helpless with an active enemy above them. There was nothing left for them to do save to surrender or be slaughtered. The fainting Broke retained consciousness long enough to hand over the command to his second lieutenant—his first had been killed in the moment of victory, possibly by a shot from his own ship—while his third lieutenant secured the prisoners and took charge of the prize. It was all over in a quarter of an hour; the wondering pilot who had brought *Chesapeake* out saw, from the deck of his cutter, the two ships come together, heard the thunder of the artillery and the smoke of the cartridge explosion, and then saw the two ships sail off before the wind together in silence.

There was the wildest exultation in England when the news reached there from Halifax. Captain Capel, to whom, as senior officer present in Halifax, Broke addressed his report, began his covering letter with the comparative restraint of "It is with the greatest pleasure . . ." but then he went on with something like bombast regarding Broke's achievement, and, oddly enough, Broke's report displayed taste a little worse, in contrast with the dry wording of so many official reports telling of stupendous victories. He wrote of the "proud old British Union" floating triumphantly over the American flag, and of the "irresistible fury" of "our gallant bands." The fact that Broke, of all men, could let his pen run away with him in this fashion was the clearest proof of the tension the British navy had undergone during the period of defeat, and of the influence upon Broke of the preceding anxiety of the British press and of the Admiralty.

The bad taste went unnoticed; the British press, even the professional press, was guilty of a good deal worse. The series of American victories had been interrupted at last, at a time when it had begun to seem as if America possessed some special secret formula for victory; the present generation can remember when tides of German and Japanese victory were flowing and the fainthearted began to fear that nothing could check them either. Now a British ship had captured in fair fight an American ship of a force considerably superior and whose superiority was vastly exaggerated in the estimates of the battle. The sober *Naval Chronicle* called the feat "the most brilliant act of heroism ever performed," although Wellington, learning the news during the delirious days after Vittoria, wrote of it merely as "a most fortunate event." Broke was made a baronet, when even knighthood was a rare reward for a successful single-ship action. His two surviving senior lieutenants were both promoted to commander; usually only the first lieutenant was promoted—incidentally, Wallis, one of the two, survived to be an admiral and a centenarian. There were illuminations and banquets; it is no exaggeration to say that the adulation heaped upon Broke exceeded that which Jervis and Duncan had received after St. Vincent and Camperdown.

The self-criticism of the Royal Navy became far less urgent, but, to the credit of the service, it did not end. After the recent moral upheaval men were willing to learn from victory as well as from defeat. It was noticeable how ready thoughtful sailors were to admit that Broke was an exceptional captain who had trained an exceptional crew, and it was agreed by many that Broke's system and discipline must be generally imitated, both for the future safety of England and to complete the immediate and urgent task of compelling or persuading the United States to agree to peace.

In America the shock was naturally severe, although it was softened by numerous explanations—only to be expected—to the effect that *Chesapeake's* capture had been the result of a whole series of unfortunate accidents. At this very moment new pressure was being applied by the British navy, and in a fashion of which an important part of the country could not but be aware. All New York knew of the presence of Decatur and his squadron, the *United States*, the *Macedonian* (now an American ship of war), and *Hornet;* it could not be otherwise, seeing that Decatur and his men had been welcomed by a public reception. But with the passage of the weeks it became obvious also that Decatur was finding difficulty in getting away from New York. He dared not push out beyond the Narrows, for there was a powerful British squadron off Sandy Hook, and the state government was concerning itself feverishly with the defenses of the city against a British attack—Washington could offer only derisory help.

Then the three ships were seen to make the passage of Hell Gate; if their way was barred at Sandy Hook they could surely take the Long Island route. The hope did not endure for a week. At the same moment as came the news that *Chesapeake* was lost the newspapers carried the appalling information that

Decatur was blockaded in New London, lightening his ships to drag them up the Thames out of reach of the British and endeavoring feverishly and with small means to fortify the mouth of the river. Decatur had indeed had a lucky escape; venturing out of the Sound with a favorable wind, and relying on the knowledge that British ships of war had been seen south of Montauk Point well out of his course, he had been surprised by the sight of yet another squadron right ahead, off the Rhode Island coast in the neighborhood of Block Island. He had hastily turned about; he had nearly been trapped, for the squadron off Montauk was beating up to intercept him, and he was only just able to claw back to windward to the doubtful shelter of the Thames.

Here, as was obvious to all, he could be closely watched, even if the British did not arrive from out of the Atlantic with an amphibious force to storm the place, as was perfectly possible. In any case, the Montauk exit from Long Island Sound was now closely blockaded in overwhelming force, as was made apparent by the complete severance of all sea connections between New York and Rhode Island and by the rise in the price of wine to twenty-five dollars a gallon. If any further demonstration of the influence of sea power was needed, it was given later in the war by the return to New York of Decatur and his men, not in their own ships, and not heralded by music, but after a land march and a furtive voyage down the Sound in coasters, for *Macedonian* and *United States* now lay abandoned and dismantled in the Thames. The crew of the *Macedonian* was to be transferred to the Lakes, and that of the *United States* to another American ship in New York to make another attempt to break out through the blockade.

There was other bad news during that summer, to add to the depression occasioned by the depredations of the British squadrons in the Chesapeake and the Delaware. Commodore Rodgers in the *President* had indeed contrived to slip into Narragansett, returning from the Atlantic, but the news he brought was disappointing, almost ludicrous. Rodgers had been out for five months. He had crossed and recrossed the Atlantic; he had even penetrated into the North Sea, north about via the Shetlands, and in all that time he had taken only twelve prizes, none valuable, none with specie on board.

Rodgers had in fact strangely held back, as he had done previously, at a moment when he might have done great damage. His hesitation is hard to explain, particularly as in his official letters he showed that he was aware that the most fruitful area for captures was British home waters. He had barely touched on the fringe of them during this voyage, while *Congress*, which had gone out with him and had then separated, returned two months later (after seven months out), having captured only three prizes in making the circuit of the whole North Atlantic via the Cape Verdes and Brazil.

One other ship of the United States Navy had been meanwhile really doing damage in British home waters and exciting consternation in London, but the eventual result was depressing while her earlier achievements were unknown. *Argus* had slipped out of New York soon after Decatur had given up the attempt. She was under the command of William Allen, who had received his promotion as a result of the capture of the *Macedonian* by the *United States*, whose first lieutenant he was. She was fast and handy and of small draft, which accounts for her evasion of the blockades both of New York and of the French Biscay coast; she landed a new American Minister at L'Orient and came out again four weeks after leaving New York.

Allen pushed boldly into British waters, into the English Channel, and into the Irish Sea, wreaking havoc on the unconvoyed British shipping plying round the western extremity of England and across to Ireland. She lasted for thirty-one days, during which she took and burned nineteen vessels, and it is generally understood that her career need not have been cut short as it was if her penultimate prize had not been carrying a cargo of wine which proved too great a temptation to her crew.

The British brig *Pelican* was one of the vessels sent out by an exasperated Admiralty in search of the raider. She had come into Cork from the West Indies, had found orders waiting for her there, and had sailed again at once. For beacons to guide her to her quarry she had pillars of smoke by day and pillars of fire by night—the abandoned and burning vessels which *Argus* was leaving behind her. They led *Pelican* across St. George's Channel toward the Welsh coast, and off St. David's Head at dawn on the second day out she sighted *Argus* and her latest prize. There was no question of *Argus* evading battle, although it was easily in her power to do so with her superior speed; a raider— as Hitler's orders clearly laid down in 1939—is not being employed to best effect when fighting a ship of anything like equal force, or indeed when fighting any ship at all. If it is the business of the belligerent whose communications are being attacked to engage the enemy whenever found, it is the business of the raider to avoid such engagements unless there is some powerful other factor, moral or political, to be considered.

Allen commanded the most suitable ship possible for commerce destruction, and he would have been well advised to employ her solely for that end. If he had put his helm up and fled before the wind as soon as he had identified the *Pelican* there might have been some small jeers in the British press, some small disappointment in the United States; but if, having run his enemy below the horizon, he had then appeared to harass the Liverpool shipping, vanished again to raid the Nore, shown up later in the western approaches, the jeers would have been speedily drowned in cries of consternation. His appearance in Irish waters had already sent up insurance rates; a phantom raider, flitting from one area to another, would have sent them higher still. Rising insurance rates would be more likely to achieve the object of the war—to cause Great Britain to moderate her demands at sea—than would the capture or destruction of a single brig of war.

Presumably, in these the last hours of his life, Allen gave no thought to columns of figures in shipping merchants' ledgers. He waited for *Pelican* to come up to him, allowed her to retain the weather gauge, and began a hammer-and-tongs battle as the vessels came within range. On this day the American gunnery was comparatively ineffective; perhaps the crew was indeed drunk. The British gunnery was at least of the standard that had brought victory in a hundred battles against the French. In the first few minutes Allen went down, his thigh shattered. His first lieutenant was wounded; *Argus* had her rigging badly cut up. *Pelican* tried to cross her stern, was balked when the second lieutenant handled *Argus* brilliantly, received a raking broadside without vital damage, and continued the action until *Argus*' rigging was so damaged that she could not evade the next attempt to cross her stern. Raked again and again, *Argus* suffered severely. It might have been possible for *Pelican* to continue to battle her helpless antagonist from a point of vantage, but, as was frequently the case when two ships were engaged within a few feet of each other, they came together and *Pelican* lost the advantage of her maneuverability. It did not matter, as it happened, although a determined effort by the American crew in a hand-to-hand struggle might still have saved the day. As it was, *Argus* surrendered at the first threat of boarding. One quarter of her crew was killed or wounded, her decks were encumbered with wreckage, and the survivors were demoralized by the loss of their officers and by the pounding they had received; before any word of condemnation is uttered it must be remembered that they had been under fierce and effective artillery bombardment for three quarters of an hour. The ineffectiveness of the American gunnery was proved by the small British loss of two killed and five wounded.

Maples of the *Pelican* brought his prize into Plymouth, and the British press had the satisfaction of recording "another event in every way honourable to the British arms." Allen died of his wounds; the American surgeon had amputated his thigh imme-

diately after the battle, but gangrene set in and, although transferred to a British hospital, he lived only a week. The British
buried him in Plymouth with every possible military honor,
with eight captains R.N. as pallbearers, two companies of Royal
Marines under a lieutenant colonel as guard of honor, the surviving officers and men of the *Argus* as mourners, along with
the American Vice-Consul and his staff and "a very numerous
and respectable retinue of Inhabitants."

It was the usual British generosity to a fallen foe, unrelated
to the very important fact that British self-confidence was fast
returning. It would have given small satisfaction to America,
coupled with the news that another of her ships had been beaten
in fair fight by a vessel slightly inferior. But as it happened, that
news passed almost unnoticed on its arrival, for it had been
anticipated by other news much more cheerful.

Chapter XIV

WHILE YEO AND CHAUNCEY were feebly contending for the mastery of Lake Ontario, the command of Lake Erie above them was held by the British by a small superiority of force which any minor accident or any success by the Americans in the shipbuilding race could change into an inferiority. At the western end of the lake General William Henry Harrison faced General Procter; the mobility of both depended on water communication down the lake. Oliver Hazard Perry arrived in early 1813 to take command of the American naval forces; Captain R. H. Barclay, R.N., arrived in June of the same year to take command of the British naval forces—one British captain had already imperiled his career by refusing the appointment. Perry enjoyed the advantage that at least some of his necessary supplies could reach him via Pittsburgh; everything that Barclay needed had to travel via Ontario. Perry was a man of energy, and his shipbuilders were men of ingenuity; the concluding months of the winter saw construction proceeding apace at his shipyards. They were queer ships which were taking shape there, built of green timber, shallow of draft, and held together by wooden pegs; although wooden pegs were freely used in normal contemporary ship construction, the shortage of nails on Lake Erie compelled their use there for construction at points where nails were considered essential in seagoing ships. There were lake schooners which could barely carry their armament, not being designed for such concentrated and lofty loads, and which were likely to upset when their guns were fired. Even the ships built with fighting in mind were flimsy in construction on account of the haste with which they were built as well as on account of the shortages—they represented a compromise between delay and security—and their necessarily shallow draft made them even more uninhabitable than ordinary ships of war and more perilous to fight in. They were armed with whatever guns could be dragged over the endless trails and floated along the endless waterways that connected Presqu'ile with the foundries on the eastern seaboard; Cockburn's bold exploit in the summer of 1813 when his landing party destroyed the foundry at Frenchtown came too late, for Perry had by that time collected the guns which won the battle, borrowed from the army as well as supplied by the navy, and dragged up French Creek during fortunate freshets.

Seamen to man them could come only from the Ontario fleet, which Chauncey was striving to maintain at an equality with Yeo's. The importance of the command of Ontario was so obvious that Chauncey dared not part with many men; Perry, engrossed with his own problems, was inclined to attribute Chauncey's reluctance to timidity or jealousy or something even worse, and at the crisis of the campaign was held back from resigning his command only by a remarkable display of firmness on the part of the Secretary of the Navy.

On the English side the difficulties were of the same nature and even more acute. Everything for use on Eric had to come from Ontario; there was no alternative line of communication whatever, and at the farthest end of the difficult line was Procter with an army and a horde of Indians who had to be fed and supplied. The briefest loss of command of the lake meant serious trouble at its western end, where Harrison could at least keep his army together in a threatening attitude without American command of the lake. Barclay, arriving in the spring—

he encountered some difficulty in making his way along Ontario at the time of Chauncey's temporary command of that lake— was kept aware of this by ceaseless complaints and warnings from Procter, as well as from Prevost, the commander in chief; but Barclay stood in exactly the same situation to Yeo as Perry did to Chauncey, and Yeo proved to be even more reluctant to part with men or material than Chauncey was. The building program initiated on the British side was less ambitious than the American program; there was only the ship-rigged *Detroit* under construction, and guns for her could not be coaxed from Yeo on any terms. She was necessarily built without her designers knowing what armament she was to carry, and the armament she eventually received was largely made up from field artillery borrowed from Procter, supplemented by whatever else could be found—there were six different types of cannon among the nineteen guns she carried, with a complication of the ammunition supply in action that can hardly be imagined.

Barclay, as has been said, met with even more difficulty in persuading Yeo to part with seamen than did Perry with Chauncey, and another of Barclay's troubles was of a nature that Perry hardly encountered; most of the seamen under his command were Canadians, not too ready to submit to naval routine, and their numbers in any case were astonishingly small. Indeed, it is very much to Barclay's credit that he succeeded in winning the devotion of the motley force under his command.

The misfortunes that befell Barclay were to a considerable extent the result of his own personal errors. They began almost immediately after his arrival. On his very first voyage he crossed the lake to intercept the vessels set free by the American advance in the Niagara peninsula, and he failed to do so. There was thick weather, and the American ships clung to the shallows and reached Presqu'ile. Perhaps the failure to destroy them on their passage was excusable, but Barclay was aware that they were going to make the attempt—he had seen with his own eyes what was happening at Niagara—and it is hard to believe that with diligence and vigilance he could not have detected them.

Even now there were opportunities to restore the balance already disturbed. Presqu'ile was not a very secure base; its militia garrison was unreliable, seamen were lacking and the shipyard workers discontented and weakened by disease. Two powerful ships of war were under construction there which would confer superiority on Perry even after *Detroit* should be completed. The importance of these two ships can best be understood when it is realized that their entry into service trebled Perry's strength and certainly made him twice as strong as Barclay without *Detroit*. There were the same advantages to be gained from a blow at Presqu'ile as had offered themselves a few weeks before to Chauncey regarding an attack on Kingston. Barclay was aware of them, but he did not succeed in gaining Procter's co-operation.

Procter employed the mobility conferred on him by the last fleeting weeks of the British command of the lake to make an attack on Fort Meigs; the attack failed, despite the fact that Procter cut up a relieving force and inflicted terrible loss. The troops and siege equipment employed at Fort Meigs could have been far more usefully employed at Presqu'ile, but the full realization of the fact dawned upon Procter and Barclay only after the moment had passed; it would take time to prepare a fresh expedition, and when that time had elapsed Presqu'ile was regarded as too strong to be meddled with—perhaps not a correct conclusion.

Yet there was still another opportunity, even after Perry's two new ships were launched at Presqu'ile. They had to be brought out onto the lake, and there was a bar to be passed, for Presqu'ile suffered under that disadvantage; the vessels had to be lighted to a draft of five feet, not only emptied of guns and stores, but hoisted over by means of "camels," and during their passage they would be utterly defenseless. Barclay could not help being aware of Perry's difficulty; he could have guessed it if he did not hear about it through spies or careless gossip, and it was to his obvious advantage to be ready to attack the American ships as they passed the bar, helpless and unarmed. As long as he maintained his squadron within striking distance of Presqu'ile and kept the place under observation, Perry would not dare move. Barclay's actions showed that he understood the situation. He arrived off Presqu'ile on July 20 and watched the place. As it happened, he was not even imposing delay upon Perry at that moment, because the final reinforcement of seamen which Chauncey had brought himself to spare was on its way and Perry had decided not to move until it arrived.

American accounts lay stress on the vulnerability of Presqu'ile at this moment and suggest that Barclay had only to send in his boats to destroy the whole American squadron, but they do not make sufficient allowance for Barclay's numerical weakness. He had less than four hundred men on board, and he could not have scraped together a landing force of as many as two hundred men. Perry had guns mounted on the beach, and his ships had their batteries on board. Even before Perry's reinforcements arrived, and even though the regular American soldiers had been recalled and the militia were worthless, Barclay would have had no chance of success in a landing without troops to aid him, and he had no troops because Procter was now meditating a further futile offensive, against Sandusky.

The other side of the argument is that if Barclay took no action his situation was bound to deteriorate, so that the most desperate attempt could be justified. Even if an attack by brute force was hopeless, there might have been other means employed. It might have been possible for a boat to creep in under cover of darkness to attempt to set the anchored ships on fire —not a promising line of attack, but anything would have been better than inaction; the present peril was obvious, and ultimate disaster was likely.

What little opportunity Barclay had for offensive action was greatly diminished within four days of his arrival off Presqu'ile, for the reinforcements from Chauncey began to come in at last, a hundred and thirty seamen whose quality Perry deplored, but men at least—and men who, as the event was to prove, were prepared to face enormous losses. Their presence made it more necessary still that Barclay should maintain his close watch over Presqu'ile, and he did not do so.

The motives that carried Barclay away from his blockading position are impossible to discover at this late time; they were not stated in any of the documents surviving or in the records of the official inquiries held after the event. It can only be said that on the day that the last of Chauncey's reinforcements arrived the Americans, looking out across the lake, could see no sign of Barclay. He had sailed away. Perhaps his motley crews were restive; perhaps his own patience had been exhausted by ten days of waiting. Perhaps he was running short of food; provisions were continually in short supply on the British side even when they commanded the lake, but if lack of food forced Barclay to retire he was to blame—a shortage in ten days' time should have been foreseen and provided for. It may have been any other kind of trouble; with those makeshift ships and makeshift crews anything might happen, of a nature no one can guess at nowadays.

With the coast clear, Perry plunged into the business of getting his ships out over the bar; the necessity had been foreseen and arrangements already made. Barclay sailed on July 30. On the night of August 1 the movements started; during August 2 they continued. The weather was kind, but the lake was not—the depth on the bar had diminished from five feet to four. There was a perilous moment when the first of the big ships grounded and had to be refloated. They worked through the night, and by the morning of August 4 she was over the bar together with the smaller vessels, and her guns and ammunition were being hurried on board. At that moment

Barclay's sails appeared over the horizon again. It was Barclay's last chance. He might have attacked forthwith. The Americans could not have been in very good order, and their second large ship was still within the bar. But all Barclay could see was that they were in "a most formidable state of preparation," and he turned away. On August 6 Perry took his fleet out on its first cruise, and Barclay was not there to oppose him. He was sheltering at Malden, waiting for his own big ship to be completed.

And Perry was growing stronger yet, for another hundred seamen arrived from Chauncey; it is hard to overestimate the magnitude of the sacrifice Chauncey was making, because it was at this very time that he and Yeo were in presence on Ontario, facing each other with approximately equal forces. Chauncey was taking a serious risk, for a disaster to him on Ontario could nullify any gains won by a victory on Erie. Perry remained unappreciative; he could hardly spare sympathy for Chauncey when he was bitterly conscious that his own fleet was inadequately manned by any normal standard. Harrison found him more men—a hundred Kentucky riflemen, volunteering for an adventure that must have been a novelty even to those adventurous figures.

Perry commanded the lake. He swept down it to Malden, looking at the British ships inside, returning more than once from his usual anchorage in the Bass Islands, thirty miles from the British base and dominating the narrow western end of the lake. No British vessels could venture through the blockade that he instituted; the British, cut off at the far end, were immediately conscious of the resultant shortages. Even Barclay's own men were put on reduced rations during the weary days while the new ship was being fitted out. The British military position was in the gravest peril, and it could be restored only by the reconquest of the command of the lake. Nothing else would make it possible to transport the daily twenty thousand rations needed by the troops, by the Indians and their families,

and by the sailors cooped up there; it was of no importance
that the tactical situation still gave the British naval command
of the straits of Detroit and of Lake Huron, for all that wilder-
ness to the westward produced no flour, and cattle in insufficient
quantity. Barclay could come out and fight or he could abandon
his ships and carry off his crews with the British army in its
retreat, and he made the obvious choice. His newest ship was
ready for service just in time, when the flour remaining in store
was on the point of exhaustion. He sailed out from Malden
on September 10 in a desperate mood.

Oliver Perry at twenty-eight was a man of strong emotions,
fiery and energetic and yet with that vein of sentiment that
often makes itself evident in such men. His last big ship was
about to be launched at the moment when the dreary news
reached the Lakes that *Chesapeake* had been captured and that
Lawrence was dead. Perry was deeply moved, caught up in the
wave of emotion that was sweeping through much of the
United States. His new ship was christened *Lawrence* at her
launching. Press and public were repeating the words "Don't
give up the ship," which the dying Lawrence had breathed as
he was carried below. The expression caught Perry's fancy
too. He had a blue flag made on which the words were sewn in
white, after the fashion of the flag Lawrence had hoisted in
Boston; the existence of this flag is worth remembering. The
slogan would not commend itself to modern experts in propa-
ganda; it was negative and not positive; by its very wording it
admitted the possibility that the ship might be given up; and it
could hardly fail to remind the public that the ship, in the end,
had actually been given up. It might instill a mood of desperate
resignation, but that is a dangerous mood from the point of
view of the propagandist, who would fear lest the resignation
might eventually combine with the despair to induce apathy.
But it was to serve its purpose at that moment; certainly it was
a more appealing battle cry than "Free Trade and Sailors'

Rights," with its windy suggestion of legal and economic arguments.

Perry's second large ship was the *Niagara,* named for the recent successes won while Chauncey held the command of Ontario; the third largest, and much less important, was the *Caledonia,* the vessel that had been captured from the British by the prompt and vigorous action of Elliott the preceding autumn. In addition Perry had a number of schooners which were to play an important part in the battle to come, but the two large vessels comprised two thirds or more of his fighting strength. Perry enjoyed five weeks of command of the lake before the day of battle; it was a long enough period to exercise his crews, and it was also long enough to enable him to make his plans for the coming action, especially as he was able to form a close estimate of the force that would be opposed to him. Possibly he thought too long over his plans; possibly they were too rigid; possibly his exact information tempted him to be too mathematical about the battle; possibly his orders were worded too strictly to allow of the flexibility necessary in an action between fleets with its unpredictable conditions of wind and weather; possibly Perry did not exert himself to win the whole-hearted devotion of his next senior officer, Elliott, who had once been senior officer on Lake Erie, who had distinguished himself by the capture of *Caledonia,* and who now found himself under the command of Perry, who—as was known—owed his appointment to the representations of the senior senator from Rhode Island and had no distinguished fighting record behind him. These were all small factors, but, acting together, they came near to losing the battle.

Barclay's biggest ship was the *Detroit*—named after the British victory—comparable in size with *Lawrence* and *Niagara,* but far inferior in force. He had the *Queen Charlotte* (the last *Queen Charlotte* had been the three-decker flagship of the Mediterranean fleet, destroyed by fire at Leghorn), smaller but more adequately armed although still greatly inferior to

Niagara, and smaller vessels inferior in total weight of metal to Perry's. Arithmetically his squadron may have been two thirds as strong as the American squadron, certainly not more. The arithmetic is complicated by the differing proportion of long guns and carronades, and still more by the fact that it is impossible to arrive at exact figures regarding the number of men on each side fit for duty. Certainly the numerical odds that Barclay came out to fight were considerably greater than those Nelson faced at Trafalgar, and Barclay was no Nelson, as recent events had already shown. Nor was Perry a Villeneuve, as the battle was to prove.

On September 10 the chances of the weather favored America. The wind that brought Barclay down upon Perry (and that might have imposed upon the latter a roundabout exit from his harbor that would have delayed the battle) shifted at the right moment to enable Perry to come out, and with the weather gauge. He could bear down with the wind abeam and enter at once into action. He could see Barclay's two large ships stationed in the British line with a smaller vessel ahead, astern, and in between, and Perry's orders and order of sailing allotted *Lawrence* to fight *Detroit* and *Niagara* to fight *Queen Charlotte.*

As soon as the battle began Perry and the Americans faced the tactical problem which had plagued attacking fleets ever since they first formed in line. Were they to follow their leader so that the heads of the two lines would come together first, with the respective rears still far apart, or was each ship to make the best of her way into action against her opposite number? The first method might give the fleet to leeward the chance of doubling upon the leading attacking ships, and certainly might lead to indecisive action; the second was more difficult to put into practice. Even Lord Howe, a disciplinarian and a tactician, had not succeeded in bringing all his ships into close action at the Glorious First of June. And when there was doubt as to which method was in the admiral's mind, and when

that doubt was increased by the memory of the rigid convention of the line ahead, there was likely to be indecision and
disorder, as Byng found in the unlucky action that cost him
his life. And when one of the subordinate officers is sulky or
stupid, disaffected or resentful, there is likely to be entirely
disjointed action. This was Mathews' experience in 1744, when
he engaged without any assistance whatever from his second-
in-command, Lestock, who could still plead—as he actually
did at his court-martial—that he had obeyed his orders to the
letter.

Perry in the *Lawrence* found himself in close action with the
British squadron, while Elliott in the *Niagara*—representing at
least a third of the American strength—was still at long range.
The battle was ferociously contested, both sides enduring losses
of proportions that in many previous battles had ended the
fighting. Barclay's Canadians and soldiers and handful of seamen stood to their guns with a bravery that was equaled only
by Perry's Kentuckians and soldiers and handful of seamen.
Along the line there were local superiorities and inferiorities,
where in one case there was distant action with long guns
against carronades and in another close action with carronades
against long guns. The *Detroit's* guns were not equipped with
locks. Apparently she had no port-fires, even, and the guns
were fired by snapping pistols over loose powder piled in the
touchholes. They were served bravely enough, and effectively
enough, in any event. Even in small vessels the Americans had
a superiority and made good use of it, one or two of the gunboats being employed in the most effective manner for such
craft, raking the larger British vessels with their long guns
from good tactical positions ahead and astern, although in the
end the inexperienced crews mishandled their artillery and
overcharged their hot guns, so that *Scorpion's* gun leaped from
its carriage and fell down the hatchway, while one of *Ariel's*
guns burst.

In the heat of the battle Barclay's second large ship, the

Queen Charlotte, moved up in the line and brought her guns to bear on the *Lawrence* in addition to those of the *Detroit.* Perry's flagship was shot to pieces; one credible estimate states her losses in killed and wounded as 80 per cent of her total crew; the wounded had to be summoned back from the cockpit to help handle the ship. On the British side the losses were heavy; in the two big ships the captain and lieutenants were all killed or wounded, Barclay (who had lost an arm at Trafalgar eight years before) being wounded in five places. From a statistician's point of view it is a pity that no analysis of the nature of the British casualties has been preserved, for it would be informative regarding what proportion of hits was scored by the Kentucky riflemen; but there is the negative evidence of the absence of British complaints in the matter, and it is not unreasonable to conclude that small arms played a very minor part in the battle.

The vital point was that Perry survived, unhurt. If he had fallen along with the four fifths of the men around him, this battle of Lake Erie might conceivably have ended in a bloody reverse for the Americans. The fact that he survived, the fact that in the midst of all the din and destruction he kept his head clear while his fighting spirit was at fever pitch, saved the day. Elliott in *Niagara* was still at long—and ineffective—range. There can be no doubt about the fact, even though the possible explanations are numerous enough. There was the fluky wind, there were Perry's orders, there was the fact that *Niagara's* next ahead, the *Caledonia,* was slow and unhandy, and Elliott was under orders to keep in line with her. There was the possibility that *Caledonia,* badly handled, had actually balked *Niagara's* efforts to get into action. The most obvious explanation is that Elliott, resentful of being under Perry's command (or perhaps of some imagined slight), chose to interpret his orders to the letter and hung back in consequence. No actual proof has ever been put forward of this, and it is far too grave a charge to be accepted without proof. But so matters stood;

more than two hours after the fighting began, *Niagara* was still only distantly engaged, while *Queen Charlotte* had pushed into the heart of the battle and the American flagship was being overwhelmed.

Perry decided to transfer himself to the *Niagara*. There were numerous precedents for such action—in the Anglo-Dutch wars both British and Dutch admirals had frequently shifted their flags in the heat of battle from disabled or beaten ships. He started off on the long pull; it was as fortunate for America that the *Lawrence* still possessed a boat that would float as it was that Perry had not been hit. He took with him his "Don't give up the ship" flag, which may explain the British accusations that Perry absconded from his ship after it had surrendered; if that flag had been flying during the action and had then been hauled down for Perry to take with him, the British had grounds for thinking the surrender took place then, especially as the *Lawrence* actually struck immediately after Perry left her.

The firing died away. The Stars and Stripes had been hauled down in the *Lawrence*. The disabled British *Hunter* was drifting off to leeward; so was the *Lady Prevost*. The small craft were still exchanging occasional shots. Guns were being fired from *Detroit* and *Queen Charlotte* at Perry's boat, but they missed—Perry was luckier than Sir Edward Spragge, who had been killed in exactly the same circumstances in action with Van Tromp. There was some small cheering in the British ships, but the men were weary; *Detroit* and *Queen Charlotte* fell foul of each other, disabled as they were, and it was no easy matter to separate them, for the men were without officers. The expectation, even the certainty, among the British was that *Niagara* would lead the schooners astern of her away from the battle, acknowledging defeat and leaving the British in possession of the field of battle and of their hard-won prize.

Perry had nothing of the sort in mind. He boarded *Niagara*; the fluky wind was strengthening, which had made his pull all the longer. There were no recriminations at that moment;

both Perry and Elliott were determined to see the battle through. Perry took command of the *Niagara;* Elliott set off by boat to bring the schooners along as well. The wind remained favorable, and the British, exhausted and leaderless, saw the *Niagara,* fresh and uninjured, bearing down upon them. Despite the strain of the past hours Perry was still in good fighting condition and handled *Niagara* excellently—it might almost be said cold-bloodedly. He swept round the bows of *Detroit* and *Queen Charlotte,* raking them with his broadside of nine carronades; Elliott brought up the gunboats to fire into their sterns; *Caledonia,* still in good fighting condition, closed in as well. British resistance ended abruptly; *Detroit* and *Queen Charlotte* could only surrender; *Lawrence* was recaptured; *Lady Prevost,* unmanageable with her rudder shot away, hauled down her colors under the fire of *Niagara's* guns; so did *Hunter; Chippeway* and *Little Belt* tried to struggle away but were caught by the fresh gunboats and compelled to surrender. It was annihilation, disaster as complete as the French had experienced at San Domingo or Cape Ortegal, more complete than the Nile.

Perry kept his head as clear in the moment of victory as he had done in the heat of battle. General Harrison on shore must be informed that the Americans had undisputed command of the lake, and Perry did not lose an hour. "We have met the enemy and they are ours," he wrote. Those words told Harrison that his army was free to move forward, that the British army could only retreat. Within three weeks of the battle, despite the damage received there and further damage suffered in a storm, Perry had troops on board to ferry across the narrow end of the lake, and Procter was in full retreat, with his army starving. He could not, or would not, retreat fast enough. Overtaken by Harrison's forces, he turned to fight and was badly beaten, his forces almost annihilated. Tecumseh, the leader of his Indian allies, fell in the fighting, and his death and the British defeat meant the practical cessation of dangerous

Indian hostility to the Americans. Detroit was in American hands again; American soil was clear of British invaders; an American army was established on Canadian soil; American mastery of Lake Erie was undisputed; and along with all this, to the clear-thinking mind, American expansion to the Northwest was an obvious certainty.

Chapter XV

THE VICTORIES of the Thames and of Lake Erie effected an important change of mood in the United States. They were victories of annihilation, indisputable, whose consequences were obviously far-reaching; nor was it so obvious that they had been gained by a vast superiority of force. They proved that the United States could launch fleets and put armies into the field that could defeat the British, ever victorious until that time. They were victories won by national forces in the widest sense of the term and could hardly fail to stimulate the development of a national spirit, even though the opposition press still continued virulent attacks upon the administration and local bodies continued to pass resolutions condemning the action of the government. The growth of the national spirit was unmistakable; so was the change in the public mood. "Don't give up the ship" was replaced by "We have met the enemy and they are ours"—a change of slogan of the clearest significance.

The national spirit needed to be of sturdy growth in view of the disasters and humiliations that were to follow on the Lakes frontier, where Chauncey and Wilkinson (Harrison had resigned and Perry was detached at his own request for service at sea) mismanaged the operations on Lake Ontario and the St. Lawrence with the blundering co-operation of the Secretary

of War. The winter of 1813–14 found even Prevost and Yeo
able to make head against their enemies, to score some petty
but irritating victories in a campaign marked by some outrages
and counteroutrages that served to embitter the struggle in a
marked degree. Prevost's efforts had the unexpected additional
result of developing in America a new generation of military
officers worthy of their commands, who built up an American
army that could fight and march, could endure hardship and
neglect and disease, and could meet British regulars in fair
fight and give as good as they received. Napoleon's marshals
could not boast of that.

The outrages of which both sides complained did not diminish the strict courtesy with which the armed forces of the
two countries treated each other. There was a code of manners
which was very generally adhered to, more punctiliously than
by French and British officers toward each other—French
officers were likely to give vent to revolutionary sentiments
and to display a *brusquerie* that caused them to be suspected of
not being gentlemen, and Bonaparte's conception of total war
did not admit of any exchange of prisoners; the polite con-
ventions maintained between British and Americans survived
all the rude shocks of unexpected victories and defeats.

At Lawrence's first funeral at Halifax his pall was borne by
the six British captains and commanders who could be assembled there. One of them was Commander Samuel Blyth,
who had just arrived; he had been appointed nearly a year
before to take command of H.M.S. *Boxer* on the Halifax station and had only now succeeded in bringing his ship across
the Atlantic. He had been six times wounded and had won his
last promotion (and had been awarded a French officer's sword)
in a desperate action with French gunboats on the Dutch coast.
Blyth felt a grievance about his command; she was a 14-gun
brig of a class until recently reckoned a lieutenant's command.
But the Royal Navy had plenty of captains at this time; to find
them all employment it had recently been decided to appoint

captains to vessels as small as 20 guns. As a result there were far fewer commands available for commanders; Blyth waited a whole year after his promotion and then found himself given the *Boxer*, which a few years before would have been considered a poor reward for a lieutenant. It is a curious aspect of total war as waged at that time that England, fighting for her national existence, should find herself allowing young and vigorous men (Blyth was twenty-nine) to remain unemployed for these long intervals as a result of their having distinguished themselves.

Blyth's crew numbered some seventy men; he sailed from Halifax immediately after Lawrence's funeral, under orders to harry the coast of Maine. He spent nearly three months in these waters, taking a couple of prizes and incidentally capturing a small boat with a party of ladies on board, including a colonel's wife. He released boat and ladies, a courtesy acknowledged by the colonel in an advertisement in the press. At dawn on September 6, 1813—Perry was waiting at Put in Bay for Barclay to come out—*Boxer* was lying at anchor close inshore when she sighted a strange brig heading up the coast.

Lieutenant William Burrows was one of several officers of the United States Navy who had gone on furlough during the period of recrimination before the outbreak of war, and he had accepted civilian employment in the mercantile marine. His first voyage ended in his being taken prisoner while on his way home from Canton. After he was taken into Barbados the mutual courtesy between the opposing forces allowed him to go home on parole, and in the spring of 1813 his exchange was arranged and he was free to serve. His record was good although not distinguished—he had won the approval of Preble and Bainbridge and Lawrence—and he was given command of the *Enterprise*, which, since the days when she had distinguished herself as the fastest vessel in the Mediterranean and had won her reputation for good luck, had been altered from a schooner into a brig with the loss of much of her speed, although her offensive power at close quarters was greatly increased. She now carried, instead of the twelve six-pounders for which she was designed, fourteen 18-pounder carronades and two nine-pounder guns. A similar change in her sister schooners had been fatal to all of them—the British had captured every one—and now she was only a slightly larger and slightly more powerful example of the detestable British gun brigs, crammed with men —over a hundred—and most uncomfortable.

Burrows took her out from Portsmouth and headed along the coast. He was looking for action and could not doubt that he would find it soon, where both privateers and Royal Naval vessels clustered thick. He found the *Boxer* off Penguin Point, not far from Portland, Maine. Blyth stood out to meet her; it was a day of fine weather and fluky winds, and until midday the two vessels lay becalmed just out of range of each other. When at last a breeze sprang up, *Enterprise* had the weather gauge, but Burrows held off for two whole hours, apparently to test the sailing qualities of his converted schooner against those of the British brig. He had shifted one of his long nines aft from forward, pointing it through his cabin window, possibly because he could envisage a tactical situation in which it would be desirable to have a gun bearing right astern, or possibly to alter *Enterprise's* trim and improve those sailing qualities which he was now testing.

It was two in the afternoon before he decided to close, and then he went straight into action with Blyth awaiting him. There was no attempt on either side to gain any special advantage during the minutes of the approach; each side held its fire with admirable discipline until close alongside, within "half pistol shot"—say ten yards, hard though that is to believe. According to *Enterprise's* senior surviving officer, the crew of the *Boxer* then gave a cheer and fired a broadside, and the crew of the *Enterprise* cheered and fired a broadside in return. It may indeed have happened in this fashion; more likely cheers and broadsides were nearly simultaneous on both sides.

Those first discharges, aimed by unshaken men, were likely to be deadly, and indeed they were. Blyth received an 18-pounder shot through the body and fell dead; Burrows received a grapeshot in the thigh and fell dying. With each ship firing as rapidly as possible, *Enterprise* drew ahead of her opponent; for a moment the nine-pounder which Burrows had shifted aft played with effect, raking the *Boxer*, which must have been in confusion as a result of the death of her captain, because she could have crossed *Enterprise's* stern and raked her even more effectively. As it was, *Enterprise* was able to swing round and cross *Boxer's* bows, raking her repeatedly. The battle was won; badly crippled aloft, and with one third of her men killed or wounded, *Boxer* surrendered—she had to do so by hail because her colors were nailed to the mast. Thirty minutes' firing had beaten *Boxer* into a wreck; *Enterprise* was not nearly so severely damaged.

There had been some misbehavior on board the *Boxer*, a master's mate and three seamen having left their posts and run below to get out of the fire; a rare enough occurrence to call for comment. The guilty men (all with English, Welsh, or Irish names) did not avail themselves of exchange and stayed in the United States to avoid trial. Nevertheless, the British court-martial frankly attributed the defeat, in addition to "the superiority of the enemy's force," to "the greater degree of skill in the direction of her fire"—an admission that must have been painful to make but was highly indicative of the changed professional attitude of the Royal Navy. The far larger casualty list of the *Boxer* was incontestable proof that *Enterprise* had hit more often than she had been hit; some of the excess was due to the advantageous tactical position that *Enterprise* secured halfway through the battle, but the published report of the carpenter of the *Enterprise* regarding damage received left no doubt that after the first two broadsides *Boxer* hardly scored a hit at all.

McCall, the senior surviving officer of *Enterprise*, took her and her prize into Portland, Maine. It was the opportunity for the armed services of the United States to return the courtesies of the British navy toward Lawrence's and Allen's remains. The bodies of Burrows and Blyth were buried with all the ceremony that the city of Portland and the local military and naval authorities could extemporize at short notice. Twelve marshals, "under the direction of Robert Ilsley and Levy Cutter, Esquires," guided the procession. The troops included the Portland Rifle Company as well as regulars. The two bodies were brought ashore from their respective ships amid the discharge of minute guns, were landed at Union Wharf and borne along Fore Street and Pleasant Street, High Street, Main Street, and Middle Street to the Reverend Mr. Payson's meetinghouse, and thence to the cemetery, accompanied not only by Isaac Hull and the crews—captive and free—of the two ships, but by everyone of note in official positions, from the selectmen and the sheriff, the collector of the port, the superintendent general of military supplies and the judiciary, down to the presidents, directors, and officers of the banks and insurance offices and citizens in general. Blyth was buried beside Burrows, and his ship's company put a stone over his grave.

It was a civilized gesture in a war that threatened to become uncivilized. The accusations of reciprocal atrocities were the least significant symptoms. There was a growing exasperation in England which the victories of Perry and Burrows did nothing to allay. A nation which had pulled down from his throne the greatest conqueror since Alexander was not unnaturally infuriated at the refusal of a small and upstart state to acknowledge defeat at the same hands. Bonaparte's abdication did not take place until early April 1814, but once Leipzig had been fought and won in October 1813 it was obvious that at least he would be beaten into submission and that England would be able to turn all her strength against America. A large section of the British public clamored for extreme measures. It was soberly put forward in public prints that the "arrogance of the American government" must be chastised. To humble its proud spirit it should be made "to kiss the rod." In the event of a refusal on the part of America, "let havock, with all its horrors and devastations, be carried into her interior. Bombard her towns—abolish her works—burn her shipping." The only fear of this writer was that the British government "will probably still vacillate, will further forbear."

There were, indeed, counterarguments put forward. The *Naval Chronicle* in a lengthy editorial—long enough to need publication in installments—roundly condemned the legality of the Orders in Council according to international law and admitted that before the outbreak of war many of the acts of British naval officers in American waters were inexcusable. While maintaining the British attitude regarding naturalization, it pointed out that the American legislation prohibiting the employment of foreigners in American ships should put an end to British demands regarding impressment, and it also pointed out—it was a new contribution to the controversy—that American naturalization had been abused by English shipowners to save their crews from impressment. It quoted Burke at length regarding the spirit of the American people, and expressed a conviction that the American people would rather endure the calamities of war than the indignities of peace.

The British press revealed the difficulties faced by the British government. They had to reconsider their war aims, and they had to reconsider the methods by which they could achieve them. They could still fear humiliation or annoyance, but not national disaster. They had the national dignity to consider, to balance the possibility of concessions against prestige. They wanted to terminate the pestilential nuisance of the American war, but they wanted to avoid all appearance of doing so under compulsion. Future disputes with minor powers would be far harder to settle if the notion got abroad that Britain would sooner yield than face a small war. Yet how was the naval and military power of Great Britain to be exerted in order to induce

America to accept the minimum of concession? It was not an easy question to answer, and the government received only cold comfort from Wellington when they consulted him on this professional matter. Wellington, in a letter that has already been quoted, went on to say, "In such countries as America, very extensive, thinly peopled, and producing but little food in proportion to their extent, military operations are impracticable" without river or land transport. Landings upon the coast "are liable to the same objections, though to a greater degree, than an operation founded upon Canada." Then came the final dash of cold water: "I do not know where you could carry on such an operation which would be so injurious to the Americans as to force them to sue for peace." The British government therefore were aware of the definite opinion of their most brilliant soldier that the United States offered no decisive military objective; their memory of the War of Independence, when the occupation of New York, of Boston, of Philadelphia, did not bring about submission, might have told them as much in any case. Wellington did not touch on the naval side, but the British blockade, although it had reduced American sea-borne commerce to negligible proportions, had not so far brought America to sue for peace, and most certainly had not put an end to the maddening activities of American privateers.

The knowledge did not simplify the British problem. Perhaps it is to the credit of Lord Liverpool and his Cabinet that they did not abandon the search for a solution. They determined on further, greater efforts, to continue and to magnify their offensive against America, and to search with all their strength and ingenuity for a method of dealing a mortal blow to their enemy. The sprawling republic along the far shore of the Atlantic might have a vital spot, even though Wellington had pointed out that it had neither a heart to be pierced nor a head to be battered in.

As early as the autumn of 1812 the Czar Alexander of Russia had expressed an interest in terminating the Anglo-American

contest. There had been a considerable trade between his country and America which he wished to see revived, but with
Bonaparte in Moscow his other interests were far more pressing;
he could not afford that his principal ally should be distracted
from the European campaign. He was, moreover, a man of
vague humanitarian impulses with a wavering but genuine desire for peace. He offered his good offices, through John
Quincy Adams, the United States Minister at St. Petersburg.
It was a long journey from St. Petersburg to London; far longer
to Washington. It was not until March 1813 that the offer
reached Madison, a month after he had received the appalling
news that a British squadron had entered the Chesapeake and
the equally appalling news that Bonaparte's invasion of Russia
had ended in disaster.

Yet it cannot be said that Mr. Madison was willing to make
sacrifices in the cause of peace. He was ready to discuss it, but
the reader of his state papers cannot fail to be impressed by Mr.
Madison's readiness to discuss any matter. He was willing to
nominate commissioners, but in his instructions to them he was
emphatic that the United States government would not yield
in the slightest regarding the point at issue, the question of impressment. At least nominally that was the question about which
the two nations had gone to war. England had been ready to
fight rather than yield, and America had been ready to fight
rather than relinquish her demand that England should yield.
Madison's express instructions maintained the American demand. The British—as had appeared when Warren had first
made overtures to Washington—had no intention of yielding.
The deadlock was obvious from the start; when the Russian
Minister in Washington conveyed his imperial master's wishes
to Warren in the Chesapeake the only immediate result was the
leakage of military information to Warren through the unguarded gossip of the intermediaries.

Nevertheless, Madison named his commissioners and dispatched them on the long journey to Russia, despite the re-

calcitrance of the Senate in the matter of confirming Gallatin's appointment. Madison's motives are hardly susceptible of analysis. They are of direct military interest, for the British warlike effort was necessarily directed (even if unconsciously) to inducing Madison to refrain from backing by war his demands for the cessation of British practices of impressment. The raids upon Maryland villages, the encouragement of Federalist discontent, the blockade of the Atlantic seaboard were all aimed, directly or indirectly, at breaking down what the British believed to be Mr. Madison's unreasonable, wanton—even criminal—obstinacy regarding impressment. There had been numerous examples, in the old days, of deliberate laying waste of a potentate's dominions in order to induce that potentate to change sides or policy; the present war might provide another.

It does not appear that the possibility influenced Madison as yet. He did not admit any weakening of his resolve to his friends; apparently he did not admit it to himself either. He still was not fully aware of the damage that war might inflict; he was aware of the victories won by Bainbridge and Hull and Decatur. He was a man of rectitude; it would be hard to induce him to abandon principle for expediency. He was a man of firm will; it would be hard to induce him to abandon a policy entered upon after deep consideration. In any event, it was his duty to strike a balance between the material loss to his country through war and the moral loss through abandonment of principle, and to do so called for both time and experience. His nomination of commissioners, in accordance with the Russian invitation, may be construed as the effort of a conscientious man to omit no part of his duty, which was to prevail on Great Britain to agree to his demand, however hopeless appeared the present means. It is possible enough, all the same, that even without admitting it to himself he was influenced by the thought that should he, inconceivably, change his mind the means would be ready and available by which he could put the new policy—whatever it might be—into effect.

In one respect his attitude had certainly changed. There had gradually faded out from his correspondence all mention of what might be termed the hoped-for by-products of the American entry into war. He had ceased to dream of a second Peace of Paris and a liberalized or a revolutionized British government; the unwavering attitude of the British Cabinet and Bonaparte's behavior had brought about a change in his opinion both of the solidity of the British constitution and of the desirability of any alteration of it under French influence. The emancipation of Canada—as he thought of it—did not seem either as desirable or as practicable, thanks to the evident willingness of the Canadians to fight and the disaster of Detroit. Nor did the humiliation of England—despite the capture of the *Guerrière*, the *Macedonian*, and the *Java*—seem as important in face of the humiliation of America with British topsails in sight of Baltimore and Washington and Philadelphia. To this extent, then, the British had achieved success in the war so far, whatever disasters they had experienced and whatever losses they had suffered. The possibility of increased American demands had been greatly diminished. The point at issue in Mr. Madison's mind was now only the matter of impressment, even though that was hardly realized as yet by Mr. Madison and his entourage; the Liverpool Cabinet could not be expected to appreciate the change in the atmosphere.

Certainly the British Cabinet did not read any sign of yielding into Madison's move. Castlereagh as Foreign Secretary took up the strong position that, as the point under dispute was a question of British internal administration and legislation, the mediation of a third party was undesirable; the flank of that position could have been turned by simply pointing out that the practice of impressing men from foreign ships was one that concerned any nation with ships at sea, but Alexander and his ministers refrained from making use of this maneuver even if they saw that it was possible. Castlereagh could continue to employ his first argument, so that any subsequent agreement to negotiate would be a condescension.

In any case, travel was slow and communication difficult and European events far too exciting to admit of much interest being taken in a war three thousand miles away. It was not until the end of July 1813 that Gallatin and Bayard reached St. Petersburg, and at that time all Europe was gathering its strength and making the diplomatic moves that were to culminate on August 15 in the termination of the armistice of Plasswitz and the initiation of the Leipzig campaign. During that convulsive struggle the Czar could be expected to give little attention to American affairs and, typically, he gave none; the commissioners were to spend six weary months in St. Petersburg and achieve nothing. At the end of the year, when they eventually left the city, the allies were on the Rhine and the British position was enormously strengthened.

Nothing had been achieved by the commissioners; nothing had been done by Alexander since he took the first step. Yet everything necessary had been done, strangely enough, to make peace possible. The mere nomination of the commissioners, the mere mention of peace by Alexander had sufficed to set up the international machinery, even though it stayed idle, clogged by the deliberation of cabinets and the difficulties of transatlantic communication. Castlereagh and the British Cabinet had been compelled to move. Whether the point under dispute was solely of domestic interest or not, whether to meet the Americans was a condescension or not, the British Cabinet could not face the world, Parliament, and the British electorate under the suspicion that they had not grasped any and every opportunity for peace. Eight months after his nomination of the commissioners—in November 1813, in fact—the vital dispatch reached Madison and informed him that British negotiators would meet with the American ones. The machinery for making peace was now set up. Its existence would in itself be a factor in the making of peace.

Meanwhile the British government bestirred itself. The ostensible war objective was to induce America to drop her demand for the cessation of impressment; apparently it was only by blows that it could be achieved. There was a body of opinion which in addition desired to avenge the naval defeats; there was a body of opinion which desired to re-establish British naval prestige—between these two there was obscurely a distinction as well as a difference, but it was clear that these objectives could be attained only by vigorous action. Another body of opinion clamored for the conquest, the partition, the utter reduction of the United States.

There was also, as has been mentioned, a strong body of opinion inclining toward peace on any honorable terms, even at the price of concessions, but for the present at least the British government decided rightly or wrongly for vigorous action. With this policy determined upon, means had to be found to implement it, despite Wellington's discouraging comments. The imminent fall of the French Empire, or at least its reduction to impotence in the event of a compromise peace, would set free the best, although nearly the smallest, army in Europe, as well as the greatest navy the world had ever seen. How to put these military assets to best use might remain a matter of debate, but on one point it was easy to agree. Admiral Sir Borlase Warren's command must end. He had been given an enormous force and a practically free hand, and yet America seemed to be as full of fight as ever, American privateers were actually becoming more destructive, and units of the American navy were still emerging from and returning to American ports. The instructions he had originally been given to endeavor to make peace seemed to have influenced his feelings; he did not seem to be the man to wage a vigorous war of the kind contemplated. There was an opportunity available of removing him from command, for he had complained of the burdens of his duties and had actually recommended—unlike the great majority of commanders in chief—that his command be reduced by the separation from it of the West Indies. The opportunity was taken; Warren was removed and a successor selected and appointed.

This was Vice-Admiral the Honorable Sir Alexander Cochrane, K.B., a younger man, though not markedly so, for he was nearly fifty-six. But he came of a family noted for its originality and activity; he was the brother of the ninth Earl of Dundonald, a man in advance of his time, whose interest in the development of commercial chemical and manufacturing processes was reducing the family fortunes while meriting better success. The ninth earl's son—Alexander Cochrane's nephew—was that "Cochrane the Dauntless" whose exploits as captain of the *Speedy* and at the Basque Roads marked him as one of the most brilliant of British naval officers; an inventor, too, whose suggestion of the use of compressed air was put into practice much later during the construction of the first Hudson River tunnel. One member of the family was involved in a famous fraud; many of them had distinguished careers in the army and navy. In fact, Alexander Cochrane had a family interest in America; his cousin, the seventh earl, had been killed at the siege of Louisburg fighting side by side with Americans, and ungratefully the Americans had killed his own brother, Charles, at Yorktown in 1781—a fragment of family history worth bearing in mind.

Alexander himself had had a long and distinguished career as a naval officer, colored by all the varied experiences that fell to the lot of the Royal Navy during twenty years of war. As captain of the *Thetis* in 1796 he had brought the *Prévoyante* to action off the Capes of the Chesapeake and captured her. As captain of the *Ajax* in 1801 he had been responsible for the landing arrangements in a most successful amphibious action—Abercromby's landing in Egypt—and had gone on to head a brilliant little operation when the small craft of the fleet broke into Alexandria harbor. When he reached flag rank he was given the command in the Leeward Islands; with his flag in the

Northumberland he took part in the battle of San Domingo and drove ashore and destroyed the *Impériale*, reputed to be the finest three-decker afloat. In 1809 he commanded the fleet in another brilliantly successful amphibious operation, the reduction of Martinique; he was marked as a lucky man, as well as active and able and original, and he had had more experience in combined operations than falls to the lot of most. Along with all this was his very definite rancor toward America, which may perhaps be explained by the fate of his brother; expressions in his correspondence are reminiscent of the violent outcries in some of the British press, but they may, however, merely be echoes of them. With twice the naval force Warren had disposed of and with a well-trained army at call, he might be a dangerous enemy.

Cockburn was retained as his second-in-command—he had displayed under Warren the desirable quality of relentless activity—but with the transfer of command a belated change was made; Yeo on the Lakes was made independent. It was an obvious and necessary item in the agenda of reorganization, but it remained to be seen whether Yeo would be more successful in extracting the necessary support from the Admiralty rather than from a commander in chief, and, if he did so, it remained to be seen whether he would employ it to good purpose. Yeo's retention of the command after the defeat on Lake Erie is hard to understand, but he wrote remarkably telling reports of his operations and plans, and that may perhaps account for it.

And so the stage was set for the next act in the tragedy. While, with horrifying slowness, the peace commissioners were drifting toward a meeting, England was gathering her strength to bludgeon America into submission, and the British Cabinet was organizing as great an effort as they believed the British taxpayers would endure. Lawrence and Blyth, Burrows and Allen had been buried with international ceremony, but they were dead men, and other men were to die by the thousands as well with less attention paid to their graves.

Chapter XVI

DURING THE WINTER OF 1813–14, while the British navy was endeavoring to keep a close watch on the coast of America, contending with all the difficulties of the geographical and meteorological conditions there (a hurricane came as far north as Halifax and did considerable damage), a unit of the United States Navy was engaged upon an enterprise at the farther end of the world of remarkable interest; it would be worthy of study if only because it gave training in war to Farragut, who as a child of thirteen served as a midshipman on board and even had an experience in independent command.

Captain David Porter of the *Essex* was, before the outbreak of war, perhaps the best known to the British public of all the American naval officers, thanks to various bloodless but vigorous clashes with the Royal Navy. He was "that boisterous champion of free trade and sailors' rights"; in America he was perhaps best known as having, in his capacity of first lieutenant of the captured *Philadelphia*, organized the prison school for officers in Tripoli. He had held captain's rank only since 1812, but he had had command of the *Essex* since 1811—somewhat against his will, incidentally, as he mistrusted her sailing qualities and disliked her armament, which consisted in forty 32-pounder carronades and only six long 12-pounders. Nevertheless, he had distinguished himself in the opening weeks of the war by surprising and capturing the British sloop *Alert*—not too alert—before sailing from the Delaware on October 28, 1812, with the intention, already mentioned, of joining Bainbridge in the South Atlantic.

The arrangements for concentration failed; *Constitution* fought *Java*, *Hornet* fought *Peacock*, and both returned home, and Porter far to the south at the last rendezvous (by posing as a British officer he had picked up the messages left him by Bainbridge with the Portuguese authorities) deduced from the rumors which reached him that he was alone and independent. He decided to make for the Pacific, and the correctness of his decision was never questioned, not by the authorities at home nor later by historians. The capture of a British mail packet with fifty thousand dollars in gold and silver on board had already provided him with the money he would need and may have been the deciding factor in his choice of route. Yet it can be pointed out that he did not capture another prize until March 1813, so that for three whole months he was doing no damage at all. The British whalers he intended to harry were not numerous (although individually considerably more valuable than the average run of prizes) and they were by no means a vital part of the British mercantile marine. On the other hand, he could count on the news of his arrival in the Pacific forcing the British into a dispersion of force which could be inconvenient at least. The real justification of the enterprise lies in the fact that it would excite apprehension in the minds of the British authorities as to where American activity could be looked for next; well executed, it could be counted on to have the moral effect which was the objective in going to war, and its nuisance value would be magnified in the imagination of the enemy.

Certainly the enterprise was executed astonishingly well. Before he set out to round the Horn, Porter saw to it that *Essex* was as well prepared for the stormy passage as she could possibly be, stiffened by reducing the top hamper and by striking the ammunition below, and new sails and cordage replaced the old. With reduced rations from the start she could be confident of not being inconvenienced by shortage of food and water, and precautions were taken against scurvy, including the pathetically useless one, practiced in most ships of that day, of boiling vinegar between decks—the only result being the masking of one stench by another. The Horn was rounded without incident save for the anticipated storms, and the *Essex* attained the distinction of being the first American ship of war to sail that Pacific Ocean in which so many victories were to be won a hundred and thirty years later.

Fresh provisions were picked up, and *Essex* entered Valparaiso on March 14, 1813. It was necessary to gather information and to give all hands a run ashore, but it was certain that the news that an American frigate was in the Pacific would be hurried in every direction, over the Andes to Buenos Aires and northward to Panama and the Caribbean, as soon as the Stars and Stripes were sighted. The question of neutrality in this Spanish possession was more complicated even than usual, because Chile had already made the first moves toward independence of Spain, while the Viceroy in Peru was interpreting his duty as an ally of England as necessitating the commissioning of privateers against American commerce—American whalers, in fact.

Porter, his crew refreshed and his provisions completed, sailed again with commendable promptitude. He found and captured a Peruvian privateer, disarmed her, and sent her in to Callao with his interpretation of the neutrality laws for the benefit of the Viceroy. He recaptured some of the prizes she had taken and obtained a few men from their crews. He went on northward to the Galápagos Islands, and by remaining in their neighborhood he captured twelve British whalers which sailed into his hands as they sought to renew their provisions and water. Yet it should be borne in mind that to effect these captures *Essex* was cruising round the Galápagos for five whole months, and it was during that very period that *Argus* captured nineteen prizes in thirty-one days. Not merely that, but *Essex* now needed refitting, and the next three weeks were spent unproductively in a passage to the Marquesas, and there she stayed until mid-December. The visit of the *Essex* to the Marquesas was a romantic episode with its feasts among the coconut palms and its little native wars and its Polynesian beauties, but it was nothing more.

What is most instructive about the whole cruise is Porter's ability as an administrator and leader. His losses in men, from disease and desertion, were extraordinarily small; in fact, by recruiting from the American whalers, he actually had more men under his command at the end of it than at the beginning —something unique in the naval history of the period. *Essex* was hove down in Nukuhiva, in true buccaneering fashion, her bottom cleaned and her rigging new set up; Porter maintained his ship at sea as a fighting unit from October 1812 until March 1814, for seventeen months continuously, his crew in health and discipline, without once calling at a home port. Drake and Anson could hardly boast of more in that regard.

He showed marked ability and ingenuity in employing the prizes he took as tenders; the sturdily built whalers—most of them already mounting a few guns—were the merchant ships most easily adapted as ships of war. His tenders extended his horizon and were useful for gathering news, and conceivably they might be of some value in a battle. On the other hand, he was reckless in the matter of trying to send his prizes home. All the three that made the attempt were recaptured, involving the loss of the prize crews who could have been more usefully employed. It would have been better to burn the ships and retain the men; the prisoners could have been landed on the South American coast without undue hardship.

With his ship refitted, Porter decided to return to Valparaiso; it was a strange decision, for he had already received from there, through his tender *Essex Junior*, positive information of the pending arrival of a British naval force and even of its probable strength, which was superior to that of the *Essex*. It appears obvious that Porter deliberately went to fight a battle; well enough if he could count on a certain and easy victory, bad if there was a chance of being seriously crippled, and suicidal in the circumstances. Perhaps he hoped to snatch a victory over the British ships by falling on them separately, but it was too great a risk for a raider captain. An American frigate at large at the ends of the earth was worth certainly four in a home port —as the year was to prove—and, considering the size of the British navy, she was worth at least ten British frigates. It was Porter's duty to avoid any sort of equal battle. By his own account he left Nukuhiva provisioned for six months. He could have rounded the Horn and reappeared in the South Atlantic, leaving the British squadron at Valparaiso cooling its heels and out of the war; *Essex* off the Cape of Good Hope or St. Helena might have done serious damage. Or he might have continued his westward course. His appearance in the China Seas or the Indian Ocean would not have failed to excite consternation. There was a neutral port in Macao available. Whatever happened to him could not have been worse than the actual result, and his cruise might have continued in glory instead of ending in glorious disaster.

Porter reached Valparaiso on February 3 and stayed there until the eighth without sighting an enemy. His stay there is a final proof that he was looking for a fight; he could have completed with provisions and water and vanished out to sea again if he had wanted to. On the eighth there arrived the British squadron; *Phoebe* under Captain Hillyar, more powerful, thanks to her long guns, than *Essex* at long range, and at short range far inferior, thanks to the carronades of the *Essex;* and in addition the sloop *Cherub*, far inferior to *Essex* but likely to turn the scale if all three ships were in action together. Hillyar misjudged his distances as he entered—easy enough there, with fluky winds and a shore steep-to. There was a moment when the two ships were almost in contact and when Porter could have fired a raking broadside into *Phoebe*, with the likelihood of an immediate close engagement and a fair chance of victory. He refrained, on Hillyar's verbal assurance that he would not attack. Presumably Porter was actuated by the desire to respect the neutrality of the port. That neutrality was doubtful; Spain was an ally of Great Britain; if Chile was in rebellion against Spain she was an enemy of Great Britain. Porter had enjoyed the hospitality of the harbor, which certainly influenced him, but an untenanted harbor and one suddenly invaded by a hostile force are two different things. Most important of all, he was a citizen of a country that had gone to war on a point of international law, and he had to respect the forms of law. Yet it is most unlikely if anyone would have condemned his action had he opened fire in those particular circumstances, with a hostile vessel close on board. He need not have awaited or listened to Hillyar's assurance that he would not attack; it is hardly straining a point to say that he should not have done so.

Whether Hillyar should have given that assurance is another matter, although he was clearly speaking in all honesty when he declared that he had no intention of attacking; if he had entered the port with that intention it would have been obvious. It is hard to condemn a man for hurried words spoken while his ship was in imminent danger of collision, but Hillyar was indiscreet. He had come in to clear up the question of neutrality and to arrange for the battle that Porter was so clearly courting, and he spoke hastily with those arrangements in mind which he did not think about quickly enough to admit of alteration. He did not have immediate and informal battle in mind, and he spoke to avoid that in just the same way as he was avoiding a collision, and he may have had the question of the safety of the town in mind as well. Perhaps he regretted his words later, when he realized what construction might be put on them, but there was no question of treachery or even of a *ruse de guerre* hurriedly contrived for the occasion.

Subsequently Hillyar and Porter met on shore and entered

into a verbal agreement regarding the neutrality of the port. Certainly they agreed not to fight in Valparaiso roadstead, where stray shot could injure the town. What else they agreed upon is a matter of some dispute, as might be expected of a verbal agreement. It is hard—it is almost impossible—to believe that Hillyar expressly agreed to respect the neutrality of all the thousands of miles of desert coast; most probably the matter was not even mentioned. It would appear sufficient to arrange for the safety of the inhabitants of the town; with that settled, there seemed no need for further discussion. In addition it is clear that, by having any contact whatever with Hillyar, Porter showed that he did not believe him to be guilty of sharp practice in that much-debated matter of the hail during the first meeting of the ships; he would never have addressed a word to him if he had thought Hillyar guilty. And the existence of the agreement, undisputed, necessarily involves a fresh start in the relationship between the two; the incident of the hail was now closed. It is nonsense to accuse Hillyar of ingratitude, even if gratitude were compatible with the execution of a naval officer's duty; to speak of "Hillyar's deliberate and treacherous breach of faith," as Theodore Roosevelt does, is to cast the wildest and most vicious aspersion without any justification at all. Hillyar completed with water and then took his ships to sea, cruising off the bay, and Porter had to review his proposed course of action. He had come to Valparaiso courting a battle; now, in a more sober moment, he was anxious to avoid one except in favorable conditions. That meant a close action with *Phoebe*, with *Cherub* out of the way; not so easy to achieve, as Porter discovered in a preliminary sally, for *Phoebe* kept close to *Cherub* and exit was impossible without action with both of them. Porter waited for three weeks after this, while Hillyar kept the roadstead closely blockaded—no easy feat on that precipitous coast with the treacherous winds blowing down savagely over the hills above the town. To have maintained station for three weeks without once being taken unawares was a remarkable achievement on Hillyar's part.

In the end it was Porter who was forced into action in unfavorable circumstances. A fierce gust of wind swept the roadstead. One of *Essex's* cables parted; the second anchor dragged. Finding himself drifting out to sea, Porter acted promptly; five minutes brought about the change between lying peacefully in Valparaiso roadstead and being in imminent peril. He cut his remaining cable, set and reefed his topsails, and made a dash for the westerly point of the bay, hoping to squeeze between it and the British ship. Hillyar headed him off, and at that moment another gust carried away *Essex's* main-topmast. There was no hope now of even beating back to the town. Porter went about and headed easterly, with Hillyar close upon him. Three miles from Valparaiso, Porter anchored close inshore, and Hillyar came in to attack.

This was in Chilean waters, but far enough from Valparaiso for the town not to be endangered by cannon shot. The attack was a violation of Chilean, or Spanish, neutrality. It might be expected to incur Chilean, or Spanish, resentment, although there is no record of any resentment being aroused—after the action Hillyar made use of the facilities at Valparaiso without opposition. Already the neutrality that had permitted *Essex* to lie for eight weeks continuously in territorial waters had been proved to be inadequately enforced; a neutral has obligations as well as rights. It was not for America to feel aggrieved with England at the violation of Chilean neutrality, unless, indeed, Hillyar had promised Porter never to attack in Chilean waters, and that is so inherently improbable as to be dismissed as impossible. Hillyar clearly believed any obligation he had incurred was ended as soon as the town was free from danger. Porter clearly believed he would be attacked. One hundred and one years later, almost to the day, the German light cruiser *Dresden* was attacked and destroyed in South American neutral waters and in similar conditions, having taken advantage for weeks of the neutral's being unable or unwilling to enforce her neutrality.

Porter fought well. At anchor, with the wind offshore, *Essex's* vulnerable stern was turned to her opponents. He hurriedly shifted three of his few long guns to cover the weak point. Hillyar did not allow him time to put springs on his cable, which would have enabled him to haul his ship round and present his broadside to the enemy. Porter made the attempt, but *Phoebe's* fire frustrated it repeatedly; Hillyar's long guns were more effective than he knew at the time. Hillyar closed in twice and each time had to retire; he had received some damage aloft and he had no springs ready on his cable—he could not be expected to have, seeing how the battle had started. When they were ready he closed for the third time, intending to anchor out of range of *Essex's* carronades and to make use of his springs to bring his long guns to bear. But Porter came out to meet him; he hoped that under way he might achieve close action even though his rigging was already badly damaged. Hillyar kept clear, handling his ship remarkably well; this action was unlike the majority of actions in that at no time were the ships in contact. *Phoebe's* long guns, well served, caused frightful havoc in the *Essex* during half an hour's bombardment; *Cherub* (whose captain was wounded) contributed to some unknown but probably small degree to the damage. The losses on board the *Essex* were appalling; there were something near a hundred and twenty casualties, more than half the ship's company; the British ships were firing into her hull with a steadiness and accuracy comparable with the best of American gunnery. Porter tried to beach his beaten ship and was balked by the wind; he tried to anchor, and the cable parted again or was shot away. Some of his men swam ashore with his permission, and then he hauled down his colors and ended the slaughter. The British casualties in both ships were fifteen altogether.

So ended an episode in American naval history whose importance springs mainly from the romance that surrounds it. Porter and Hillyar agreed to neutralize the *Essex Junior* and to send her to America with the prisoners on parole (including

Porter and young Farragut), and so the last of the prizes *Essex* had taken ceased to be of value to America. *Essex* had sailed on October 28, 1812; she was captured on March 28, 1814. In seventeen months she had captured fifteen prizes, and she ended in the enemy's hands. Commodore Rodgers' voyages have been sometimes criticized as unproductive and ineffectual; they were not as long, they captured more shipping, they forced a greater dispersion of the British naval effort, and they did not end in disaster.

The British reaction to the news of the capture of the *Essex* was astonishingly sober, compared with the reception of the news of the capture of the *Chesapeake* a year earlier. By mid-1814 England had recovered her self-respect and had freed herself from apprehension. Hillyar began his report laconically with "Sir, I have the honor to acquaint you," and ended it without one single expression of delight. Nor did the press indulge in any extravagances. "An event," said the *Naval Chronicle*, "of comparative insignificance," in which "owing to our superiority of force we have nothing to boast."

Chapter XVII

ON THE OUTBREAK OF WAR the Administration of the United States had taken in hand a shipbuilding program with considerably more foresight and good management than had been bestowed on the army; perhaps not the highest praise that could be accorded. Three ships of the line were begun, but, owing to the length of time consumed in building them, they never saw service. A good many small craft were purchased and commissioned as ships of war; in 1813 the victories of the heavy frigates suggested the construction of more of the type, named for their captures. They also never saw service during the war, and one of them met with a disastrous fate. Three other vessels were also begun, and, to judge by the success achieved by two of them, it might have been better if the Administration had employed the labor and materials consumed by the larger ships on the construction of many more. They were heavy sloops, designed to be as superior to the British brigs and small ship sloops as the heavy frigates were to the British frigates. In Doughty the Administration was successful in discovering an able designer; the ships—*Wasp*, *Frolic*, and *Peacock*—were both fast and powerful.

Frolic was the unlucky one. Built at Boston, she got away in March 1814. She had several narrow escapes in encounters with British frigates, took one single prize, which she burned; she met a Spanish-American privateer—a significant encounter, for with the movement for independence in Spanish America privateers were putting to sea soon to degenerate into pirates and sank her. Then in the Florida Strait she sighted a British frigate and an armed schooner to leeward of her. Her captain, Joseph Bainbridge, brother of the commodore and brought up in the same service, failed to make the best use of the qualities of his ship. The schooner weathered her as she clawed to windward; the frigate overtook her. Bainbridge lightened his ship, threw his lee guns overboard in order to be able to carry a greater press of sail close-hauled, and yet—perhaps he was balked by the schooner; not many details are available—did not shake off the frigate. He surrendered when he was under her guns. "A remarkably fine ship, and the first time of her going to sea," was the British captain's comment.

It was a depressing beginning for the new sloops; *Wasp* was more fortunate—if a ship can be termed fortunate whose ultimate fate can never be known. She was built in the Merrimack River, commissioned at Portsmouth, New Hampshire, with a New England crew under Master Commandant Johnston Blakely—another officer trained under Preble, one who had recently distinguished himself in command of *Enterprise*—and she sailed on May 1 on her brief career of five months. Her orders took her to the approaches to the Channel; the successes of *Argus* and of the privateers had called attention to the possibilities of that hunting ground. By the end of June she had taken seven prizes before she sighted, on June 28, one of the ubiquitous and feeble British brigs of war—*Reindeer*, Captain Manners; he had been sent out from Plymouth less than a week earlier to take part in the search for the vessel whose depredations had exasperated London.

Manners fought well, as might be expected of one in whose veins ran the blood of the Marquis of Granby. He contrived to do some damage to *Wasp* during the minutes of the approach, even though his ship was the one that approached; he brought a single light gun to bear at a time when *Wasp* could use none of hers. Then the ships closed and in a desperate battle *Reindeer* was beaten. Manners, with the calves of his legs shot away, kept his men to their work until he was killed by musket shots from *Wasp's* tops. The British attempted to board and were beaten back; the Americans followed them up and won. Of the British crew, far more than half were killed and wounded, including all the officers; the American loss of fifteen per cent was far higher than that suffered in most American victories. As a gruesome sidelight on the fighting it is noticed that a British seaman was shot through the head with a ramrod which some American small-arms man had forgotten to withdraw after charging his piece; the wounded man recovered.

Blakely burned his prize and went into L'Orient to refit, taking prizes on his way. Peace between England and France had been made long before, and France was now a neutral in all except good will. News traveled slowly along the long roads between Brittany and Paris; instructions traveled slowly back and then had to be reinterpreted. Despite the protests of the British Ambassador, Blakely was permitted to stay for seven weeks; it must be added that the long delay was caused by the difficulty of effecting repairs.

When he emerged he was already in an area in which he could be dangerous. He took three prizes in four days, one of them in spite of the efforts of a British ship of the line in charge of a convoy. At nightfall on September 1 he sighted four sail, closed with the one farthest to windward, and began an action in darkness, with a strong wind blowing and a considerable sea running. His opponent was another British brig, *Avon,* and the conditions of the encounter were such as to afford the greatest scope for American superiority in gunnery and fire control as well as greater fighting power. In three quarters of an hour *Avon* was a sinking wreck, beaten into surrender, with one third of her crew casualties. Before Blakely could take possession, two other British ships were at hand. There was a brief exchange of shots with one of them; *Wasp's* rigging had been badly cut about, although she had suffered almost no other damage, and she had to be put before the wind, while her pursuer was recalled by *Avon's* distress signals—luckily for her, most likely, as she was only one more of the vulnerable brigs.

On board *Wasp*, at the time of the battle, there were the captains of the recent prizes, who brought the news to England when they were sent there in a neutral. Their report of the small damage *Wasp* had received and of her few casualties (they said five; actually there were only three) had to be accepted as truth and not as American boasting; it is significant that the reaction in England was that it showed "the necessity of immediately building vessels capable of carrying more men and heavier metal"; the necessity for improved gunnery was already being lost sight of. And a rumor reached England at the same time that the *Wasp* had sunk as well; a strange anticipation of events. For *Wasp* continued on her southward course, picked up one or two more prizes, took on board, in the latitude of the Azores, two lieutenants of the *Essex* making their way home in a merchant ship from Buenos Aires, and then disappeared. She vanished from all knowledge from that day to this, lost at sea.

The third of the three sloops had the most spectacular and successful career of them all—the *Peacock*, named after Lawrence's prize. She was built at New York and escaped through the blockade of that place in March 1814 under the command of Lewis Warrington, another of the young officers (he was in his early thirties) who had been trained under Preble in the Mediterranean and with a good record behind him as first lieutenant of various of the large frigates; in *Congress* he had accompanied Rodgers during the first of the latter's cruises. *Peacock* had a secret rendezvous with *President*, which had not succeeded in escaping, and Warrington, after delivering the stores he had to carry to St. Mary's, decided to while away his waiting time among the Bahamas. The good fortune which *Pea-*

cock was always to enjoy showed itself early, even though the first two or three weeks brought no prizes. Warrington had it in mind to meet the Jamaica convoy, from which he hoped to capture prizes despite its heavy guard. Instead he ran into a small convoy out from Havana; the escort—*Epervier*, one more of the unfortunate British brigs—was carrying a hundred thousand dollars in gold and silver, private and not government property.

Despite this responsibility her captain, Wales, turned to fight, perhaps judging that by so doing he would minimize the loss; perhaps, and most probably, hoping for a victory. He rounded to on a parallel course, firing to cripple the *Peacock*, and succeeded in his object, but *Epervier* was crippled as well, not only aloft, but below, where her carronades were proving unsatisfactory. Wales had held his command for the last year; it is a curious indication of the amount of gunnery practice he had carried out that the defects had neither been detected nor remedied. *Peacock* maintained a heavy and well-directed fire, and *Epervier* hardly hit her at all after the first broadside. Wales announced his decision to board, but—it is a British admission— his men flinched and he had no opportunity to make the attempt. The losses, although heavy—almost twenty per cent— were not nearly as great in proportion as in many other actions, so it is likely that Wales had not won the devotion of his men. It was a bad ship, badly found, badly commanded, and badly manned, that surrendered to Warrington.

Very much to his credit, Warrington kept his prize afloat and succeeded in bringing her, gold and silver and all, into Savannah even though chased by British frigates. He replaced his damaged spars, sailed again, and headed for British home waters, to Ireland, to the Shetlands, south again to the Bay of Biscay. *Peacock* took fourteen prizes during July and August, by coincidence replacing *Wasp*, which at that time was lying in L'Orient. Warrington returned by the southerly route, avoiding the prevailing westeries, and completed a remarkably successful voyage by running the British blockade into New York in October 1814, having sighted none of the patrolling squadrons of brigs of war which the irritated Admiralty was hurrying to sea.

It should be remembered that *Wasp* and *Peacock* were not the only vessels harassing British commerce in British home waters during 1814, although their presence, as ships of considerable fighting value, complicated the problems of patrol and escort to a vast degree. American privateers had discovered the profits to be made in the same area, and by now sufficient time had elapsed for ships actually constructed for the business to be available. Powerful vessels, armed with twenty or even thirty guns, with crews of two hundred men, were penetrating the Irish Channel and the North Sea and taking numerous prizes. In British home waters the shipping routes were so diversified and the traffic so heavy that it was impossible to provide convoy for more than a minute fraction of the trade. Patrol had to be substituted, and any privateer captain worth his salt would learn soon enough about the routine of patrol.

The losses, the delays, the inconvenience, and the expense were all serious. It was exasperating to the British public and to the British mercantile community to find that insurance rates—the surest indication of the perils of navigation—were actually higher than they had been during the long wars with France, when England had faced the world in arms and the far side of the Channel had been in the control of a malignant enemy. The losses and inconvenience had a secondary yet vast importance. Peace reigned in Europe; countries deprived of luxuries and necessities for so long under the continental system were eager to enjoy once more the fruits of trade; commerce was reviving, and profits were to be made. This was the golden moment, and the American war was hindering England from taking advantage of it, while neutrals were not hampered at all. Continental merchant shipping was reviving. With far lower insurance rates and more certain delivery, there was a growing danger that foreign vessels might cut into the British carrying trade and that French and Spanish and Dutch colonies, now in the process of being handed back to their original owners, would supply the "colonial produce" so much in demand, to the detriment of the trade of the British colonies.

In Wellington's correspondence—Wellington was now Ambassador in Paris—we can find a striking example of the inconvenience caused. The Prussian government had commissioned a monument in Carrara marble to the memory of the late heroic Queen Louise; it was shipped in a British merchant vessel, the *Alexander*, from Livorno, and vessel and monument had fallen into the hands of the American privateer *Leo*, one of the best remembered of American corsairs. So we find Wellington, with the Congress of Vienna in session and the reconstitution of Europe in progress, having to occupy himself with regrets to the Prussian Ambassador in Paris and with promises to do his best to recover the monument.

It is small wonder that British public opinion was exasperated by a thousand similar annoying incidents and that public outcry grew more clamorous, even though it took divergent directions, with one party demanding peace even at the price of concessions and another demanding the immediate and overwhelming defeat of America, one party guiltily admitting that England's pre-war attitude had been incorrect and the other boldly declaring that as England had destroyed Bonaparte she had the right to dictate her terms to any other power on earth.

The British Cabinet, as has already been indicated, was determined to employ further force, possibly fearing that any relaxation of effort would be interpreted as weakness during the approaching negotiations, possibly hoping to add fresh conquests to the Empire, possibly in the mere hope of revenge for what many English people still thought of as an unwarranted stab in the back during the death struggle with Bonaparte. With Cochrane in command they could hope for a bold and relentless offensive against America. Troops were streaming across the

Atlantic; with a respectable force assembling at Montreal that city was now safe, for the first time since the war began, against a determined American advance, and there was every promise of an opportunity of an invasion of America; and the accumulation of naval force on the American coast meant tighter constriction of the American circulatory system, with the possible gangrene of secession.

Significant items appeared in the British press; one mentioned the appointment of "Captain Bartholomew to the Erebus (fitted to throw Congreve's rockets into the American towns, for which purpose she will shortly sail)." There was a pitiful list of the captures effected by a single ship, H.M.S. *Plantagenet*, during three months off the American coast—twenty-five names, sloops and schooners of thirty or fifty tons, with total crews of two hundred men, brought prisoner to Bermuda. There was the proclamation of a strict blockade of the whole American Atlantic coast, from the Canadian line to Florida. There could be no mistaking the indications of the gathering storm.

It was at this moment that Mr. Madison admitted defeat. There was a gloomy Cabinet meeting in Washington on June 27, 1814, the day before *Wasp* fought *Reindeer*, the day that *Peacock* arrived off Cape Clear, two weeks before Porter brought the news of the loss of the *Essex*. It was not naval news that occupied the attention of the Cabinet. Dispatches had arrived from the commissioners in Europe. They were seven weeks old, being dated May 6. Bayard and Gallatin were conveying their impressions of London, whither, with British permission, they had made their way after their weary wait in St. Petersburg, and where they were now waiting for Castlereagh to decide about entering into serious negotiations. The dispatches left no doubt about the ascendancy of Britain in Europe. She was at the height of her prestige and power. She alone had never bowed to the Corsican tyrant. She had fulfilled Pitt's prophecy and had not only saved herself by her exertions but had saved Europe by her example—and by more forceful means still, for her army had won victories unequaled since the days of Marlborough, her fleet had kept the tyrant confined, and her subsidies had set on foot the armies that crossed the Rhine. Nine tenths of the crowned heads of Europe were hastening across the Channel to share in the bounteous entertainment offered by London. By virtue of British co-operation Bourbons sat once more on the thrones of their fathers in Paris and Madrid, and a Kingdom of the Netherlands was taking shape in the Low Countries. Her intrinsic strength and the extent of her influence were obvious. America had not a friend in the world and she had a very powerful enemy.

There was no blinking this truth. The British victory in Europe had been far more sweeping and decisive than any imagination could have envisaged in 1812. The memory of those early hopes of another Peace of Paris must have been bitter. The blow had been surprisingly sudden; three months had sufficed to reduce Bonaparte from a solidly established potentate to a helpless individual dependent on the bounty of his late enemies. Until the arrival of these dispatches with the eyewitness accounts of reliable Americans there had been room for hope; now there was none, and the reaction was severe. Hostile armies were gathering at Montreal and Bermuda; hostile fleets commanded the Chesapeake and Long Island Sound.

Nor was there any money. The Treasury was empty. As nearly all the revenue had been derived from import duties, and as there were no imports, revenue had fallen away to nothing. It was hard to raise loans in anticipation of nonexistent revenues. The navy had suffered crippling delays and inconveniences from shortage of cash. Mr. Madison, driven by the need to stop trading with the enemy, had imposed an embargo on all sea-borne trade—he had even, in consequence of the refusal of Congress to co-operate, imposed it by his executive authority at a painful cost to his conscience. By the time he had won over Congress to endorse his action, the protests—and threats—of the

New England states had forced him to discontinue it, so that now, besides being penniless, the executive was faced by unrest which had already won significant concessions.

So there was nothing to do but yield, as far as Mr. Madison could see, before worse should befall. On the very day on which the vital Cabinet meeting was held, the Secretary of State wrote to instruct the commissioners to agree, if necessary, to a treaty of peace without any stipulations regarding impressment. It was surrender; America had gone to war on this one point and now would forbear to press it. England had won the war. It was not known as yet to anyone except Mr. Madison and his Cabinet, but it was an accomplished fact.

England had suffered numerous tactical reverses, but she had overawed her enemy by sheer strategical action; it might well be said that she had won the war with America in France, for it was the fall of the Empire that broke down Mr. Madison's obstinacy. True, the instructions to the commissioners laid it down that the concession was not to be made unless it should prove indispensable to a treaty of peace, but how long would it be before the negotiations would reveal the change of instructions? The event was to prove that it would not be very long, and could not be very long. England had won the war by a display of overwhelming force and by its partial employment. It was unfortunate for Sir John Borlase Warren that, having held the command in chief directing the operations against America for nearly two weary years, he should have been suspended at the very moment when his operations might be crowned with success.

Mr. Madison had given way before threats. He already could form a fair estimate of the worst that blockade could do his country. He knew about the local shortages, the cessation of trade, the hardships that the mercantile community were enduring, and the lesser hardships of the general public. But he could see that in a country as little advanced in the industrial revolution as was America in 1814 suspension of trade could be endured. No one was actually starving. It was the thought of the possible further action that England, unhampered by European complications, could take that broke down his will; he did not wait to see England's forces in action, nor to see if Europe might not once more distract her. When Monroe wrote, "Let a strong force land anywhere, and what will be the effect?" he did not know the answer to his question. Ten weeks later Washington and Baltimore would have supplied him with two answers, both encouraging. Washington was occupied—and evacuated again—with singularly few ill effects, and Baltimore defended itself effectively. The British army at Montreal appeared menacing, but what did the menace imply? Madison might be forgiven for not foreseeing the victory of Lake Champlain, but even if that victory had been a defeat, even if the British army had succeeded where Burgoyne failed, and had marched to New York, would that have been fatal to the United States? The War of Independence (as Mr. Madison could well remember) had seen New York and Philadelphia and Boston in British hands at various times and for prolonged periods, but the war had continued. Mr. Madison had not the insight of Wellington expressed in the already quoted words, "I do not know where you could carry on such an operation which would be so injurious to the Americans as to force them to sue for peace." Mr. Madison overestimated the discontent of the New England states. It was vocal, and it was expressed eloquently by the leading politicians of the area, but it seems a fair assumption that the mute mass of the people by 1814 was ready to fight, perhaps had been ready since 1812, and more certainly since Lake Erie had substituted "We have met the enemy and they are ours" for "Don't give up the ship." The Hartford Convention later was to offer indisputable indications that the leaders of the discontented party did not command the devotion of as strong a following as Mr. Madison feared. If the war was worth fighting in 1812 it was worth fighting in 1814, and Mr. Madison might have called the people about him and

announced his intention of dying in the last ditch. He might
have fought, like Hitler in Germany and López in Paraguay,
to the last man and woman, but it did not occur to him to
attempt it; it is just possible—although it is very hard to find
any indication of it in the bulky volumes of Mr. Madison's
works—that he had changed his mind about whether the war
was worth fighting.

In one respect Mr. Madison was, however, seriously to blame.
He did not wait to see how long England's happy condition of
freedom from other perils would endure. With his long experience as Secretary of State and as President he should have been
aware of the possibility of new European tensions. A week
after he made his decision *Wasp* was being well received in a
French port. At the very time of making his decision Europe
was already covertly amused at the petty humiliations England
was undergoing at the hands of the American navy and privateers. All through the autumn of 1814 Wellington in his
capacity of Ambassador in Paris was protesting, bitterly but
hardly effectively, against French breaches of neutrality. "I
trust Your Excellency will take measures to prevent the har-
bours of France from being the ports in which American vessels
of war and privateers are fitted, manned, and armed." "I beg
to draw Your Excellency's attention to the following reports
which I have received of American privateers in the ports of
France." "It is obvious that the conduct of which these papers
give the reports deprives the ports of France of all character of
neutrality." These are extracts from letters written several
weeks apart. The French government, even under a Bourbon
king, was not ill disposed toward a nation which was deflating
the overweening pride of the mistress of the seas.

The benevolence of French neutrality, though important,
was not as important as the other factors in the European situation. The allies had been united enough in May, when the
commissioners addressed their dispatches to Washington; they
had fallen apart by October. In a situation which finds a sig-

nificant parallel in 1945, western Europe was suddenly horrified at the inordinate power of triumphant Russia. There was already a shifting of alliances; secret agreements were being hurriedly made as some of the powers—England and France among them—banded together in opposition to Russia's claim to the lion's share of the spoils and to Prussia's claim to the jackal's share. War was actually contemplated; Castlereagh, deeply concerned with the re-establishment of the balance of power, and already regretting the absence of the tried battalions so recently shipped across the Atlantic, heard with delight from the commissioners at Ghent that America was ready to yield the point for which she had gone to war. Peace could then be made, without England having to make a single concession, without any diminution of her prestige in Europe, and leaving her free to give her undivided attention to and to throw her whole weight into the new negotiations.

It would not do to make too easy a peace; some concession would have to be made to that noisy section of public opinion that clamored for the utter humiliation and even for the partition of America. There was certainly the question of making Canada and the communication with Montreal secure from invasion. Some small cessions of territory and some positive agreements regarding armaments on the Lakes would contribute to the solution; perhaps a buffer Indian state in the Northwest. Castlereagh, happy in the knowledge that Washington had fallen to a British army, instructed the British commissioners to make their demands along these lines and, employing the usual bargaining tactics, to ask for as much as possible in order to give an appearance of concession in the eventual compromise. It was this situation that faced the American commissioners when, having conceded the vital point, they continued their sessions with the British commissioners in the knowledge that peace could certainly be made.

Chapter XVIII

DURING THE EARLY MONTHS OF 1814 the Royal Navy had maintained as considerable a pressure on the American coast as the weather conditions would permit. The escape of *Wasp* and *Hornet, Peacock* and *Adams,* and of the numerous privateers might convey an incorrect impression of the severity of this pressure. The long lists of captures help to correct that impression. There was no place on the coast that could feel secure. As early as April a British expedition pushed eight miles up the Connecticut River and burned the shipping sheltering there. In June another force, sailing up the whole length of Buzzards Bay, pushed into the farthest extremity and burned the shipping there. In these two holocausts forty sea-going vessels were destroyed; the number has only to be given and the terrifying effect can be appreciated, and this number was far surpassed by the total of captures and of ships destroyed in ones and twos, along the whole extent of the coast from Passamaquoddy Bay to St. Mary's River.

Meanwhile the whole seaboard waited in apprehension for the even heavier blows which were likely to be dealt as soon as the British army crossed the Atlantic. It was in the expectation of these blows that Mr. Madison had yielded and had privately admitted defeat on June 27. To guard against them the means were pathetically small, and the Administration made them appear more pathetic still; Mr. Madison found it impossible to reconcile his prejudices against a strong central government with the organization of a determined defense. With Mr. Madison's difficulties with the militia this history has no great concern.

He made one bold appointment, nevertheless, when he gave Joshua Barney the local command on the Chesapeake, over the head of a naval captain—Barney had distinguished himself during the War of Independence and, during the last two years, as captain of the successful privateer *Rossie*. As a vigorous and unorthodox seaman he could be expected to make the most of the means at his disposal, and then it appeared that those means amounted to three of the unhappy gunboats of an earlier era and ten barges with guns mounted in them. Even Barney could do nothing with such a force when opposed to a squadron of ships of the line; he was instantly bottled up in the Patuxent, the inlet next north to the Potomac, and could only lie there, watched by a small British force, until the inevitable moment when the British should bring troops up to destroy them.

Down below the mouth of the Patuxent lay Cockburn, anchored as conveniently, almost, as in Spithead; to him came Cochrane as soon as he had persuaded the reluctant Warren to hand over his command. Four good battalions of Wellington's army arrived at Bermuda—no one troubled to inquire into their feelings when they found themselves, after six years of continuous campaigning, sent off to fight in a new war without a glimpse of their native land; the hardest-driven American divisions in 1945 had seen no more than two and a half years of service in Europe at the time when it was proposed to employ them against Japan. There was available the small force which had already been employed in the Chesapeake, and when the whole arrived at Tangier Island the shipping was an imposing sight, four ships of the line, twenty frigates and sloops, and more than twenty transports. The ships of war provided a battalion of marines; the landing force was now slightly more than four thousand strong, and to command them was Robert Ross, perhaps the most brilliant of Wellington's brigadiers.

From Tangier Island, Cochrane could threaten a dozen points at once, to the confusion of the defense, and he acted vigorously and with remarkable promptitude. His force was concentrated on August 16. On the seventeenth he sent small forces up the Potomac and the Chesapeake, and on the eighteenth he struck with the rest of his force. The transports went up the Patuxent and saved the troops two days of marching. From Benedict, where they landed, they covered the ground at a prodigious pace, in the best tradition of the Peninsular army which had outmarched the French during the famous advance to Vittoria. By the third night Barney's force was menaced; Barney had to destroy his ships and retreat with his men toward Washington. One objective had been achieved.

Until this moment the American defenders had been on the horns of a dilemma—as Sherman's opponents were to be so often later—not too sure about which objective Ross and Cochrane would select. There was no time to arrange a solid defense once the British continued their advance; the British marched too well, and there was a new dilemma, for there were two roads toward Washington. Along one of them the British continued their prodigious march. They covered twelve good miles by noon and found at last a force of bewildered militia in position at Bladensburg—their commander in chief had retreated by the other road and arrived only as the fighting began. The British attacked instantly, over the river and up the hill. Barney's men stood to their guns and inflicted some casualties, some few marines made a stand, but everyone else ran away. Barney was wounded and taken. The delay had been short; the British went on marching and entered Washington that night. Most of the troops had covered more than twenty miles that day as well as having fought a battle. This was August 24; they had only begun to land on the nineteenth, over fifty miles of bad roads distant from the capital.

Cochrane in his proclamations had breathed fire and slaughter; his family, as has already been indicated, had a blood feud with America, but his bark proved to be far worse than his bite. He destroyed those of the public buildings which the Americans did not burn, and when he did so he had fair justification under the laws of war, even if the Americans had not set the example at York. Yet he could have held his hand; the ultimate objective of the war was to induce America to agree to peace, and a merciful forbearance, decently publicized, might have brought that objective nearer. Certainly he could have spared what he described in his report as "the President's palace." He burned one private house, but as a shot had been fired from it he had every justification for doing so. Of outrages there were remarkably few. There was neither rape nor rapine; the iron discipline that Wellington had established held good. The few horrible outrages of which the British army had been guilty—at Badajoz and San Sebastian—report of which, much exaggerated, had preceded them to America, had been perpetrated in the heat of battle by the residue of bad characters present in every army. In the absence of any serious opposition the British were astonishingly well behaved; by comparison it might be instructive to imagine what would have happened in Washington if Jubal Early had succeeded in entering the city in 1864. The naval objective of the campaign had been conclusively achieved; the Americans themselves had put the torch to the navy yard, and the heavy frigate *Columbia* and the sloop *Argus* had gone up in flames.

During his second night in Washington, Ross began his retreat. Once more the British army maintained its prodigious rate of marching. By the twenty-ninth Ross was putting his men on board the transports again. Eleven days only had sufficed for the whole expedition; the army was ready to strike again in some other direction—a brilliant example of the use of an amphibious force, a central position, and command of the sea.

One of the subsidiary movements had met with more success than it deserved. Captain Gordon, R.N., took two frigates and five bomb vessels up the Potomac. Gordon's energy was highly creditable. He put in ten strenuous days working his ships up against contrary winds over the unbuoyed Kettle Bottom Shoals, during which time he declared (perhaps with unconscious and pardonable exaggeration) that all his seven ships were aground twenty times. In any case, he was too deeply preoccupied with his problems of navigation to pay any attention to one of the numerous houses on the bluffs, owned by Mr. Bushrod Washington, called Mount Vernon—no mention of the place appears in his report.

His bomb vessels opened fire on Fort Washington. The officer commanding there, with a minute garrison, had been warned not to allow the place to be captured, and he solved his problem by blowing up the place, spiking his guns, and retreating—an act that later cost him his commission. Above Fort Washington lay Alexandria; the very day that Fort Washington fell a British naval officer entered the town under flag of truce. The Common Council of the town had some days earlier decided to offer no resistance in the event of the approach of a British force and had even named delegates to conduct negotiations. Consequently agreement was easily reached. All vessels lying there were to be handed over, and they were to be laden by the citizens themselves with the merchandise awaiting export, in addition to the naval and ordnance stores; even vessels that had been sunk were to be raised again, while British treasury bills were to be accepted in payment of refreshment supplied to the British force—the Common Council meanwhile hurriedly circularizing the other local authorities lest the arrival of American armed forces should imperil the agreement.

Gordon swept the place bare. Twenty-two vessels were loaded—some of them refloated and rigged—during the three days he was in occupation, and then he effected a brilliant retreat. Three commodores of the United States Navy—Rodgers, Perry, and Porter—had been sent to intercept him. They had the militia at call, some seamen, and a plentiful artillery, but Gordon fought his way past the batteries they erected, towed off the fire ships sent against him, clawed his way down the shoals (U.S.S. *President* had once passed these only by taking out her guns), and got clear away, prizes and all, the ship *Baltic Trader* and the schooner *Wicomoco* and all the others. He was back in the Chesapeake on the ninth of September after twenty-three days during which his men had spent only two nights in their hammocks, with a total casualty list of only forty-two.

Yet vigorous and successful though he was, he still had not been quick enough. Cochrane down at Tangier Island had been waiting for him since August 29, eleven long days, unwilling to undertake any new action lest Gordon should need assistance in his descent of the Potomac. Eleven days, when every day meant a new redoubt on the outskirts of Baltimore, another blockship sunk off Lazaretto Point, and a few more hundred musketeers and riflemen added to the garrison. Maryland was fully armed now; the other diversion that Cochrane had launched at the time of the march on Washington had had unfortunate repercussions. Sir Peter Parker had been sent up the Chesapeake in the *Menelaus;* landing with a small party, he had been ambushed and had lost his life. His body at the moment still lay in his ship and was eventually to find burial at St. Margaret's, Westminster, where his tomb may still be seen.

The raid and the petty success acted as a stimulus to Baltimore. So did the news from Washington, and so, especially, did the news from Alexandria. The city government, unlike that of Alexandria, had already made plans for its own defense, and during the seventeen days that followed the fall of Washington energetic action was taken. Earthworks and batteries were completed, and perhaps ten thousand men assembled—

significantly there were contingents present from other states
—stiffened by a few regulars and some seamen commanded by
Rodgers, who hurriedly transferred himself from the Potomac.
Cochrane indeed wasted not a moment after Gordon rejoined
him. He sailed instantly; by September 11 he was at the mouth
of the Patapsco, fifty sail of ships of war and transports. Long
before dawn on the twelfth his troops were landing at North
Point, field artillery and all, and pushing up the watery peninsula toward the city. Two brisk skirmishes drove the defenders
back in something very like rout to their final line of defense
across the Philadelphia road; it might have been Bladensburg
over again. It is humanly possible that if the impetus of the
attack had been maintained the British infantry might have
broken the line and entered Baltimore on the heels of the
militia. But Ross was dead, brought down by a sniper's bullet,
like Brock. The impetus was lost, and the opportunity with
it. There was the inevitable delay following on a change of
command, and Ross's successor, Brooke, had none of his invincible energy. The army halted and called on the navy to
turn the flank of the defense.

Cochrane brought his ships up the Patapsco, among the
shoals and the sunken blockships. His bomb vessels opened
fire, but from beyond decisive range. Behind solid earthworks
the militia did their duty. Brooke made a feeble demonstration;
a tentative landing by the seamen in the darkness was repulsed,
and it was all over. By September 14 the British army was
marching back to their transports, and the ships of war were
dropping down the Patapsco, and Francis Scott Key was writing some lines of verse, set to a popular drinking song, about
the bombardment of Fort McHenry by the bomb vessels and
rocket ships the night before.

Chapter XIX

IT WAS WHILE SIR ALEXANDER COCHRANE, from the quarter-deck of the *Tonnant*, was examining through his telescope the lay of the land about the mouth of the Patapsco on the morning of Sunday, September 11, 1814, that one of the decisive battles of American history was being fought between fleets neither of which carried, all told, nearly as many guns as were mounted in the *Tonnant* alone.

Lake Champlain had so far figured curiously little in the history of the war. In previous wars Montcalm and Abercromby and Amherst and Burgoyne, Ethan Allen and Benedict Arnold had all fought on its surface or around its shores. It offered one hundred and seven miles of navigable water in almost a direct line from Montreal to New York; on that route the Hudson River offered a somewhat longer stretch of navigable water. For much of the rest of the route the Richelieu River, despite its falls and cataracts, was of importance for the transport of heavy materials; Lake George, at the cost of a brief portage from Champlain, provided another thirty miles of navigation. Land transport between Montreal and New York was necessary, then, only on the gap between Lake George and the Hudson. Burgoyne had met his fate there, but another British general might have better fortune. Wellington had already written that in a thinly peopled country like America "military operations are

impracticable unless the party carrying them on has the un-
interrupted use of a navigable river."

But during the first two years of the war the American
government had ignored the possibility of cutting off the
defense of Upper Canada at its root by a direct advance on
Montreal, and the British, deeply involved at Niagara and on
the Lakes, had had no resources to spare for a thrust down
this obvious line. Until the British had a powerful army at
Montreal, the command of Lake Champlain was of no importance to them, but the moment they had, it became of supreme
importance, for the lake would provide easy transportation for
the whole army train for eight long marches in a country of
few and poor roads. The fact could have been foreseen and
precautions taken to ensure the command of the lake, but with
the balance of power so uneasy on Lake Ontario (all through
1813 and 1814 Yeo and Chauncey had faced each other across
the lake, making feeble raids and counterraids during momen-
tary superiority of force), almost nothing was done to establish a solid dominating fleet on Champlain. In any case, the
British had command of the lake from June 1, 1813, for on
that day two of the three American sloops on the lake rashly
pursued a British force into the Narrows at the Canadian end
of the lake, were caught by a contrary wind, and forced to
surrender to British land forces with artillery on the banks.
The transfer of these vessels to the British service conferred
numerical superiority, which was strengthened on one occasion by the transfer of the crew of a British sloop of war, lying at Quebec, to the lake. With efficient crews on board the
three British sloops swept the whole lake, destroying barracks
and stores on both the New York side and the Vermont side
while Macdonough, the senior American naval officer present,
could only look on helplessly. The lesson was lost on Yeo; it
was taken to heart by Macdonough.

Lieutenant Thomas Macdonough as a midshipman had been
with Decatur in the *Intrepid* on the occasion of the burning of

the *Philadelphia;* later, during the gunboat attack on Tripoli, he had, while boarding a Tripolitan gunboat, seen his cutlass blade break off during the hand-to-hand action and had wrenched a pistol from his enemy's hand and killed him with it. His appointment to command on Champlain carried with it some of the unreality that distinguished much of the Administration's management of the war; he reported direct to Washington, but Washington believed him to be under Chauncey's command. He was dependent for most of his supplies on the captains of the navy yards at New York and Boston, but at the southern end of the lake there were some manufacturing resources on which he could draw. The success of his operations hinged largely on the assistance of the army; a blow at the British base might secure permanent command of the lake, but military co-operation could be secured at first only by appealing to the Secretary of the Navy to use his influence with the President to give directions to the Secretary of War to give orders to the local generals—to Hampton, Wilkinson, and Dearborn, whose names have only to be mentioned to convey an impression of Macdonough's difficulties.

Macdonough established a secure base for himself up Otter Creek in Vermont, where the narrow channel could be guarded against British raids, and devoted himself to the shipbuilding race. The results were curiously small, bearing in mind the efforts being made at the same time on Lake Ontario, where a three-decker ship of the line was under construction at Sackets Harbor. Macdonough had to compete—there is no other word for it—for men and stores with Chauncey; an appeal made in person in Washington by Macdonough's second-in-command resulted fortunately in the transfer of Noah Brown to Otter Creek as chief constructor. Brown built and launched (in April 1814) the 26-gun ship *Saratoga,* altered a steamer under construction into the schooner *Ticonderoga,* of 14 guns, and completed in the nick of time the *Eagle,* of 20 guns. To man and arm these ships Macdonough was dependent on what he could glean after Chauncey had reaped the harvest; it is worth noting that some of the guns he obtained were columbiads, neither long gun nor carronade, of the type that innovators in England were advocating during the period of self-examination after the early defeats.

The British appeared off the American base before these ships were completed, but the shore defenses were too strong for them; with the completion of *Saratoga*, Macdonough enjoyed numerical superiority and put it to effective use, sweeping down the lake in co-operation with the army, now under the command of a capable officer, Izard, with a capable subordinate, Macomb. Water-borne transference of troops and stores permitted the solid establishment of an American force at Plattsburg on the New York side, well up toward the Canadian border and on the invasion route, but by now there was a sufficient accumulation of British troops at the British base to make an assault upon the latter inadvisable. Macdonough could now only await the next British move; his position was rendered precarious by the transfer, under orders from Washington, of Izard with four thousand men from Plattsburg to Niagara—a three weeks' march—leaving Plattsburg defended only by a skeleton force under Macomb.

On the British side the efforts put forth had been culpably feeble. Yeo was as obsessed with the importance of Ontario as was Chauncey, and remarkably little in the matter of men and stores was allotted to the British base at Ile aux Noix. He was on bad terms with the local commanding officer—Pring— whom he superseded at the eleventh hour, and also with a far more important figure, Prevost, who united in his own person the appointments of governor general and commander in chief. As head both of the army and of the civil government Prevost enjoyed an authority many generals have yearned for, but his lack of control over the navy as well handicapped him. In any case, neither he nor Yeo displayed any vision regarding the importance of the command of Lake Champlain; they went on

living in the fool's paradise of the temporary command enjoyed in 1813 and early 1814, until Macdonough's sortie disillusioned them. It was only then that new construction was
undertaken, and only to the extent of building a single ship,
the *Confiance*, which, as time was to show, was not sufficient
to confer on the British the necessary superiority of force. No
explanation can be offered for this extraordinary lapse, save,
as already suggested, the complete lack of any foresight on the
part of Yeo and Prevost, added to their lack of agreement.
Prevost and Yeo between them—especially after Yeo was
made independent of the Atlantic commander in chief—could
have put through the construction and fitting of three ships
the size of *Confiance*, with good will and prevision; Ile aux
Noix had no worse—possibly better—communications with the
outer world than had Kingston, where Yeo was building his
three-decker.

A certain date now became of towering importance. Prevost
was informed that *Confiance* would be ready for service on
September 15 and that command of the lake could not be
counted on until then—and if then. To Prevost the news was
irritating. By mid-July he had in hand at Montreal a respectable corps of Wellington's infantry; by mid-August he had
thirty thousand good troops under his command; he could
concentrate fifteen thousand men easily with which to strike
at New York. Yet even mid-August was late in the year to
begin the endless march over the divide and down the Hudson; and here was Yeo announcing that a start could not be
made until mid-September. Burgoyne's campaign had consumed a whole season, from early summer until its disastrous
end in October. A September start involved an element of risk;
no one would willingly be caught with an army in the field in
the center of New York State in November. Prevost not
unnaturally fumed at the delays. The time already lost could
not be regained. A determined effort to build ships at the
Canadian end of the lake during the preceding winter would

have made matters much more simple; but the preceding winter Bonaparte had not yet fallen, Wellington's army was fighting desperately in southern France, and the present situation could only have been foreseen by a man of considerably greater ability than Prevost. He could now only wait; impatiently. His large forces were being fed on beef driven to his headquarters by Americans attracted by the high prices he offered—Wellington had had a similar experience in France, where the French peasants sold him their cattle rather than have their stock fall into the hands of their own soldiers. The completion of *Confiance* may have been delayed by Macdonough's action in intercepting a complete set of lower masts and topmasts prepared by unpatriotic Vermonters and actually on their way into Canada. Their loss at the eleventh hour certainly added to Yeo's burden and probably did not moderate his bad temper. Prevost and Yeo and Pring were at odds, each with the others. Yeo brought up a new captain, George Downie, senior to Pring, to take over the command on Lake Champlain; he did not arrive until the beginning of September, completely new to lake conditions and unfamiliar with the strategical situation.

On August 25 *Confiance* had been launched. For a crew she was dependent on drafts from the ships in the St. Lawrence, and as these were insufficient, a detachment of infantry was sent aboard. She had to be rigged and equipped, her powder got into her, and her artillery mounted, while she herself had to be dragged out of the channel in which she lay into the Lake—an operation that consumed two whole days. And the moment Prevost knew of the launching he set his army in motion. He quitted the St. Lawrence on August 31; in two days he was over the border, pushing steadily southward and brushing aside the slight opposition of the militia. While shipwrights and riggers and gunners were laboring over *Confiance* he reached the shore of Champlain; on the night of September 6 he marched into Plattsburg, one week before (according to his information) *Confiance* would be ready for action—presumably he had discounted something of what the sailors had told him. Macomb had established his forces in a strong position covered by earthworks well furnished with artillery, his flanks resting on the lake. Prevost refused to launch an immediate assault; the obvious alternative was a siege, with parallels and batteries—an operation of two weeks at least.

And lying in the bay behind Macomb was Macdonough with his squadron. Prevost may have heard that on the very day his advanced guard reached Plattsburg the *Eagle*, of 20 guns, had arrived, with shipwrights working on her as in *Confiance;* certainly he knew that reinforcements were coming in to Macomb by water. A formal siege would take too long, and the siege of a place with communications open by water was proverbially difficult. There were no weeks to spare. There were no days to spare. If there had been, everything might have been easier. Prevost could have drawn his lines round Plattsburg, and Downie could have blockaded the place with his squadron. In that case Macdonough would have been forced to come out and fight; a very few days of that pressure could hardly have failed. Until he should come out Plattsburg would be isolated and Prevost's water-borne communications secure; if Macdonough had emerged for a battle in the open lake the eventual result might have been the same, but it could never have been worse.

Yet Prevost would not delay for a week or a day or even an hour. Apparently what he envisaged was the entry of the British squadron into the bay, the destruction of the American squadron, and then an immediate assault by his troops drawn up in readiness. The American troops, disheartened by the loss of the ships and knowing themselves isolated, could be expected to be only halfhearted. With Macomb's army destroyed and the lake communications secure, Prevost could march the next day for New York with no more of these maddening delays. From the moment of his arrival in Plattsburg he sent a series of letters to Downie, each one something more insulting than the last, with the result that Downie, who was only a commander, was driven into attacking against his judgment, although he was not actually under Prevost's orders.

Macdonough had lain at anchor in Plattsburg Bay for the past several days and had taken every precaution against an attack; it should be remembered that Macdonough had no certain knowledge that such an attack would be delivered—and if it had not been, those precautions would hardly have received two lines of notice in a detailed technical history. Even so, it was the measures which Macdonough took that made the subsequent victory so decisive, and it is all the more to his credit that he took precautions against an event that might never occur.

They were the precautions of a thoughtful and well-educated officer. He anchored his squadron inside and close to the southward-pointing Cumberland Head that delimited Plattsburg Bay. The British would be approaching from the north —the wind usually blowing along the length of the lake—so that they would have to round Cumberland Head and then enter into battle close-hauled to the wind; there would be little chance, therefore, of his windward flank being turned as Nelson had turned the French windward flank at the Nile. His two big ships, *Eagle* and *Saratoga*, were at the windward end —the line of four extended north and south—so that his principal strength was mobile. He not only had springs on his cables, to enable his ships to turn through a considerable arc without setting sail—that was an elementary precaution—but he went to the trouble of laying out kedge anchors on either bow with cables laid out to them from *Saratoga's* quarters; with these, given time and good organization, he could turn his ship completely round. There might possibly be some advantage in that, in various not too obvious eventualities. His ten gunboats, with their oars to move them about, were distributed as a rather feeble reserve to reinforce the line.

Downie, to Prevost's unconcealed rage, was delayed for a day by contrary wind; it meant a second day in which to exercise his crew at their stations, another day for the carpenters and riggers to continue their work. During the night of September 10–11 the wind changed, and Downie got under way. At dawn he hove to outside Cumberland Head and rowed round in a small boat to examine Macdonough's dispositions. It was a beautiful day of early fall; the sun rising over the Green Mountains and lighting up the Adirondacks must have been a lovely sight. Downie was probably more interested in the fact that the wind was fluky. He could identify Macdonough's four ships, including *Eagle*, which he had never seen before. He could neither see nor hear as yet any sign of activity on Prevost's part, although the last letter he had received from him announced that the troops were waiting to make an assault, while the squadron had announced its coming by firing blank charges from Cumberland Head. In any case, there could be no more delay. Downie had himself rowed back to the squadron, issued his orders, and advanced to the attack.

In tonnage, in numbers, in men, and in guns—even in the debatable matter of carronades and long guns—there was little to choose between the British and American squadrons. *Confiance*, two thirds of Downie's strength, had been hardly exercised at all; *Eagle*, one third of Macdonough's, had been exercised rather more. With a force approximately equal in strength—four larger vessels and twelve gunboats against four larger vessels and ten gunboats—but probably inferior in efficiency, Downie was going in to attack an enemy in his chosen position; possibly the fact that he was taking the offensive and might choose—as far as conditions would allow—the point of concentration of his attack would swing the balance in his favor.

It did not do so; everything went wrong. Downie came round the headland, his four ships abreast, his gunboats pro-

longing his line to turn the American southward flank. Close-
hauled on the starboard tack, he tried to close with the head
of the American line, but the wind was erratic and *Confiance*
did not succeed in closing to the point where her concentrated
power would be most effective; most certainly she did not
cross the head of the American line as had been hoped. Downie
nevertheless handled his ship coolly despite the damage she
was receiving; he anchored and opened a fire most destructive
considering the long range, five hundred yards, and in fifteen
minutes he was killed.

The *Chubb*, with her 10 guns, contrived to reach the American line, but, badly cut up by the American fire, with half
her crew casualties, and commanded by an officer who did not
keep a cool head, she did not succeed in anchoring, and fell
into American hands. The *Finch*, also of 10 guns, did not succeed in closing at all; despite only trifling loss she drifted use-
lessly in the failing wind and eventually ran aground well out
of the fight. The *Linnet*, 16 guns, under Pring's command,
reached her station and fought a desperate battle. Of the British
gunboats, half were well handled; they forced Macdonough's
weakest ship, *Preble*, out of line and kept *Ticonderoga*, the
next weakest, too busy to play any part in the main battle. The
other half were feebly led—their senior officer flinched and
later deserted to avoid trial by court-martial.

Macdonough in the *Saratoga*—his Sunday prayers had hardly
been completed when the firing began—therefore found himself along with *Eagle* fighting *Confiance* and *Linnet*, with some
considerable help from the gunboats at his end of the line. The
united American strength in this vital section of the battle was
appreciably greater than the British, and Macdonough's personal example and remarkable control over his men helped
to wear the British down. He was hurt more than once by
flying fragments and falling spars, but he lived; a most important factor in the battle. The British gunfire, at first very effective, fell away rapidly in efficiency, mainly through lack of

control—the death of Downie and of several others of his officers accentuating the poor drill of the men. *Eagle* cut the cable at her bows, anchored again by the stern, and by so turning presented a fresh broadside to the enemy, at the cost of losing ground to leeward which she could afford, being at the head of the line. For *Saratoga* to have done the same would have been tantamount to withdrawal from the battle; but her starboard side guns were rapidly being silenced, through their own defects or the enemy's fire. To bring his port broadside to bear Macdonough made use of the kedge anchors laid out on his bows. It was a complex maneuver, calling for a clear head and accurate timing, dropping an anchor astern, hauling up on one kedge, passing the stern cable to the bows and then hauling in on it; luckily the British fire was so diminished while this was being done. *Saratoga* came slowly round and opened fire with her undamaged broadside of 13 guns. No shot carried away a cable in the way Porter's springs had been shot away at Valparaiso. The surviving lieutenant of the *Confiance* was attempting to turn his ship as well; the losses had been frightful, the ship was filling with water—the wounded down below in actual danger of drowning—his spare anchors had been shot away, and of course he had only a spring to his anchor cable to use for the maneuver. The effort was worse than useless; *Confiance* turned only far enough to allow herself to be raked, and she would turn no farther. Helpless, she could only surrender. Macdonough could now transfer the cable from the other kedge to the opposite quarter and haul in on it. This brought his broadside to bear on *Linnet*, which could only surrender as well, isolated, helpless, and sinking, after one of the most desperate defenses in history.

It was the end of the battle; the British gunboats withdrew unpursued, but Macdonough's battered ships and his patched-up prizes now dominated the lake; nothing could be more evident. To Prevost it certainly was. He halted the feeble demonstration he had been making against Macomb's works, and that night he marched back to Canada. Any invasion of the United States by the northern route was now impossible, at least until the Royal Navy, starting with nothing, could build up a superior fleet on Champlain, and that would be never if the Americans knew their business as well as they appeared to know it.

Chapter XX

THE COURSE OF THE WAR had been profoundly affected by the death of two British soldiers and by the survival of two American sailors. Brock had lived long enough to prove his energy and ingenuity and ability. Had he lived longer the British army on the Lakes frontier would certainly have been brilliantly handled, and during 1813 the Americans under Dearborn and Wilkinson would have had rough treatment. It is fair to assume, knowing what we know of his brief career in command, that Brock was fully aware of the importance of command of the Lakes and that he might perhaps have instilled some energy into Yeo and might have guided his efforts into effective channels. Brock's prestige would certainly have made Prevost's meddling unlikely.

The consequences of Ross's death are more incalculable; but no army could have been led with more energy than the one that captured Washington. It really seems more likely than not that had he not been killed that same army might have overrun the defenses of Baltimore before the defenders had time to settle into them. The point can be debated, but the behavior of the American militia during the skirmishes in which Ross lost his life did not promise well for a determined defense had they been hotly pursued. A Bladensburg might have been expected and not a New Orleans.

The two American victories on the Lakes were due in very large part to the personal exertions of the American leaders. If Perry had fallen on the quarter-deck of the *Lawrence* and the chances were about three to two that he did fall—the battle of Lake Erie might well have ended in a repulse for the American squadron, with the *Lawrence* left in British hands to carry with her superiority of force as soon as she could be patched up. If Macdonough had been killed by Downie's opening broadside—as were one fifth of his men while he himself was hurt—the *Saratoga* might not have fought so hard; she could certainly not have been handled more methodically. Downie was killed during the first few minutes. We learn little about him during his brief nine days of command, but we do know that before his death *Confiance's* fire was highly effective and that it fell away steeply after it. With Macdonough dead and Downie alive, the battle of Lake Champlain might have ended like some of the battles between the English and the Dutch, like Parker's Dogger Bank action, in a drawn battle with the two opponents too exhausted to fight on.

Statistically minded historians have devoted much space to minute analyses of the forces engaged in the various battles, without making allowance for the profound truth stated by a master of war that in war it is not men but one man that counts. America owes much to Macdonough and Perry; perhaps as much, too, to Preble and Rodgers, in whose school they received their professional education; and perhaps as much again to the two riflemen who brought down Ross and Brock.

The consequences of the victory of Lake Champlain and of the fiasco at Baltimore were important. The news reached Ghent three weeks after the arrival of the news of the capture of Washington; the whole sequence of events is interesting. The American commissioners had already yielded on the one vital point. They had given way regarding the British claim to the right of impressment, which was the original cause of the war, but with the understanding that the final treaty should contain no reference to the matter, thus saving America from the humiliation of a public acknowledgment of defeat. On the other hand, they had stood firm, with laudable good sense, regarding the British proposal for a buffer Indian state between Canada and the western United States. To a later generation that knows of the fate of Indian treaties and the temper of the pioneers who flooded westward after the war it is obvious that any such arrangement would have led to ceaseless friction and probably to renewed hostilities. Agreement to drop the project was reached in the nick of time; the very next day arrived the news of Washington, and the British attitude stiffened. From that date, September 27, until October 21, the British were inclined to demand conquests, both to gratify that section of the British public which desired the humiliation of America and to secure the Canadian frontier. The American commissioners could only oppose these demands with a hopeless obstinacy, mindful of the appalling disasters which this obstinacy might occasion to their country. And then came the good news. Prevost had been foiled; no British army would ever march down the Hudson. Baltimore had withstood the advance of British forces; the clearest proof that the country had not disintegrated as some had feared and others had hoped. Perhaps just as important was the negative news. The capture of Washington had been followed by no serious consequences. The President and the Administration were back in the capital, and the government of the country was proceeding in no worse fashion than before.

The British press offered a profitable study. Cochrane's official letter regarding Baltimore could only offer, as justification and compensation for the British efforts, the inconvenience to which America had been put in concentrating the militia around the city. Yeo's covering letter to Pring's report on Lake Champlain was obviously bad-tempered. When he wrote, "I have good reason to believe that Captain Downie was urged, and his ship hurried into action, before she was in a fit state to meet the enemy. I am also of opinion that there was not the least necessity for our squadron giving the enemy such decided advantages," it was clear that he was in the midst of a bitter quarrel with Prevost; an official letter of this sort could only lead to a court-martial (Prevost died before it could take place), and if the British leaders were wrangling with each other like this there was hardly likely to be danger on the Canadian border. A correspondent wrote, "Our war with America has been one of disaster and misfortune." An editorial note said, "Nor do we see any advantages in the peace, to the United States, that are not equally available to the United Kingdom."

The British public had suddenly realized that despite peace in Europe they would have to go on paying, in 1815, the hated income tax of no less than ten per cent, while—as has already been indicated—insurance rates for the Irish Sea were three times as great as they had been at the height of the war with France, and in both respects the press comments were bitter. There was even a lesson to be learned from the reaction of the British press to the opening words of Macdonough's report on Champlain—"The Almighty has been pleased to grant us a signal victory"; it would be hard to decide which aspect of this innocent expression exasperated the British most, that Macdonough should use somewhat similar wording to Nelson's famous opening words in his memorandum after the Nile, that he should lay claim to the assistance—or at least the countenance—of the Almighty, or that he should announce a victory at all.

There were symptoms of war weariness to be observed everywhere, despite the bellicose phrasing of some of the pronouncements of the British press; nor could acute observers like Gallatin and John Quincy Adams fail to note the signs of uneasiness displayed in the negative fact that Wellington was not appointed to the command in North America despite the popular clamor that he should be, and in the positive fact that Lord Hill had been appointed and that his appointment had then been canceled. The commissioners stuck to their guns and refused to consider any cession of American territory, and they were supported by positive instructions to that effect from Mr. Madison.

On the other hand, it might not be well to be too inflexible on less vital points. There were still disasters to be recorded, and there might be more. The same mail which had brought the news of Baltimore and Champlain brought also the unpleasant news that a British amphibious force had penetrated into Maine. Bangor and Machias were in British hands—indeed, the British commander in chief announced his occupation of the whole of the country as far as the Penobscot—Americans were taking the oath of allegiance to His Britannic Majesty, and an American frigate, the *Adams,* had had to be destroyed by her own crew, having been caught unluckily in the Penobscot at the moment when there was a British landing force available to compel her destruction. Cochrane still had his troops and his transports and his command of the sea; from his central position in Bermuda he could strike again and perhaps—perhaps—more effectively than he had at Baltimore. The blockade of the American coast was still effective; the Treasury was still empty. American merchants were as anxious as the British to share, unhampered by war, in the world trade at last possible. There were powerful arguments, therefore, in favor of being accommodating.

The British had the same information as had the Americans, and more as well. Lord Liverpool was fully aware of the objections being raised to the continuance of the income tax, of the depredations of American privateers, and of the consequences of the battle of Lake Champlain. He also knew that he had offered the American command to Wellington and had met with something as nearly resembling a refusal as the Duke's sense of duty would allow him to make.

Wellington had pointed out that if he were given the command the British government would be committed, because of his enormous prestige and reputation, to a war which would demand nothing less than complete victory; and he had reiterated his opinion that complete victory was impossible over an unorganized country like America. Liverpool had sought for another commander in chief; there were two very capable soldiers to be found Lord Hill, Wellington's second-in-command, and George Murray, his quartermaster general—and then it became apparent that they would not be available. The European situation had deteriorated to the danger point. A new war, between the recent allies, was an actual possibility. With half the British army across the Atlantic, the British military position was weak; with a war on her hands, England's political position was also weak, for she could not take a firm attitude in negotiations while the other parties could threaten a display of sympathy for England's active enemy, based on the unresolved difficulties of the legality of blockade. Wellington and Hill and Murray were all needed in case of a continental war, and that made a resounding success in America unlikely. Castlereagh urgently needed peace with America in order to free his hands in Vienna.

In these circumstances, military and political, neither side wished to delay the conclusion of peace, and peace was concluded with a rapidity and a display of common sense that did credit to all concerned. With no mention of the vexed questions of blockade and impressment, America was saved from public humiliation; with no other concessions on either side, national dignities were preserved. The preamble of the eventual treaty was unusually truthful—"His Britannic Majesty and the United States of America, desirous of terminating the war which has unhappily subsisted between the two countries, and of restoring, upon principles of perfect reciprocity, peace, friendship, and good understanding between them . . ." The sentiment was quite genuine, even if it arose from a realization —most unusual in belligerents—that they were engaged in a war which could profit neither and was harmful to both. So acutely did both sides become aware of this, once their attention was called to it, that nothing was allowed to delay the conclusion of peace.

The object of every war, or threat of war, is, in a final analysis, to bring about such a state of mind in the other party that he does not want to make war. The will of the enemy is the ultimate objective, as Hitler was never tired of preaching and as Clausewitz understood in those moments when he was not engrossed in the means to the exclusion of the ends. By 1814 both England and America had reached that state of mind. Mr. Madison's conversion was the product of many factors: the failure of the invasion of Canada, the emptiness of the Treasury (resulting from the British blockade), and the fall of Bonaparte —it must be remembered that Mr. Madison took the important step of waiving his demands regarding impressment in June 1814. Yet it would be hard to withstand the conclusion that the greatest factor was the presence of a British squadron in the Chesapeake; it was with those topsails almost in sight that Monroe sent off the crucial dispatch. Naval and military factors brought about the British change of heart, the defeat at Lake Champlain, and the repulse—almost bloodless though it was— at Baltimore, and the continued presence of American privateers in British home waters. Finally it was the threat of further military operations—the continuance of the blockade and the menace of Cochrane's roving army—that kept the American commissioners amenable and facilitated the negotiations.

Once peace came to appear desirable, every step was taken to hurry its coming. Debatable questions were ignored or postponed for future discussion. Two hundred written words, even with all the "whatsoevers" and the legal redundancies, affirmed the peace; hardly more were necessary to settle the very difficult questions arising out of a definition of the war's end in all parts of the world, and a hundred words decided the fate of the prisoners. By contrast it took some thousands of words to set up a future commission to clear up the debatable points left over from the Peace of Paris, now thirty years old. The question of the Indians was solved—or postponed—by specifically including them in the treaty of peace, in two brief paragraphs.

One single article, of fifty words, made declaration of the intention of the United States to abolish the slave trade; its presence was an indication of the power and determination of the benevolent enthusiasts of Britain as compared with the more fitful influence of the war party.

The shelving of the debatable points was denounced by some intelligent people on both sides of the Atlantic, on the grounds that it would lead eventually to a renewal of the war. They were proved in the event to be wrong; the memory of the profitless damage done by the war persisted and was as influential in the minds of those responsible for keeping the peace as the knowledge of it had been in the minds of those responsible for making the peace. The boundary questions were settled amicably, and from there it was an easy step to the neutralization of the American-Canadian border, an achievement in the cause of peace so beneficial, and so far ahead of its time, as almost to justify the bloodshed and misery of the tragic war.

And less than fifty years was needed to prove to both belligerents that a foreign country is not always led to adopt a policy out of sheer wickedness. Mr. Lincoln's proclaimed blockade of the southern states would hardly have borne examination in the light of the principles laid down by Mr. Madison. The wild outcry in Britain when an American ship of war removed two American citizens from a British merchant ship came strangely from a public whose grandfathers had fought to maintain both the right of impressment on the high seas and the impossibility of a change of allegiance. Attitudes had changed with the times since Christmas Eve, 1814, the very appropriate date which brought peace to the whole of the civilized world.

Chapter XXI

Seven weary weeks elapsed before H.M.S. *Favourite*, bearing the treaty of peace and a British chargé d'affaires, clawed her way across the Atlantic in the teeth of westerly gales and reached New York, but fast horses carried the vital papers from there to Washington, and only six days passed before the treaty was ratified and the war officially ended, the Senate raising singularly few difficulties. Almost two years, from March 11, 1813, to February 17, 1815, had passed since Mr. Madison's nomination of commissioners to treat for peace.

It was during this period that patriotic Americans had been forced to endure the sight of British ships of war in American waters, not only in the Chesapeake and Long Island Sound, but up the Connecticut River and the Penobscot, the Potomac and the Delaware. Their sublime immunity must have been infuriating, and every ingenious mind in America set itself to devise means to put an end to it. The leading spirit was Robert Fulton, the "American adventurer" as the British press not unfairly described him. After studying, and abandoning, portrait painting as a profession in England, he had devoted himself to mechanical invention, working on various British canal projects and then turning his attention to the problems of underwater attack on ships of war and of steam navigation. He had tried to

interest both Bonaparte and the British government in his in-
ventions and, failing, had returned to America—after an absence of many years—and had started the Hudson River steamboat service—engined by the English firm of Boulton and Watt
—which was later to prove so useful to Chauncey in the transport of his material to the Lakes. The presence of British ships
of war in American waters revived interest in his ideas. He devised both fixed "torpedoes"—later called mines—and floating
torpedoes; "fish torpedoes" they were called by a later generation. The fixed torpedoes, fastened to piles driven in the channel
bottom, suffered from the disadvantages of the small technical
progress made to that date. It was hard to make either water-
tight joints or an efficient firing apparatus. But as far as can be
ascertained at the present day, the knowledge of their existence
did exert a certain extremely minute influence in restraining
the activities of the British ships; Fulton busied himself mostly
in the neighborhood of New York, and even Long Island
Sound was not nearly so promising a field for these mines as
the Potomac or the Patapsco would have been—if Cochrane's
Tonnant had run upon one outside Baltimore, later developments might have been greatly accelerated. The fish torpedoes
were intended to be towed; barrels of gunpowder floating
awash on a raft, to be dragged by the towing vessel—under oars,
naturally—against an anchored ship. The plan was that, by
crossing the prospective victim's bows, the towing cable could
be drawn across the ship's anchor cable. The towing vessel
would be carried down one side of the ship and the torpedo
down the other. Then, by pulling on a line loosely fastened
along the tow rope, the trigger of a musket lock inside the torpedo could be tripped and the torpedo set off; alternatively
the far less ambitious and less efficacious plan might be adopted
of merely exploding the torpedo against the anchor cable,
thereby setting the ship adrift.

Equally interesting were the towing vessels devised for the
purpose; they were meant to be trimmed nearly awash, with

only eighteen inches of freeboard, and covered over with a turtle deck armored against shot; the motive power was provided by paddle wheels driven by men within. Perhaps these vessels embodied the earliest germ of an idea which was to bear important fruit later, but it should be remembered that at the same time the British government had also under consideration an actual submersible boat—already called a "submarine"—for use during the war.

Neither fish torpedoes nor mines scored any success, but one fish torpedo in Lynnhaven Bay, devised by Edward Mix, U.S.N., exploded only a hundred yards from H.M.S. *Plantagenet*, occasioning some alarm. Some ingenious people in Connecticut, however, devised a means that killed a few British seamen—they allowed small merchant vessels, filled with produce and abandoned by their crews, to be captured. Then either a time fuse or a tripping line concealed in the cargo set off an explosive charge which it was hoped would destroy the ship lying alongside; nine British seamen were killed in such an explosion on board the schooner *Eagle* three hours after her capture.

The British termed mines and torpedoes and booby traps alike "infernal machines" and expressed equal horror at the employment of all three of them as being equally contrary to the laws of war; their employment embittered the later months of the war—Sir Thomas Hardy's attack on Stonington, Connecticut, the motives for which have so often been misinterpreted, was inspired by the belief that the place was a center for the manufacture of torpedoes. To the historian of the present day the main interest in that affair now lies in the profound difference between the official accounts on either side; the reader can hardly believe they are describing the same action.

One other of Fulton's activities came to fruition too late; Fulton was dead and the war was over before his steam frigate *Demologos* (later christened *Fulton*) was launched. Fulton was hampered in this case again by technical difficulties. He had no facilities for rolling iron armor and had to be content with building timber sides five and a half feet thick; his engine was unsatisfactory, with ten pounds to the square inch the greatest pressure that could be raised in the boiler. This gave the ship, nevertheless, a speed of four miles an hour, from a central paddle wheel situated between two separate hulls. Thirty-two-pounder guns were the largest she could carry, so that, until an efficient shell gun could be devised, she was not likely to be a serious menace to ships of the line. She was only a portent, and not a power, deeply though she impressed post-war British observers; but with slightly accelerated construction and a few technological advances in America, Long Island Sound might have witnessed something like the first day of the battle of Hampton Roads with no *Monitor* on the way to redress the balance.

One of the British periodicals, discussing in January 1815 the possibility of peace with America—which had already been signed—passed on to an ominous piece of news. "The American ships, of which Sir George Collier is in chase, are supposed destined for the British Channel." The "ships" were really only one ship, the *Constitution*, now under Charles Stewart's command, although some American privateers took advantage of Collier's absence to escape from Boston as well. So far Stewart had had no opportunity to shine, although when the war began his reputation had stood very high. As captain of the *Constellation* he had been blockaded in Norfolk; transferred to *Constitution*, he had already made one unsatisfactory cruise in 1814, returning prematurely when he discovered that his ship was ill found. For the rest of the year he had lain in Boston, watched by the British squadron. Not enough attention has been paid—it may be added parenthetically—to the remarkable seamanship displayed by the Royal Navy in maintaining the blockade of the New England coast. Meteorological and geographic conditions there presented difficulties even greater than were evident in the blockade of Brest; the maintenance of the blockade with astonishingly few losses was a proof both of seamanship and of the ability to endure hardship.

But in December 1814 one of the westerly gales blew Collier from his station and enabled Stewart to emerge with *Constitution;* Collier on his return had no difficulty in detecting her absence. Collier headed for the Channel, he hoped in pursuit, but at least hastening to cover the most important strategical point, but Stewart had turned south, celebrating Christmas—and, without knowing it, the conclusion of peace—in the neighborhood of Bermuda. He found only a single prize there and crossed the Atlantic on the southerly route to Lisbon and off the Portuguese coast captured an important prize—a laden Indiaman. The news of his presence would attract every ship in the neighborhood, and he rightly decided to head for a different area where other possible prizes might be making their landfall. It was by the purest chance that he sighted the British ships of war *Cyane* and *Levant* on February 20, some distance to the northeast of Madeira. Three days earlier Mr. Madison had ratified the treaty of peace, but seventy men were to be killed or maimed that day.

The *Levant* was of the lightest class of ship-rigged vessels; the *Cyane,* classed as a corvette, was a somewhat more powerful vessel; neither of them could compare as an instrument of war with *Constitution.* The total of their combined crews was far less than *Constitution's;* the total of the combined weight of their broadsides was almost equal to *Constitution's,* but it came mostly from carronades, and it was *Constitution's* long 24-pounders which were to decide the battle. The two ships were on their way to the American station; when *Constitution's* ignoring of the private signal revealed the fact that she was an enemy, the two captains decided to fight. In view of *Constitution's* sailing qualities they could hardly have hoped to escape in any case.

It was fine weather—a moderate breeze and a moderate sea, enough to test the seamanlike qualities of the contestants while leaving as little to chance as in any sea battle. The first sighting took place at 1 P.M.; the British ships, at first widely separated, closed up into the traditional line ahead with half a cable's length interval before Stewart could engage them. It was 6 P.M., after sunset, before the firing began, and the battle continued in ever growing darkness relieved by a clear moon. Stewart had no hesitation in engaging the two ships together; he had the weather gauge—the ships had the wind abeam—and could choose his range. He began at 250 yards, distant enough for his long guns to have a distinct advantage over the enemy's carronades; Stewart fought the whole battle with a coolness and a readiness of resource that can hardly be overpraised. He checked his fire when his gun smoke, drifting to leeward, hid his enemies, and caught sight of them again just in time to see *Cyane*, the aftermost ship, luffing up to cross his stern. He balked the maneuver by throwing his sails aback—*Constitution's* crew was amply large enough to work the ship and both broadsides simultaneously and rapidly—battered the *Cyane* nearly into silence, and then, setting sail again, he caught *Levant* trying to wear round to re-enter the battle and raked her from astern, destructively. *Levant* drifted out of the battle, her rigging cut to pieces, and Stewart rounded on *Cyane* again, raked her, closed with her, and forced her into surrender. He put a prize crew on board without wasting a moment and headed before the wind in search of *Levant*. She had re-rove her rigging and was beating back toward the scene of the action when *Constitution* came down on her in the faint moonlight. She could see no sign of her consort and could only guess the worst. She fired her broadside into her tremendous antagonist as she passed and received a far worse one in exchange; then she held on in the hope of escape, but Stewart swung round in pursuit, caught her an hour later, and compelled her surrender as well.

The *Naval Chronicle* announced the defeat "with considerable mortification and regret," but the British ships had fought well; against any antagonist other than Stewart and his highly efficient crew they might have stood a chance of success. Stewart took his prizes into Porto Praya in the Cape Verde Islands, under Portuguese sovereignty; when he reached there the news of the ratification of the peace still had not arrived, even though it was now a month old. The very next day Collier's squadron came in sight, and Stewart, mistrusting the ability of the Portuguese to enforce their neutrality, got under way in haste; it was a very creditable feat to get clear of the roadstead, prizes and all, before Collier was within range—the discipline in *Constitution* must have been of the highest order. Collier bungled the tactical pursuit and thereby discounted the credit he could have claimed for having made contact again with an enemy who had disappeared from his knowledge three thousand miles away.

Constitution made her escape, cutting away her boats and lightening ship so that her last action in the war echoed her first; the cold-blooded naval historian may regret the fact that the pursuit was not effective enough for her to have been tested against one of the spar-decked frigates in pursuit of her which had been built for the express purpose of engaging vessels of her class. *Cyane* escaped as well; *Levant*, headed off, ran back into the unavailing shelter of Porto Praya, where Collier came in and seized her—the Portuguese government later paying compensation to the United States. *Cyane* came sailing into New York on April 9 and anchored in the North River, with a salute to the authorities; the British blockading squadron had dispersed some weeks before, naturally, and *Constitution* had a similar easy re-entry (after a call at a Brazilian port) for Stewart to receive the rewards undoubtedly due his skill.

It was a month after Stewart's escape from Boston and more than three weeks after the signature of the peace treaty that Decatur endeavored to make his escape from New York in the *President*, on January 14, 1815; he had with him the crew of the *United States*, victors over the *Macedonian*, brought down from New London. A northwesterly gale was blowing, bring-

ing snow with it, dark and bitterly cold; the misery endured
by the crews of the blockading vessels endeavoring to keep
close into shore is better imagined than experienced. Hayes, the
senior officer of the British squadron, had under his command
the cut-down battleship *Majestic*, the big frigate *Endymion*,
and the lighter frigates *Pomone* and *Tenedos*. The gale—one of
those that delayed H.M.S. *Favourite* in her passage across the
Atlantic with the peace treaty—blew him from his station off
Sandy Hook down to the southeastward during the night of the
thirteenth, and the next morning Hayes had to decide on a new
course of action as the gale moderated. Sooner than claw back
to the Hook in the teeth of the gale, he stood close-hauled to
the northward through the day and the night to close the gap
between him and the Long Island shore; he left *Tenedos* to the
southward in case the enemy should after all try to slip out
round behind him. It was a sound piece of work, to which
Hayes did not fail to call attention when he wrote his official
report.

Decatur had been unlucky. With a brig carrying reserve provisions in company he had left his anchorage off Staten Island
during the night of the fourteenth and had grounded on the
bar owing to a pilot's error. He drove over after nearly two
hours' pounding, stripping off some of his copper and hogging
his ship and twisting her masts; the loss of those two hours was
of equal importance. There was no returning against the gale
that was blowing. Decatur was committed to the attempt to
reach the open sea, and he did as Hayes expected—he headed
along the Long Island shore. He had crossed the bar about 10
P.M. About 3 A.M., somewhere off Fire Island, he altered course
a little to the southward. Two hours later, in the very first light
of the wintry dawn, he sighted the British squadron, almost
within range; he had nearly run into their arms. At least he was
to leeward—he had just escaped through the cordon, in other
words—and if it had not been for the two-hour delay on the bar,
perhaps if it had not been for his unlucky but somewhat reck-

less change of course, he would have been clear through without being sighted, despite Hayes's having adopted the best possible course.

Decatur could only turn and run along the Long Island shore. The damage she had received on the bar cut down something of *President's* speed; she was making a certain amount of water, necessitating the use of the pumps. With the gale moderating every hour, Decatur lightened his heavily laden ship, throwing overboard boats and provisions. He was given a moment's grace by the unexpected appearance of *Tenedos* to the southward; *Pomone* was detached to identify her and lost several miles in the chase. All through the winter's day the chase continued; *Endymion* overtook the clumsy *Majestic* in the chase and gradually closed on *President*. By the afternoon bow- and stern-chasers were in action; as night approached, *Endymion* was up to *President's* starboard quarter; there was no chance of *President* turning away, with the coast on her port beam. Captain Hope of the *Endymion* handled his ship well; he maintained the station he had gained, using his slight advantage in speed to yaw and fire his port broadside into *President's* quarter. *President* could hardly bring a gun to bear, and any alteration of course would enable the other pursuing ships to cut the corner and come within range. Moreover, Hope's skillful handling of *Endymion* gave Decatur no opportunity of closing—Decatur had his boarding parties mustered in the hope of suddenly overwhelming *Endymion*. The wind had dropped to a very moderate breeze; on board *President*, pounded as she was by well-aimed artillery, the heartbreaking labor had to be begun of wetting her sails, hauling sea water up to the prodigious height of her royal yards—*President* had every stitch of canvas set, including studding sails. *Endymion* was keeping up a steady fire; she was doing some damage to *President's* sails and rigging, and at any moment she might do more; *Endymion's* main-deck guns were 24-pounders, with a shattering effect nearly twice as great as the 18-pounders the big American frigates had so far encountered.

Half an hour of it was as much as Decatur would endure. It was essential that he disable this harassing opponent. He put his helm to port and swung his ship to starboard, threatening to cross *Endymion's* bows. Hope turned at once to counter this obvious move, and the two ships ran southward side by side; it was just light enough for the other British to see what had happened and to incline their course to intercept. Decatur's object was to dismantle his enemy, and it seems almost certain —there is no official word on the subject—that he made use of "dismantling shot." These were composed of bars of iron joined by a ring at their ends; they flew out during the trajectory of the projectile, which came through the air like a revolving star, intended to cut sails and rigging. The British had found some on board the captured *Chesapeake* and had noted them with the disapproval extended to all innovations, although chain shot and bar shot had been employed at sea almost since the invention of artillery. For over two hours *President* fired into *Endymion*, broadside to broadside in the darkness, far longer than was needed to shatter the *Guerrière* or the *Macedonian*. Darkness probably made the aim poor on both sides, but *President* suffered considerable damage and losses—Decatur was wounded by a splinter—while *Endymion*, with fewer casualties and without losing a spar, had her sails "stripped from her yards." This striking phrase, which occurs in more than one official statement, seems to be proof of the use of dismantling shot; the time taken to achieve the result seems equal proof of its inefficiency, in this case at least. Probably there was still a considerable sea running, and on this course the ships would be rolling heavily; with the added handicap of darkness, the poor gunnery can be accounted for.

Endymion dropped back, and Decatur turned his stern to his other pursuers and ran before the wind again. But *Pomone* and *Tenedos* had been guided after him by the flashes of the gunfire and kept *President* in sight; after two more hours *Pomone* caught her up although she had all possible sail set. *Pomone* worked up within range, took in her studding sails, and fired a destructive broadside; *Tenedos* was somewhere close—the evidence is self-contradictory in regard to exactly where, but at least was threatening to enter into the struggle.

Decatur had been hit again; three of his lieutenants were dead. He gave the order to haul down the light which, hanging at the mizzen peak, substituted for the colors in the darkness, and when *Pomone*, closing in, hailed to ask if *President* had struck, someone hailed back to say yes. *President* might have fought on for a while; she might have had a few more men killed and wounded; she might have killed and wounded a few more British seamen. She certainly was not a helpless wreck, for she had all sail set, although she had been badly battered and had lost one fifth of her men. Perhaps fatigue was the cause of the early surrender; it can be taken as certain that no one on board had had a moment's rest since the anchor was weighed thirty hours before; the labor of lightening the ship, wetting the sails, working the pumps, and handling the guns had been severe. The ship was taking in a good deal of water and the pumps were still hard at work. Decatur had been active for the last thirty-six hours at least, and he was shaken by his wounds.

On the other hand, Decatur may have deliberately decided against being the cause of further loss of life. *Pomone* was alongside, *Tenedos* closing in; *Majestic* could not be far off, and *Endymion* would be up soon—as she actually was, in less than two hours—after bending on new sails. Decatur's own expression is, "Without a chance of escape left, I deemed it my duty to surrender," which certainly implies that he was desirous of avoiding further loss of life; but his own fatigue, as well as that of his men, may have led him to the decision. His court-martial absolved him, the American public took him to their hearts on his return, and he was employed the same year in the Mediterranean in command.

The British public received the news with delight—"our hopes have been most honourably realised"—but it was hardly to the credit of the technical press that it should argue, as it did, that *Endymion* had defeated *President* in a fair ship-to-ship action; Decatur was handicapped from the start by the damage done in crossing the bar and, from the moment firing began, by the necessity of keeping ahead of his pursuers. *Endymion* was well handled in circumstances that must have been familiar, by discussion if not through actual experience, to every British captain as a result of a thousand pursuits by superior force during the preceding twenty years.

Even though peace had been signed, it had not been ratified, and the news of the loss of the *President* had a political importance, for it arrived in time to influence the United States Senate in its consideration of the peace treaty, for there was other news just arrived in Washington which might otherwise have stiffened the attitude of the Senate. Cochrane, after his withdrawal from before Baltimore, had contemplated the multiplicity of objectives still open to him, his fleet, and his army, in the light of the instructions that flowed in to him from the British government. The knowledge that he was free to strike influenced both sides during the peace negotiations; the orders to Cochrane were markedly influenced by some of the other factors that developed during those negotiations.

The most astonishing was the discovery by one party in the British government that they did not want to beat America too severely. England's recent allies were suspicious of any possible aggrandizement of British power; Spain and France, in particular, were sensitive about any action on the part of England to establish herself in the territories transferred a dozen years before by the Louisiana Purchase. Nor was Spain overfriendly toward British intervention in Florida. Mr. Madison's annexation of West Florida, made by executive order (with searchings of heart that can only be guessed at), had been confirmed by the Senate just before the outbreak of war, while Spain was

convulsively struggling against Bonaparte; but Spain was un-
friendly toward any plan made by England to regain the territory for her; Spain, flatly, would prefer to see West Florida
in American hands than in British and would not countenance
any use of her name in the struggle. In consequence, Cochrane,
if he intervened here, would be under the same handicap as
Wellington had experienced regarding anti-Bonaparte movements in the South of France in early 1814; he could make no
promises to the inhabitants, and especially to the Indians, that
they would not be handed back to the United States on the
conclusion of peace.

Cochrane's plans had been grandiose; he had contemplated
raising a servile rebellion among the slaves in Georgia; he had
contemplated arming and disciplining the Creeks and the Choctaws and striking across country to the Mississippi at Baton
Rouge, to cut off and compel the surrender of New Orleans.
Meanwhile he found his plans necessarily modified by the successive dispatches from England limiting his political objectives,
reducing the military force he had been promised, and changing
the military commander in chief. The British Cabinet, confronted with the deteriorating conditions in Europe, wished to
send no more troops across the Atlantic; they would have been
well advised to abandon the amphibious offensive if they could
not support it wholeheartedly, but they could decide on neither
course. They sent a few more men to Cochrane; they permitted
him to make use of the colored regiments garrisoning the West
Indian islands, and in default of Wellington or Hill or Murray
they sent another commander in chief, Sir Edward Pakenham,
Wellington's wife's brother. He had frequently been put in
command of a division in the Peninsula when no other major
general had been available—as interim commander of Picton's
division he had made the decisive attack at Salamanca—but he
had never been entrusted with an independent operation.

As far back as September 1812, long before there was any
question of transfer to America, Wellington had written, "Pak-

enham may not be the brightest genius"—an estimate which every student of Wellington's correspondence can understand to be a severe condemnation. But in any case Pakenham arrived only in time for the closing episode; until his arrival the British military forces were under the command of a junior major general more completely under Cochrane's influence than Downie had been under Prevost's, and until the moment of battle the responsibility was entirely Cochrane's.

During the summer of 1814 the attempt to rouse the Creeks and the Choctaws ended in a fiasco, although Cochrane sent a capable officer and considerable supplies to the Apalachicola; the restraining orders of the Cabinet would have brought this about even if Andrew Jackson's recent campaigns had not made the Indians extremely cautious in the absence of a powerful British force to support them. Cochrane still had a free hand in the matter of the selection of an objective, and he elected to make an attack on New Orleans, but with his now limited forces he could not spare a man for the contemplated move against Georgia. He transferred himself to the Caribbean, picked up reinforcements from the West Indian islands, and proceeded to launch the limited attack which was now the only one open to him.

On the American side the preparations for defense were as tardy and as disorganized as could be expected of the Administration, even though its problems were greatly simplified by the early news of the transfer of the British forces from Bermuda to the Caribbean. This made it as certain as anything could be in war that the attack would come against the Gulf coast; there was the fact that winter was close at hand to reinforce the conclusion; the Atlantic coast was likely to be unmolested. And an attack on the Gulf coast could only have New Orleans as its objective, direct or indirect. The belligerent who has to take precautions against an attack by sea usually has very dispersed points to guard, as Hitler discovered. Yet even with an easy decision to make, even with all the facilities of the Mississippi to simplify communication, little was done to secure New Orleans. Orders for the transfer of troops were given reluctantly, and the heavy artillery which would have been invaluable was not sent at all. No naval effort was made; an energetic construction program on Lake Borgne, multiplying the gunboats which on those shallow waters would have been of real use, might have foiled Cochrane altogether. It may be that the reason for all this otherwise unaccountable neglect was that the Administration's eyes were fixed on the unrest in New England, preparing at that moment to express itself in the Hartford Convention, with one of its chief grievances the extremely limited system of conscription which Mr. Madison contemplated. Oddly enough, with all its failures, the Administration had already, back in 1813, taken the decision that was to influence events around New Orleans when General Armstrong appointed Andrew Jackson as a regular major general.

Jackson had been distracted during the autumn by Cochrane's attempt to raise the Indians, even though a British naval attack on Fort Bowyer—the only place of strength between East Florida and New Orleans—had ended in a minor British disaster. Jackson had consumed some of his strength in an advance upon and the capture of Pensacola, in defiance of the government's instructions—a feat which throws a curious light upon the vexed question of Spanish neutrality and which had no effect on Cochrane's plans at all. Despite the British repulse at Fort Bowyer, Jackson felt compelled to disperse the forces he had at hand. The Gulf coast was obviously the British objective—even more obviously than was the French Channel coast in 1944—but it was a difficult task to make it all secure with a military force of no more than ten thousand men when a sea-borne army of similar strength could strike without warning at any one point. Nervous about his communications by the Mississippi, Jackson had to guard his left flank against that very attack toward Baton Rouge that Cochrane had contemplated, weakening the defenses of New Orleans proportionately; it was a typical example of the dilemma in which a force on the defensive finds itself when in the presence of superior sea power.

Nevertheless, Jackson, when he decided to repair in person to New Orleans, acted with all the fiery energy that had already made him conspicuous. He brought his small disorderly forces under discipline and set to work fortifying New Orleans. Above all, he put in order and garrisoned Forts St. Philip and Bourbon on the river below New Orleans. If Cochrane had it in mind to ascend the river to the city he would have to storm at least one of these places first—no sailing fleet could run past the forts against the current as Farragut was to do later—and this would afford Jackson time to concentrate. Jackson's activity was beyond all praise, but only after he had given up the Florida adventure; it remained to be seen if the Tennessee and Kentucky militia would arrive in time from up the river to take part in the defense.

Cochrane had been subjected to some of the irritating delays almost inevitable in the concentration of a force in sailing ships. The serious and important diversion of a threat against the Georgia coast did not take place at all. Jamaica was by no means a convenient base for an incursion into the Gulf of Mexico, in view of the prevailing trade winds, but he wasted remarkably little time. He committed himself to his offensive before the last of his reinforcements had arrived—in fact, before Pakenham had joined him. Of the various routes open to him—via Barataria, up the river, by Lake Borgne, and by Mobile—he selected that by Lake Borgne; his fleet and transports were in the sheltered anchorage off Ship Island—seventy miles from New Orleans as the crow flies—on December 8; Jackson had reached New Orleans on December 2, having stormed Pensacola on November 7. Of the seventy miles that intervened between Cochrane and his objective, sixty were water; but that water was too shallow for ships of war or for transports—the muddy, desolate lagoons of the coast. The further advance

would have to be made by the boats of the fleet. This inconvenience was the price that had to be paid for circumventing
Fort St. Philip.

It was now that five of the vast flotilla of gunboats whose construction had begun with Jefferson's administration, and whose
sister vessels had been so conspicuously useless, proved themselves invaluable. Under the command of Lieutenant Thomas
Catesby ap Jones they were watching Cochrane's fleet from the
shallows; they were a "fleet in being"—the deterrent effect of
such a fleet on a superior force meditating invasion had been
noted by Torrington more than a century before. Cochrane
felt himself obliged to deal with them before committing his
troops to their voyage in open boats across Lake Borgne. In the
country of the blind the one-eyed man is king; out of range of
the British broadsides, the gunboats—"this formidable flotilla"
as Cochrane officially termed it in strange contrast with his
allusions to gunboats in his Chesapeake dispatches—were the
most efficient fighting vessels either side possessed. Cochrane
had to swamp their opposition with an overwhelming force of
his ships' boats, no less than forty launches, and perhaps more.
Jones did not succeed in maintaining his fleet "in being"; he
did not handle his flotilla with exceptional brilliance, and he was
unlucky regarding wind and tide, but he fought a desperate
battle when he was overtaken. His boats were all captured after
inflicting considerable loss on the British. But this was December 14, six days after Cochrane had dropped anchor—and
Cochrane had been in Washington six days after he had begun
his movement thither; the gunboats had won for Jackson six
uncovenanted days to strengthen his defenses and for his reinforcements to arrive.

The delay occasioned by the mere existence of Jones's flotilla
was inevitable enough; after its destruction delay succeeded
delay. When the rapidity and energy displayed in the raid on
Washington are remembered it is hard to avoid the conclusion
that the death of Ross had deprived the amphibious force of its

vitality. The discovery was only now made—or at least it was only now that allowance was made for the deficiency—that the fleet had insufficient landing craft. The troops had to be ferried into Lake Borgne in successive echelons, assembling at an intermediate staging point at Pea Island within the lake; oddly enough, Jackson, badly served by his intelligence, remained quite unaware of this movement of several thousand men forty miles from his headquarters.

The British advanced troops suffered severely when the Louisiana weather turned to its detestable winter's worst. They bivouacked in the swamps among the alligators under heavy rain in freezing weather, knee-deep in mud and without fuel, while the army completed its caterpillar movement of bringing its tail up level with its head. Then at last they moved again, ferrying the last thirty miles across the bay and up the Bayou Bienvenu. The weather was atrocious, the vessels were repeatedly aground, and the troops spent twenty-four hours crowded in the open boats. Yet they retained enough vigor, when they landed, having pushed up the bayou as far as possible, to surprise and capture the American pickets posted there. It was dawn, and a short movement brought them to the road to New Orleans, eight miles from the city. Now it was noon of December 23. The next day—while peace was being signed in Ghent—the remaining troops were brought up, and on the next day—Christmas Day—arrived Pakenham, who, as commander in chief, now found himself joining his army, which had been landed for him—without his being consulted in the least—in the heart of his enemy's positions. Perhaps it was only natural that he should delay awhile to take stock of his situation.

Jackson had already shown some enterprise. On the evening of the twenty-third he had sallied out from New Orleans with what troops he had in hand and had beaten up the British outposts in a confused action fought in the dark, between equal numbers and with equal losses, and the United States Navy had made a fresh appearance, the schooner *Carolina* harassing with her guns—as effectively as might be in the darkness—the British troops between the Mississippi and the levee. Since that time Jackson had stayed quiescent, but that did not mean he would not oppose an advance. Two more days went by, during which the British managed to catch *Carolina* within range of their field guns, and set her on fire with hastily heated red-hot shot, but the ship *Louisiana* took her place and anchored a little higher up the river. Then at last, on December 28, Pakenham moved up the road to cover the few short miles between him and the city.

It is instructive here to compare dates. The British left Jamaica on November 26 and dropped anchor on December 8. On that latter date Jackson was in New Orleans with two weak regular battalions and a thousand volunteers and militia; his other troops were widely dispersed in the Mobile area and at Baton Rouge. Carroll with the Tennesseans and Thomas with the Kentucky militia were far up the Mississippi, and there was one single primitive steamboat on that river. It was not until December 15 that Jackson ordered the troops at Mobile and Baton Rouge to join him; had it not been for the existence of Catesby Jones's flotilla, and had the British troops been handled as promptly as they had during the Washington campaign, Jackson's small force could well have been driven out of New Orleans. Even as it was, Carroll only reached the city on the twenty-third, with the British advanced guard eight miles away. A quicker passage by the British fleet from Jamaica, a more lavish provision of landing craft, and Carroll could have been anticipated by several days. The subsequent delays on the part of the British may not have been quite so important, but at least they gave Jackson five days in which to rest his weary men and settle them solidly in their entrenchments; by December 28, when Pakenham found himself face to face with the American position, any further direct offensive was hopeless.

At this point the naval historian, having recorded the employment of sea power to secure surprise for the offensive and to force dispersion on the defensive, and having recorded how the opportunities were lost, might well be excused the melancholy task of describing the subsequent events after the armies had been brought face to face. Yet it is worth consideration that sea power and the threat of its further employment might still have saved the British army from its bloody repulse. A movement against Fort St. Philip down the river could not have failed to alarm Jackson; the fall of the fort would free the river to the British navy and expose his flank; in the face of that possibility Jackson would have been compelled to leave his entrenchments and commit himself to an offensive action against the British army in position, with possibly a different result.

As it was, Pakenham made little attempt to regain for himself freedom of maneuver. He made a reconnaissance in force against the American lines, with the result—inevitable in any halfhearted offensive—of raising the spirits of the defense; it could not be said that he correspondingly depressed the spirits of his own veteran troops, for the later assault was to prove how high was their morale. He made an attempt to employ regular siege methods against the American positions, and it was a lamentable failure; it was absurd to expect anything better— leaving out of account the absurdity of a raiding force venturing on a regular siege at all—in view of the fact that he was not equipped to undertake a siege and was opposed to a force whose communications were unimpeded. The well-served American artillery put an end to the badly judged effort in short order.

His next plan met with more success than it deserved; there is no excuse for the Americans that it met with any at all. He dug a canal from the bayou to the river and dragged ships' boats along it, and by their means transported part of his army across the river to threaten Jackson's flank. It is hard to understand how he was permitted to pass a single man across, or how, after his defeat, a single man of the detachment was ever able to rejoin the main body. Pakenham himself could have had little faith in the diversion. He did not wait for it to produce any effect; the movement was delayed by causes which might well have been foreseen, and before it was well under way Pakenham launched his main body forward in a frontal attack. It was a mad attack, so mad that the student seeks for some unmilitary reason for it—friction between Pakenham and Cochrane is the most likely one; tempers were probably short after a month of wallowing in the morass.

No man in his senses could expect Bladensburg over again; this was no bewildered militia breathlessly occupying an open hillside. There was a strong regular stiffening, and many of the militia had seen considerable service already under Jackson's command. Four thousand steady infantry packed into a front of three quarters of a mile, occupying trenches with which they had had two weeks to become familiar, their flanks secure, and with a numerous artillery, could not have been moved by a frontal attack made by four times the force Pakenham commanded; the fact that many of the American infantry were armed with rifles and knew how to use them only made the losses more rapid and more devastating. The success won on the other side of the river came too late. Pakenham's men suffered stoically the frightful losses that British infantry have suffered under dashing generals since time immemorial, and Pakenham himself paid the price of his folly in this, the classic example of sea-borne mobility thrown to waste.

It says much for the British discipline, and very little for Jackson's enterprise, that the British maintained themselves for a week in their original position, while they recovered the force sent across the river, sent back all but their very badly wounded, and then effected their evacuation with almost no loss. During the entire six weeks—from December 8 to January 18—Jackson made no threat against the attenuated British communications; save for his sortie on December 23 he maintained a purely passive defense, remarkably badly served by his intelligence. It was perhaps as well for his military reputation that he was opposed to an enemy obliging enough to move slowly and to ruin himself in useless offensives.

A final gesture displayed the advantages the British had forgotten to employ earlier, when they pounced upon Fort Bowyer, which had previously defied a naval attack, and forced a prompt surrender of the place. That was the day that H.M.S. *Favourite* at last reached New York with the news of peace.

Chapter XXII

THE JANUARY GALES that held *Favourite* back and had blown *President* over the bar blew again on January 20, and the two fine American sloops in New York sailed out in broad daylight and, thanks to their speed and weatherly qualities, went through the British cordon with no particular difficulty. One of them was Warrington's *Peacock*, refitted after two months in New York following her successful cruise of the year before when she had captured *Epervier*; the other was *Hornet*, which had captured the original *Peacock* and was now under the command of James Biddle. The captains did not know that *President* had fallen into British hands four days earlier; their orders were to rendezvous with her at Tristan da Cunha in the farthest South Atlantic. From there the westerlies would carry them round the Cape of Good Hope, and a squadron of that strength at large in Indian waters would call for a whole fleet to round them up. *Peacock* reached the rendezvous first, was blown off by a gale, and returned on March 23— a month and a week after Mr. Madison and the Senate had ratified the treaty of peace—to find that the American navy had gained another victory.

Biddle had encountered one more of the ubiquitous British brigs, the *Penguin*. The latter represented an attempt on the part of the Royal Navy to remedy some of the deficiencies of her class; she was a trifle larger, was manned by a more numerous crew, and mounted a heavier battery, with 32-pounder carronades in place of 24-pounders. She was hardly inferior in force to *Hornet*, therefore, but the ensuing engagement only served to demonstrate the fact that the Royal Navy still had not found the means to improve the quality, or at least the training, of the British crews; not even after many sharp lessons. The battle was fought in the roaring westerly weather of those latitudes, to put the gunnery training on both sides to the severest test, and it ran the course that might almost be predicted. *Penguin* ran down to engage and was badly battered in the opening broadsides, during which the British captain was cut in half by a round shot. The two ships came into contact, with *Penguin's* bowsprit caught in *Hornet's* mizzen shrouds, and the British attempt to board was beaten back by the American musketry. *Penguin* tore loose at the cost of her bowsprit, whose loss brought down her foremast; Biddle was slightly wounded while ascertaining if she had surrendered, and then within a few more minutes *Penguin* was forced to haul down her colors, a sinking wreck with one third of her crew dead or wounded; *Hornet's* loss was far less than one tenth of her numbers.

Peacock and the attendant storeship which had sailed with her arrived immediately after the battle; *Penguin* was burned, the prisoners were put on board the storeship, and the two sloops ran before the westerlies round the Cape and headed for East Indian waters, abandoning the rendezvous with *President* after waiting for her three weeks. It is an interesting illustration of the distribution of the British navy that the first sail they sighted, on April 27—more than two weeks after leaving Tristan de Cunha—should be a British ship of the line, the *Cornwallis*. Her size and sail spread led the American captains to think she was an Indiaman—74s and Indiamen were constantly mistaken for each other, partly because Indiamen had rows of painted ports—and they closed on her before they discovered their mistake.

With recognition came flight on diverging courses. *Peacock* was the faster ship and soon vanished. Biddle hauled as close to the wind as he could in the expectation that his handy ship would weather on the two-decker with ease. But *Cornwallis* was a weatherly ship which not merely was as fast as *Hornet* but actually crept up to windward of her, and this not merely in the brisk wind which was blowing at the time of the first encounter (when a big ship might be expected to have the advantage over a smaller one) but also later, when the wind moderated. There was an anxious time when it seemed as if *Hornet* would go the way of *Syren* and *Rattlesnake*—both over-taken by heavy ships—and Biddle had to throw overboard first his ballast and his boats and then his stores and then his anchors and cables and finally his guns. The chase continued into the night; Biddle tacked to throw off pursuit in the darkness, but *Cornwallis* maintained a good lookout and tacked as well. At dawn she was within range and began firing with her bow-chasers; the shot passed overhead, between the masts, without scoring a lucky hit. *Cornwallis* as well as *Hornet* was making every effort to discover which particular trim gave her the last yard of speed at this time when yards were of vital importance; the weather was squally, and with the sudden variations each ship gained on the other in turn. On board *Hornet*, muskets and cutlasses followed the other gear over the side, the capstan, the armorer's anvil, the ship's bell, and finally the topgallant fore-castle was hacked to pieces and thrown over; the crew was used as living ballast to correct the trim while anxious eyes measured the distance between the ships. For the whole of that day the chase continued, with the British scoring an occasional hit, but never a vital one. In the late afternoon a shift of the wind found *Hornet's* best point of sailing, or *Cornwallis'* worst, and *Hornet* drew away. *Cornwallis* stayed in sight through the night, but at dawn she was fifteen miles astern, and after another few hours abandoned the pursuit. Biddle could do no more than turn back for home, his ship having no fighting capacity left; at the Cape of Good Hope on May 9 he heard of the conclusion of peace.

Warrington in the *Peacock* had held on and reached East Indian waters, where Porter might have appeared with *Essex* a year previously if he had not taken his fatal decision to return and fight *Phoebe*. By the middle of June—four months after the ratification of peace, six months after the signing at Ghent—he was off the coast of Java. One war had ended and two others had begun and he knew nothing about any of these things. Bonaparte had escaped from Elba, had reached Paris, and had mobilized an army; at the very time when Warrington's men sighted the mountains of Sumatra and sniffed the scented breeze that blew down from then, Bonaparte was in full march for Belgium, and while Warrington was burning captured Indiamen, Bonaparte's army was breaking in red ruin against the British infantry at Waterloo. Not only that; America was fighting a new war. An American fleet was at sea, with Decatur's pendant flying in the new *Guerrière*. The day Bonaparte was galloping from his last defeat was the day that Decatur captured the Algerine *Estadio* in the Mediterranean, and on that day Warrington was still fighting the old war. Altogether he took, and destroyed, four valuable prizes.

On the last day of the month Bonaparte was en route to Rochefort and St. Helena; Decatur was sailing for home, his mission completed (except for the finishing touch that the Royal Navy had to give the following year), and Warrington was conning his ship into the Strait of Sunda, with Sumatra on the one side and Java on the other and Krakatoa under his lee, when he sighted his fifth sail—yet another armed brig, this one flying the gridiron flag of the Honourable East India Company. There is contradictory evidence as to what happened next; certainly Warrington was informed that peace was made, but there was the fort of Anjer to offer refuge to the stranger if she could slip into it, and Warrington would take no chances. He fired a broadside into her when she refused to surrender, and seven men died. Her name was *Nautilus;* the American *Nautilus* had fallen into British hands three years before.

A Final Note

        Mr. Madison's comments on those three years, made in his message to Congress after the ratification of peace, are interesting. The war had, he said, "been waged with a success which is the natural result of the legislative counsels, of the patriotism of the people, of the public spirit of the militia." He announced that "the causes of the war have ceased to operate" and "the government has demonstrated the efficiency of its powers of defense."

These bold affirmations were followed by a statement of what "experience has taught us"; the "us" presumably including Mr. Madison—as much an admission of shattered illusions as could reasonably be expected of a party leader. "A certain degree of preparation for war," said Mr. Madison, "is not only indispensable to avert disaster in the onset, but affords also the best security for the continuance of peace." Mr. Madison was therefore confident that "the wisdom of Congress" would "provide for the maintenance of an adequate regular force," and for "the gradual advance of the naval establishment," and for "adding discipline to the distinguished bravery of the militia." So the war had put an end to Mr. Madison's early fears of the growth of a military caste, even to the extent that he hoped Congress would provide for "cultivating the military art in its essential branches, under the liberal patronage of government."

And Mr. Madison had learned much from the wholesale defiance of the embargo and the unrest of New England; the final
solemn words of his message made a recommendation of the
deepest importance. "Let us never cease to inculcate obedience
to the laws, and fidelity to the Union."

Index

Accommodation (schooner), 141
Adams (frigate), 148, 249
Adams, John Quincy, 196
Aeolus (frigate), 53
Africa (ship of the line), 25, 28, 50, 54, 55
Alert (sloop), 71, 73
Alexander I, Czar of Russia, 195, 199
Alexander (merchant ship), 219
Alexandria, Va., capture of, 230, 231
Allen, William, 169, 171, 172, 202
Amelia (frigate), 127
Arethuse (frigate), 127
Argus (brig), 24, 27, 47, 106, 169, 229; vs. *Pelican*, 170–72
Ariel, 183
Armstrong, Gen. John, Secretary of War, 155
Avon (brig), 215

Bainbridge, Capt. Joseph, 214
Bainbridge, Capt. William, early career of, 112; in command of *Constitution*, 113–15, 117–22
Baltic Trader, 231
Barbadoes (frigate), 97
Barclay, Capt. R. H., 173–79, 181–84
Barney, Joshua, privateer captain, 88, 227
Bayard, James, 199, 220
Beckwith, Gen. Sydney, 146–47
Belvidera (frigate), 49; vs. *President*, 29–33; vs. *Constitution*, 49–55
Beresford, Sir John, 102

Beresford, Sir William, 102
Betsy Ann (schooner), 141
Biddle, James, 275, 277
Blakely, Master Commandant Johnston, 213, 215
Blockade, coastal, 134, 137
Blyth, Comm. Samuel, 189, 190, 193, 202
Bonaparte, Joseph, 81
Bonaparte, Napoleon, 11, 12, 20, 22, 73, 81, 133, 189, 193, 278
Bonne Citoyenne (sloop), 115, 122
Boxer (brig), 189; vs. *Enterprise*, 190–92
Brock, Sir Isaac, 73, 151
Broke, Sir Philip, 28–29, 49, 50, 55–58, 99, 161–66, 232
Brown, Noah, 235
Burrows, Lt. William, 190–93, 202
Byron, Capt., 29, 30, 52, 54

Caledonia, 181, 184, 186
Canada, as U.S. objective, 14–15; Wellington on defense of, 150–51; campaigns against, 156–59
Carden, Capt. John, 106–10
Carolina (schooner), 270–71
Castlereagh, Viscount, 198–99, 220, 225
Cecil Foundry, 143
Champlain, Lake, battle of, 233–44; results of U.S. victory, 246–48
Chauncey, Capt. Isaac, 76, 152–58; 174, 179, 188

Cherub (sloop), 207, 211
Chesapeake, 160–61; vs. *Leopard*, 10;
    vs. *Shannon*, 163–65, 167
Chesapeake Bay, blockade of, 134
Chippoway, 186
Choctaws, 266
Cidade de Lisboa (brig), 141
Cochrane, Vice-Adm. Sir Alexander,
    201, 202, 228–29, 232–33, 249,
    264–69
Cockburn, Sir George, 140–45, 148,
    202
Columbia (frigate), 229
Comet (privateer), 86, 88
Confiance, 237, 238, 241–43
Congress (frigate), 24, 29, 105, 160,
    169
Constellation (frigate), 23, 139, 140,
    256
Constitution (frigate), 29, 44, 46, 47;
    vs. *Belvidera*, 48–56, 112–13, 115,
    256; vs. *Guerrière*, 59–68; vs.
    Java, 118–22; vs. *Cyane* and
    Levant, 257–59
Convoy Act, 19
Cornwallis (ship of the line), 276–77
Creeks, British attempt to influence,
    266
Croker, John Wilson, 72
Cyane (corvette), vs. *Constitution*,
    257–59

Dacres, Capt. James, 48–49, 62–67
Dearborn, Gen. Henry, 45, 155–57
Decatur, Capt. Stephen, 28, 102; in
    command of *United States*, 106–
    11, 113, 167, 168; attempts escape
    from New York, 259–64
Delaware, blockade of, 134
Detroit, 175, 181–86
Detroit, surrender of, 45; recaptured,
    187
Dominica, 87
Doughty, ship designer, 213
Downie, Capt. George, 238–41
Droits de l'Homme, 45
Duckworth, Vice-Adm. Sir J. T., 91

Eagle (schooner), 235, 240–43, 255
Eckford & Brown Bros., 154
Eliza (schooner), 137
Endymion (frigate), 260–62

Enterprise (brig), 190; vs. *Boxer*,
    191–92
Epervier (brig), vs. *Peacock*, 217
Erie, Lake, British superiority on,
    151, 173; battle of, 180–87
Essex (frigate), 24, 71, 203–7, 210–12
Essex Junior, 206
Estradio, 278

Favourite, 253, 260, 273
Fernando de Noronha, 114
Finch, 242
Fisgard, 107
"Free Trade and Sailor's Rights," 11,
    163, 180–81
Frenchtown, British assault on, 174
Frolic (British brig), 98–99, 111; vs.
    Wasp, 101–3
Frolic (U.S. sloop), 213
Fulton, Robert, 253–55

Galatea (frigate), 105
Gallatin, Albert, 197, 199, 220
George Washington, 112
Ghent, peace treaty signed at, 270
Great Lakes, strategic importance of,
    151–59, 173, 174; action on, 180–
    87
Guerrière (American frigate), 278
Guerrière (British frigate), 29, 48,
    58; vs. *Constitution*, 59–68

Hampton, Va., capture of, 147, 148
Hardy, Sir Thomas, 255
Harrison, Gen. William Henry, 173,
    179, 186, 188
Hillyar, Capt., 207–11
Hornet (pilot boat), 141
Hornet (sloop), 24, 27, 113, 167; vs.
    Peacock, 122–24; vs. *Penguin*,
    275–77
Hudson River steamboat service, 254
Hull, Capt. Isaac, early career of, 47;
    in command of *Constitution*, 48–
    56, 59–68, 70; as supervisor of
    N.Y. harbor defense, 75, 92, 193
Hull, Gen. William, 45, 69, 70
Humphreys, Joshua, shipbuilder, 43,
    44
Hunter, 185, 186
Huron, Lake, British superiority on,
    151

Immortalité, 107
Indefatigable, 45
Independent (merchant ship), 141
Insurgente, 23
Iphigenia, 116

Jackson, Gen. Andrew, 267–71, 273
James Madison (revenue schooner), 97
Java, 116; vs. *Constitution*, 118–22
John Adams, 23
Jones, Master Commandant Jacob, 99, 100–2, 111, 113
Jones, Lt. Thomas Catesby ap, 269, 271

Key, Francis Scott, 232
Kingston, Ont., in U.S. strategy plans, 156, 157, 158

Lady Prevost, 185, 186
Laforey, Sir F., 87, 132
Lambert, H., 116–19, 122
Lawrence, 180, 182–85
Lawrence, Master Commandant James, in command of *Hornet*, 113, 122–25; in command of *Chesapeake*, 161–65; funeral of, 189, 190
Leo (privateer), 219
Leopard, vs. *Chesapeake*, 10
Levant (ship of war), vs. *Constitution*, 257–59
Linnet, 242–43
Little Belt, vs. *President*, 10, 23; in Lake Erie battle, 186
Lively (schooner), 137
Liverpool, Lord, 249, 250
Louisiana, 271

Macdonough, Lt. Thomas, 234–36, 239, 240–42, 248
Macedonian (frigate), 79, 106; vs. *United States*, 107–11; as U.S. ship, 113, 167, 168
Madison (corvette), 154
Madison, James, 9, 10–11, 196–98, 220–24, 226–27, 279, 280
Magnet (sloop), 79
Majalahonda, 90
Majestic (battleship), 260–61
McHenry, Fort, bombardment of, 232

Meigs, Fort, attack on, 176
Menelaus, 231
Meshouda, 23
Mims, Capt. Charles, 138
Minerva (frigate), 71
Mix, Edward, fish torpedo devised by, 255
Montagu, 123
Morris, Lt. Charles, 50, 65

Nagle, Sir Edmund, 91, 132
Nancy, 141
Narcissus, 97
Nautilus (British), 278
Nautilus (U.S. ship of war), 46, 97
Navy, Royal, 17; status of in 1812, 19–20; superiority of, 37–42; criticism of, 127–35
Navy, U.S., shipbuilding program, 43–44, 213–14; unpreparedness of, 47
New Foye (schooner), 137
New Orleans, battle of, 266–74
Niagara, 181–86
Nymphe, 105

Ontario, offensive against, 156–57

Pakenham, Sir Edward, 265, 266, 270–73
Paris, Peace of, 12
Parker, Sir Peter, 231
Peacock (British brig), vs. *Hornet*, 123–25
Peacock (U.S. sloop), 96, 213, 216–17, 275–78
Peake, William, 124–25
Pelican (brig), vs. *Argus*, 170–71
Pellew, Sir Edward, 45, 79, 130
Penguin, 275, 276
Peninsular War, 19, 20–21, 39, 84, 90
Perry, Commo. Oliver Hazard, in command on Lake Erie, 153, 173, 174, 178–86, 188
Philadelphia, 24, 99, 112
Phoebe (brig), 136, 207–9, 211
Pike, Gen. Zebulon, in attack on York, 156, 157
Plantagenet, 220, 255
Plasswitz, armistice of, 199
Plattsburg, N.Y., 236; British attempt at, 238–44

Poictiers, 102
Polly (schooner), 137
Pomone (frigate), 260–63
Porter, Capt. David, in Tripolitan
    War, 24; in command of *Essex*,
    71–72, 114–15, 203–12
Preble, 242
President (frigate), 24, 105, 160, 168,
    216, 259; vs. *Little Belt*, 10, 23;
    vs. *Belvidera*, 30–33; vs. *En-*
    dymion, 261–63
Presqu'ile, 175–78
Prevost, Sir George, 189, 236–39, 241,
    243, 244
Prince Regent (sloop), 157
Privateering, 14, 85–88, 92–96, 160,
    249
Procter, Gen. Henry A., 173, 176,
    186
Psyche (frigate), 116
Put in Bay, 190

Queen Charlotte, 181, 182, 184–86

Reindeer (brig), 214–15
Renommée, 115; renamed *Java*, 116
Resolution (brig), 123
Retaliation (schooner), 112
Rodgers, Commo. John, early career
    of, 23; at start of war, 24–25; in
    command of *President*, 30–36,
    48, 104–5, 113, 168–69, 232
Ross, Robert, 228, 229–32
Rossie (privateer), 86, 88, 227
Rover (brig), 87

Sackets Harbor, 156–58, 235
St. Fiorenzo, 116
Salamanca, 22, 73
San Domingo, 109, 140
Saratoga, 235, 240, 242–43
Sawyer, Vice-Adm., 25, 32, 72, 91
Scorpion, 183
Shannon (frigate), vs. *Constitution*,
    49–52; vs. *Chesapeake*, 161–65
Solon (sloop), 141
Southampton, 97, 98
Stewart, Capt. Charles, 138–40, 256–
    58

Tecumseh, death of, 186
Tenedos (frigate), 161, 260–63

Thames, 188
Theresa, 141
Ticonderoga (schooner), 235, 236,
    242
Tonnant, 233
Torpedoes, Fulton's experiments
    with, 254
Truxtun, Thomas, 23

Ulysses (pilot boat), 141
United States (frigate), 24, 44, 206;
    vs. *Macedonian*, 107–11; 142,
    167, 168, 259
United States, grievances leading to
    war, 10; blockade against, 134,
    137; shipbuilding program, 43–
    44, 75, 213–14; Madison's em-
    bargo, 221

Valparaiso, naval engagement off,
    141
Van Rensselaer, Gen. Stephen, 45
Viper (brig), 97
Vixen (brig), 97, 98

War of 1812, events leading to, 10;
    purpose of, 11; British sentiment
    concerning, 15–22; U.S. senti-
    ment concerning, 69–70; early
    attempt at conciliation, 79–80;
    peace commission, 196–97, 199,
    225, 250; peace treaty, 251–52
Warren, Adm. Sir John Borlase, 78–
    80, 83, 85, 88–89, 91, 104, 116,
    132–34, 137, 140–42, 146, 149, 200
Warrington, Lewis, 216–17, 278
Washington, Fort, bombardment of,
    230
Wasp (sloop), 98–99; vs. *Frolic*,
    101–3; vs. *Reindeer*, 214–15; vs.
    Avon, 215–16
Wellington, Field Marshal, 22, 39, 73,
    81, 82, 84, 90, 128, 133, 143, 145,
    195, 219, 224, 249
Whinyates, Capt., 98–101
Wicomoco (schooner), 231
William (merchant ship), 117

Yeo, Sir James Lucas, 98, 115, 151,
    158, 179, 202, 238, 247
York, Ont., 155, 156–57; U.S. attack
    on, 156–57

Miles

0   100   200

CANADA

L. WINNIPEG

L. SUPERIOR

L. MICHIGAN

MISSOURI R.

MISSISSIPPI R.

L
O
U
I
S

UNITED

NORTHWES

OHIO R.

ARKANSAS R.

MISSISSIPPI R.

TENNESSE

A
N
A

MISSISSIPPI

TERRITORY

RED R.

RIO GRANDE

M E X I C O

New Orleans

palacios

95°

Gulf o